ENDING SEXUAL VIOLENCE IN COLLEGE

Ending Sexual Violence in College

A COMMUNITY-FOCUSED APPROACH

Joanne H. Gavin, James Campbell Quick,
and David J. Gavin

JOHNS HOPKINS UNIVERSITY PRESS | *Baltimore*

© 2021 Johns Hopkins University Press
All rights reserved. Published 2021
Printed in the United States of America on acid-free paper
2 4 6 8 9 7 5 3 1

Johns Hopkins University Press
2715 North Charles Street
Baltimore, Maryland 21218-4363
www.press.jhu.edu

Library of Congress Cataloging-in-Publication Data

Names: Gavin, Joanne H., author. | Quick, James Campbell, author. |
Gavin, David J., author.
Title: Ending sexual violence in college : a community-focused
approach / Joanne H. Gavin, James Campbell Quick, and David J. Gavin.
Description: Baltimore : Johns Hopkins University Press, [2021] |
Includes bibliographical references and index.
Identifiers: LCCN 2020015933 | ISBN 9781421440156 (hardcover) |
ISBN 9781421440163 (ebook)
Subjects: LCSH: Rape in universities and colleges—Prevention. |
Sex crimes—Prevention. | Women college students—Violence against—Prevention.
Classification: LCC LB2345.3.R37 G38 2021 | DDC 378.1/9782—dc23
LC record available at https://lccn.loc.gov/2020015933

A catalog record for this book is available from the British Library.

*Special discounts are available for bulk purchases of this book. For more information,
please contact Special Sales at specialsales@press.jhu.edu.*

Johns Hopkins University Press uses environmentally friendly book materials, including
recycled text paper that is composed of at least 30 percent post-consumer waste,
whenever possible.

To honor Otto Alois Faust, MD, Class of 1915,
Johns Hopkins University School of Medicine
Mein Großvater ist immer noch mein Held
und sein Geist erhebt mich wie ein Adler!
JimC

We dedicate this book to all those suffering the trauma of sexual assault in silence and to those trying to prevent the next assault from happening. Together may we create a Culture of Intolerance.
Joanne and David Gavin

CONTENTS

ACKNOWLEDGMENTS

As we completed the research, writing, and revisions for this book, we enjoyed support and constructive feedback from a host of individuals. The several seminar presentations where we presented our prevention and response model, especially with our colleagues at the University of Texas at Arlington and the University of Manchester, UK, yielded excellent questions and comments. Jeff Orleans was gracious early in our work with his suggestions about the complicated issue of sexual assault on campus. Doctoral candidate Manisha Mohan Vaswani did an excellent job of digging out the initial set of research studies on sexual violence, summarizing key sections, and developing early stages of the prevention model. Ashton Jones produced the superb graphics in the book. Once the first set of manuscript reviews were in, Carol Byrne did a comprehensive search to recover studies, articles, books, and other sources essential to manuscript revision. Finally, John Dycus provided an exceptional set of editorial eyes as he went through the work with a fine-toothed comb to smooth some rough edges. Jim thanks Sheri Schember Quick for once again providing critical and insightful comments from a different point of view.

We would also like to thank those who took time from their busy schedules to discuss their thoughts on the topic. Dennis Murray, Deborah DiCaprio, Christina Danielle, and Ed Freer from Marist College were all very generous making time to meet with us and offering helpful insights. Finally, David and Joanne would like to thank Marist College for granting us a research sabbatical which was critical to helping us focus our thoughts around this major project.

ENDING SEXUAL VIOLENCE IN COLLEGE

CHAPTER ONE

Introduction

——————

IN THE HUNDRED YEARS since women in the United States won the right to vote, they have earned 59 percent of the master's degrees and 52 percent of the doctoral degrees awarded in this country (Perry, 2015). Women currently constitute 56 percent of college students in the United States (US Department of Education, 2019), make up almost 50 percent of the workforce, and hold more than 50 percent of management and professional positions (Catalyst, n.d.).

Despite women's gains in representation and in education, much remains to be accomplished. In 2016, among S&P 500 companies, while women held 44 percent of all positions, they held only 36 percent of first- and mid-level positions, 25 percent of executive- and senior-level positions, 20 percent of board seats, and 5.8 percent of the CEO positions; of top earners, they made up a mere 9.5 percent (Catalyst, n.d.). And despite legislation designed to address inequity in earnings, women continue to earn less than men. According to the Bureau of Labor Statistics, women earn 83 cents on the dollar to men. This figure varies by industry, with the highest being construction, 91.3 percent, and the lowest legal, 56.7 percent.

Wages and job rank are not the only important areas where women need to advance. Many in society still see women in a subjugated role from a sexual relations perspective. Women are victimized not only by sexual assault but by a culture that would rather hide the evidence than fix the problem.

Scope of Sexual Assault

When women are seen as property, they are available to be used and abused as men see fit, including sexually. Laws have attempted to limit sexual abuse in the United States, but until society, the culture, and those legislating and enforcing the laws change, the problem will never be resolved.

In the United States, 321,500 people aged 12 or older were sexually assaulted or raped in 2015 (Office of Justice Programs, 2015). That's one person assaulted every 98 seconds. Approximately 91 percent of these sexual assaults were committed against women (Rennison, 2002), and 54 percent were perpetrated against women between the ages of 18 and 34. One in every five women will be the victim of an attempted or completed rape; that number for men is one in seventy-one (Black et al., 2011).

The statistics for the LGBTQ (lesbian, gay, bisexual, transgender, and questioning) community is even more concerning. According to the National Intimate Partner and Sexual Violence Survey conducted by the Centers for Disease Control and Prevention (CDC), 46 percent of lesbian women, 61 percent of bisexual women, and 35 percent of heterosexual women experienced rape, physical violence, or stalking by an intimate partner in their lifetime (Centers for Disease Control and Prevention, 2010). The survey also found that 34 percent of gay men, 37 percent of bisexual men, and 29 percent of heterosexual men experienced rape, physical violence, or stalking by an intimate partner.

Even more troubling is the continued indifference. As recently as the late 1990s, law enforcement officers did not take seriously many claims of sexual assault. A study done by Campbell and Johnson (1997) showed that police officers thought about 90 percent of all sexual assault claims were false, while in fact only between 2 and 10 percent of such claims in the study were false (Lisak et al., 2010). With attitudes like this, accurate investigations will never occur. And certainly laws to prevent sexual assault will never be appropriately enforced if those charged with enforcing the laws believe that sexual assault claims are lies perpetrated by women who want to get back at innocent men.

The problems with adjudicating sexual assaults do not end with the officers who investigate them. Some judges have biases, too. When the bias favors acceptance of rape myths and when judges who accept these myths are hearing sexual assault cases, injustice is inevitable.

Research by Gray (2011) found that when presiding judges voiced rape myths, the likelihood of a defendant being found not guilty or receiving a lighter sentence was higher. One documented instance of a judge's bias happened in the 2007 case of *Rambold v. Montana* (Tosti-Vasey, 2014). Montana teacher Stacey Rambold pled guilty to sexual contact without consent with one of his students. Judge G. Todd Baugh sentenced Rambold to thirty-one days in jail, although Montana's sentencing guidelines required a minimum two-year prison term for the crime.

In an attempt to explain his decision, Judge Baugh exposed his rape myth bias. The student, a 14-year-old Hispanic girl, "was as much in control of the situation as the defendant," he said. Rambold was white and 49 years old (Tuttle, 2013). Baugh also said that the girl "looked older than her chronological age" and that "this wasn't the forcible, beat-up type of rape" (Serna, 2014). Following public outrage and through the efforts of chapters of the National Organization for Women in Montana and Pennsylvania, Baugh was reprimanded and suspended thirty-one days without pay. The state's prosecutor appealed Rambold's sentence and he was resentenced to fifteen years with five years suspended. The victim took her own life shortly before her seventeenth birthday, before Rambold was ever brought to trial.

Bias is not limited to those in law enforcement and the judiciary. Also hampering effective prevention of sexual assaults is the mindset of many men in decision-making positions in the public and private sectors who believe that, short of brutal rape, sexual encounters are just boys being boys or, more disturbing, that the woman "really wanted it." This promotes the culture of not holding men responsible for their actions and placing the blame on the victim. While awareness has grown, these problems are prevalent in organizations everywhere.

Sexual Assault and Harassment at Work

Most organizations are still run by men making decisions that will mostly benefit men. Whether these decisions are made intentionally or because these men simply cannot understand the issue from a woman's view is unimportant. The facts remain: the men at the top set the culture for the organization, and often it is a culture of acceptance of assault and harassment of women.

Sexual assault at work is not rare. Duhart documented that between 1993 and 1999, 36,500 US workers were raped or sexually assaulted while at work or on duty (2001). Duhart also determined that 8 percent of all rapes happen while the victim is at work. Harrell (2011) found that between 2005 and 2009, rape/sexual assault accounted for 2.3 percent of all nonfatal violence in the workplace.

In a study of employed women, 38 percent reported experiencing sexual harassment at work (Potter and Banyard, 2011). These numbers have not changed in the last nine years. A survey conducted in January 2018 by the organization Stop Street Harassment (Chatterjee, 2018) found that 38 percent of women reported being sexually harassed at work. Of these women, 9 percent reported having to either change jobs or seek new assignments at their current job due to the harassment.

Another survey, conducted in 2017 by ABC/*The Wall Street Journal*, found that 30 percent of women have experienced sexual harassment from men in the workplace and that 25 percent of those women were harassed by men who had influence over their careers (Zillman, 2017). Nearly all of the women reporting these transgressions said the perpetrators went unpunished by the organization. This survey did report some encouraging results: 75 percent of Americans said workplace sexual harassment is a problem and 64 percent deemed the problem "serious." Those numbers are up 11 and 17 percentage points, respectively, from a similar poll conducted in 2011 (Zillman, 2017).

There are financial as well as personal, social, and cultural reasons to get this workplace harassment under control. In 2015 the Equal Employment Opportunity Commission recovered $164.5 million for workers alleging workplace harassment (Feldblum and Lipnic, 2016). These were direct costs only. Few recent attempts have been made to estimate the total costs of sexual harassment, but in 1994 the US Merit Systems Protection Board attempted to estimate this cost to the US government (Erdreich, Slavet, and Amador, 1994). Over a two-year period, it added up to $327.1 million: job turnover cost ($24.7 million) plus sick leave ($14.9 million) plus loss of individual productivity ($93.7 million) and workgroup productivity ($193.8 million). The board said this was a conservative estimate and the actual cost may be higher.

While little current information is available on the economic impact of sexual harassment, considerable research has addressed impact on the victims. Merkin and Shah (2014) found that women who had experienced sexual harassment at work were significantly and negatively affected. There was a decrease in job satisfaction, greater intent to leave their jobs, and higher absenteeism. Recently McLaughlin and colleagues (2017) found that victims of workplace sexual harassment experienced immediate negative outcomes, including financial stress and diminished long-term career success.

Sexual Assault and Harassment in the Military

A study by the US Department of Defense released in May 2018 found 6,769 reports of sexual assault in the military in 2017 (Wilkie, 2018), a 9.7 percent increase from the 6,172 reported cases in 2016. In 2016, 129,000 military service members reported severe and persistent sexual harassment or gender discrimination (Brignone et al., 2016).

According to Castro, Kintzle, Schuyler, Lucas, and Warner, sexual assault and sexual harassment are more difficult to address in the military than in other settings. They found that these factors allowed sexual assaults to thrive in the military culture: regular movement of personnel, team allegiance, leadership responsibility, coed living arrangements, the military reporting system, resilience building, emphasis on training, value on performance, problem resolution at the lowest level, and the military legal system (2015). Problems in all of these arenas may be important for the military to address; several of them are relevant to college campuses as well.

Sexual Assault and Harassment on College Campuses

Several of the factors in the military that allow sexual assaults to thrive may also be found on college campuses. The most notable similarities are coed living, the regular movement of individuals, and leadership responsibility.

At one time the military was composed entirely of men, and all living arrangements were single-sex environments. Once women entered the military at all levels, even direct combat, the living arrangements became coed. Likewise, campus resident halls originally were gender segregated, with separate halls for men and for women. This changed in the 1970s, and by the 1990s most resident halls were either fully coed or gender segregated by floor. Today, many colleges offer coed rooms.

While coed living has its benefits, such close proximity during the years when hormones are most active can cause problems. Clery Act data reported in 2014 indicated that 71 percent of campus rapes and 46 percent of all unwanted fondling occurred in residence halls, and that the latter number had been gradually increasing since 2005 (Curcio, 2016). (The Clery Act is discussed in chapter 2.)

In response to the challenges of sexual assaults on campuses, Catholic University returned to single-sex residence halls in 2011 (Garvey, 2011). Garvey cites research done by Christopher Kaczor, who found that students in coed resident halls reported binge drinking more than twice as often as students in single-sex resident halls. Kaczor further reported that students in coed resident halls were significantly more likely to have had a sexual partner in the last year and twice as likely to have had three or more sexual partners as those living in single-sex resident halls.

Another similarity between the military culture and the college campus is the movement of individuals. College students do not move with military frequency, but the response to the newness of an environment for moved personnel and new freshmen is identical. Most moved military personnel do not know anyone in their new environment and want to make friends and fit in. New freshmen are in the same position—they are scared and vulnerable. New freshmen are sexually assaulted so often in the first few dangerous weeks of the first year that the period has been termed *the red zone* (Jacobs, 2014).

A third similarity is in leadership responsibility. Military leaders are responsible for ensuring that sexual assaults and harassment do not happen under their command. When these behaviors occur, those in a military leadership position may feel pressure to deny that they have taken place. College administrators are no different. The Clery Act mandates the reporting of all sexual assaults and harassment on campus, but fully disclosing this information in not in the institution's best interest. Just as it does a military leader, an incident can put a college administrator in a very difficult position.

Military Academies

Nowhere are these challenges more clearly seen than in the military academies. Military academies have a shared culture of the military and the traditional college campus. And this culture may explain why getting sexual assault under control at the military academies is proving to be so difficult despite all the resources aimed at stopping these behaviors. Taken together, sexual victimization in the US military academies is high (60 percent of cadets and midshipmen).

The number of reported sexual assaults at the US Military Academy at West Point doubled during the 2016–2017 academic year over 2015–2016 (Wilkie, 2018), the fourth straight year that the number of assaults went up. There were smaller increases at the Air Force Academy and the Naval Academy. Some military officials believe that reports of assaults, not assaults themselves, have increased in number. Regardless, the situations in military academies offer a perfect microcosm in which to study and solve the problem. The Department of Justice estimates that sexual assaults in the military academies is up 47 percent, rising from 507 reported incidences across all service academies in 2015 to 747 reported incidences in 2018 (Copp, 2019).

Six Reasons to Focus on Sexual Assault and Harassment on College Campuses

While the military academies may be the perfect place to study sexual assault and harassment, they are under the purview of the federal government, function under different guidelines from those governing nonmilitary colleges and universities, and enroll only a small portion of the college-age population. An equally compelling look at the problem of sexual violence is available on the American college campus.

The first reason why focusing on college campuses can be useful in understanding sexual assault and harassment is that traditional-age college students are still in late adolescence. Because the human brain is not fully developed until age 25 (Arain et al., 2013), these students are not fully developed cognitively. During the college years, students' attitudes can be influenced through education and socialization. As educators, we have a mandate to shape them into societal contributors.

A second reason for focusing on college campuses is that college is a time when students transition from dependent children to independent adults. While the first reason is physical—student's brains are not fully developed—the second reason is that students at this age have not yet matured and remain very vulnerable emotionally. Their same-age non-student peers are seen by society (and, often, their parents) as fully functioning adults with jobs and independent lives, but individuals in school are still in large part the responsibility of other people. Students' parents and their college or university have a sense of needing to protect them. Parents trust in the school's administration to provide a safe, secure environment and to protect their children. This trust is not to be taken lightly. Creating a safe environment can make or break an institution.

The third reason to focus on college campuses is that during college, students engage in a host of risky behaviors that increase the probability of sexual assaults. Students suddenly experience a freedom they have never known before, and they test limits. College students drink more than their same-age nonstudent peers (Carter, Brandon, and Goldman, 2010), primarily because their environment allows it. They can be with one another at any time of the day or night, seven days a week. In many colleges, fraternity and sorority houses offer a place to hold a party whenever the students want. With this kind of access and limited supervision, college campuses often amount to a party venue.

One risky behavior is the hookup, or uncommitted sexual encounter, which is becoming normative for adolescents and young adults (Garcia, Reiber, Massey, and Merriwether, 2012). Hookups include a range of sexual behaviors, from kissing to intercourse, with no promise or even intention of a romantic relationship. Research indicates a connection between hookups and sexual assault. In some of the examples studied, 78 percent of unwanted vaginal, anal, or oral sexual assault occurred during a hookup (Flack et al., 2007). While all hookups increased the probability of sexual assault, hookups with acquaintances and previous romantic partners were the most dangerous (Flack et al., 2016).

A fourth reason to examine sexual assault on the college campus is that it is a relatively closed environment. Researchers may learn more about both victims/survivors and perpetrators of sexual assault because on college and university campuses they can control for factors that are uncontrollable in other situations. Unfortunately, college campuses offer a lot to study.

Women aged 18 to 24 who attend college are three times more likely to be sexually assaulted than women of other ages (Rape, Abuse, & Incest National Network, n.d., Victims of sexual violence). Women of that same age group who do not attend college are four times more likely to be sexually assaulted than women in general. While the probability of assault for nonstudent women is higher, the "punch bowl" environment of a campus setting offers a distinctive location in which to understand sexual assault.

A fifth reason for focusing on college campuses is that students take chances that make them easy targets. On their own for the first time and wanting to be part of the crowd, they engage in behaviors such as binge drinking and extensive drug use. College women go to parties and bars in places and with people they do not know, putting them in great danger.

Jacobs's red zone (2014) is a time when college freshmen are sexually assaulted more than at any other time in their college career. The Department of Justice has identified the red zone as running from the start of school to the Thanksgiving holidays. During this time, new freshmen are the most susceptible to falling prey to sexual assault.

According to a report funded by the National Institute of Justice, 50 percent of campus sexual assaults happen during the red zone (Krebs et al., 2007). Another study found that there were significantly more reports of sexual misconduct during the early fall semester than later in the year and that such reports were more frequent from first-year students than from older students (Kimble, Neacsiu, Flack, and Horner, 2008). This study also found that the number of complaints decreased with each year in school. Several theories offer explanations for the red zone. Some believe that it is primarily a function of new students meeting new people and wanting to fit in. Unsupervised and eager for acceptance, the may engage in behaviors like drinking or drugs which they are not equipped to deal with.

Because of the dangers of the red zone and sexual assault in general, many colleges include sexual assault training during orientation. While most people support this training, others think it too little, too late. Those in the latter camp believe that to be really effective, training must begin long before students enter college. Still others believe that safety training—what to do and what not to do in those first hours on campus—continues the message of blame the victim. They believe that putting all of the responsibility on the potential victim to protect herself or himself instead of on the perpetrators to stop undesirable behaviors perpetuates the rape culture of not placing the blame where it belongs.

Clearly, blaming the victim is wrong. But leaving potential victims unaware of the high-risk behaviors that increase the probability of being victimized is wrong, too. These two schools of thought are not mutually exclusive. Education of both potential victims and potential perpetrators is critical (Senn and Forrest, 2016). Creating a culture of respect through knowledge and training is a most important first step.

A situation similar to the red zone is study abroad. Many schools encourage students to spend a semester in another country to expand their minds and their cultural knowledge. Most study abroad experiences are even less structured than a traditional college campus, however, so students, especially freshmen, who join one of these programs face a greater risk of sexual assault than while on the school's main campus (Kimble, Flack, and Burbridge, 2013). This is not an opportunity to be avoided, but one that must be approached correctly. Colleges must ensure that they take the same appropriate precautions at their international campus as they do at their main campus. Students must be educated about the risks involved in the less structured environments of many study abroad programs.

The sixth and final reason for focusing on college campuses is the minefield colleges and universities face under Title IX legislation. University administrators are bombarded with Title IX requirements, under penalty of losing all federal funding, in order to be in compliance. There are binding state and local laws as well as extensive nonbinding federal guidance. Even the most diligent administrator can get lost in this quagmire. But if higher education administrators can be helped to figure this out, what is learned in this environment may be applied to the rest of society.

Changing the Culture
Social Culture

We can work to get better laws enacted. We can educate and train as many people as possible. But if perceptions of women and attitudes toward sexual assault do not change, not much else will. We must find a way to help society, especially men in decision-making positions, see women as their equals.

Many believe that to truly implement change in the way we view each other, education must begin early. Stereotypes must be eradicated before they fully develop, and a foundation of respect for women must be built early in a child's life. A child is not born with deleterious ideas; they are acquired over time and through the influence of others. Reversing this process will not be quick, but it is essential.

Tragedies such as those involving abuse at Penn State and within the Catholic Church serve as yet more wakeup calls about the need for children to be educated about sexual assault at a much earlier age. According to the Centers for Disease Control and Prevention, prevention education should begin as early as middle school. One program in this arena is Shifting Boundaries, which teaches middle school boys and girls about dating violence and sexual harassment (Taylor, Stein, Mumford, and Woods, 2013) by promoting positive social attitudes, negative attitudes about dating violence, and positive bystander behaviors.

The CDC recommends two programs for high school training. Safe Dates (Foshee et al., 2005) is intended for eighth- and ninth-grade boys and girls and explores gender-role norms, improving peer helping, and dating conflict resolution skills. The second program, Real Consent (Salazar, Vivolo-Kantor, Hardin, and Berkowitz, 2014), is a web-based interactive model aimed at teaching young men what real consent is and how to prevent sexually violent behaviors.

Organizational Culture

A necessary step in changing culture is changing the organizational culture of institutions of higher education. Everyone must be trained to do something when they see something. Colleges and universities must become intolerant of sexual assault; they must become places where gender-role norms are equal and no one is fair game for the elite few.

One example of a culture desperately needing change was Pennsylvania State University before 2011, before the Jerry Sandusky abuse story was uncovered. Several janitors witnessed one of the rapes (Freeh, 2012). One of the janitors, a Korean War veteran, told investigators it was one of the worst things he had ever seen. But neither he nor the other janitors said anything. They feared they would be fired.

As long as the employees of an organization believe that reporting bad behaviors will not be welcomed by leadership, they will never reveal the things that leadership needs to hear. By engaging the organization's leaders and training all its employees and students, a college or university can ensure that a culture that would protect a child molester can never arise.

Scope and Dimension of This Book

This book offers a comprehensive look at sexual assault on American college campuses and offers best practices to address the issue. We present a model to prevent sexual assault at both the individual and the organizational level. The model presented in this book has three sections: primary prevention, secondary prevention, and treatment after the event. Each section covers an important part of crafting safe campuses.

In discussing primary prevention (chapters 2, 3, and 4), we focus on understanding the evolution of Title IX and sexual assault legislation. We also present our model for prevention of sexual violence and treatment of victims/survivors and communities that experience an assault. We discuss the challenges of enforcing the sexual assault legislation, from the attitudes of the individuals charged with investigating sexual assault to the risky behaviors that put college students in peril.

We then turn our focus to the critical aspects of sexual assault that need to be considered when developing a prevention plan. Consent, risky behaviors, and the challenges of protecting a school's reputation—all must be considered.

In discussing secondary prevention (chapters 5, 6, and 7), we develop educational and training programs. What are the unique challenges of creating programs that will be most effective for faculty, students, and staff? What are the challenges of athletes and athletic departments, and how can a program best address them?

We then discuss the aftermath of an assault (chapters 8 and 9). No program, regardless of how well structured, will ever be totally successful. So understanding how to respond appropriately to those who suffer a sexual assault is critical. The school sets the tone for how the victim/survivor copes with the tragedy. We also discuss the impact on the community and on those accused.

We address the importance of university leaders giving their full support to safe campus programs. We also offer a plan for creating university communities that support everyone and take an active role in healing all involved after an assault happens.

Finally, we present three case histories (chapter 10). These cases illustrate aspects of prevention, training, and aftermath of sexual assault on campus.

We want to be very clear about the terminology used in this book. In much of the writing on the topics addressed in this book, individuals who have experienced an assault are most often referred to as *victims*. We believe there is power in words, so we prefer to refer to those individuals, where possible, as *victims/survivors*. When discussing an investigation or trial, the individual who is accused of committing the assault is referred to as the *accused*, *perpetrator*, or *defendant*. The individual who brings forth the charge is referred to as the *victim*, *complainant*, or *plaintiff*.

Two Caveats

Some of the issues discussed in this book are "moving targets." For example, as of the writing of this book, no decisions have been made regarding the permanent removal, adjustment, or continuation of the guidance put forth in both the 2011 Sexual Violence Dear Colleague Letter (Ali, 2011) and the 2014 Questions & Answers on Title IX Sexual Violence document (Office for Civil Rights, 2014). Nevertheless, we include a discussion of both documents in this book. Some support removing this guidance; their objections to the guidance are discussed in detail. Others believe the country has taken a step backward in protecting victims of sexual assault. Regardless, we believe that organizations that have all the facts are best able to make decisions to ensure their campus is as safe as possible.

Statistics indicate that sexual violence in the lesbian, gay, bisexual, transgender, and questioning community is as big a problem as it is in heterosexual intimate partner relationships—if not a bigger problem. We address the problem in this community whenever possible in this book, but our discussion is hampered by the relatively limited research on this topic and the small number of available programs for this community (Rollè et al., 2018). We hope this book takes a significant step in addressing this problem as a unique aspect of sexual violence on college campuses.

CHAPTER TWO

The Evolution of Title IX

ON JUNE 23, 1972, President Richard Nixon signed into law the Education Amendments of 1972, which expanded the Higher Education Act of 1965, the Vocational Education Act of 1963, and related education legislation to address sexual discrimination. This legislation has come to be known as Title IX.

In its original form, Title IX made no specific statement about athletics. However, the law's greatest initial impact was in creating opportunities for women in high school and college athletic programs. In addition to opening doors for female athletes, it served as another platform for the women's movement, which had been reenergized, in part, by the 1972 passage of Title VII of the Civil Rights Act. Title VII prohibited employment discrimination based on gender (National Women's History Project, n.d.).

Title IX had great success. In 1966 only 16,000 women competed in intercollegiate athletics; by 2001 the number of female athletes in college had jumped to 150,000. In 1971 fewer than 295,000 women were competing in high school sports; in 2001, 2.8 million female high school athletes were participating in competitive sports (Winslow, n.d.).

While this law has been very successful in helping women achieve equal opportunities, new laws and amendments to existing laws have moved the benefits well beyond athletics and employment opportunities. Today, one of the most robust applications of Title IX is in sexual assault and harassment.

Sexual assault and sexual harassment found a home in Title IX through an interesting series of events. During the 1970s and 1980s, women's rights organizations were increasingly dissatisfied with the criminal justice system and its inability or unwillingness to prosecute "he said / she said" or "word against word" cases. So these activists sued the alleged victim's college or university under the Title IX nondiscrimination command, applying it to sexual assault and other forms of sexual violence (United Educators, 2015).

As more and more lawsuits prevailed, educational institutions and Congress had to respond. Colleges were self-imposing stricter sexual misconduct policies, and Congress began passing and enforcing additional federal laws to make women, especially college women, safer. This chapter looks at several laws and their origins to help explain how Title IX came about.

Clery Act

The Jeanne Clery Disclosure of Campus Security Policy and Campus Crime Statistics Act, originally known as Title II of the Student Right-to-Know and Campus Security Act of 1990, was signed into law as an amendment to the Higher Education Act of 1965. It was enacted to increase accountability and transparency of colleges regarding the safety of their students (McCallion, 2014).

Since 1990, new laws have effected change in the Clery Act. A major change occurred in 2008 when the Higher Education Opportunity Act amended the Clery Act by adding a requirement for all colleges and universities to develop and distribute immediate campus emergency response and evacuation procedures. The 2008 act required that colleges report bias-related crimes (hate crimes) in four new categories: larceny, simple assault, intimidation, and destruction/damage/vandalism of property. It also required that campuses with student housing develop and publicize policies for responding to reports of missing students and implement fire safety reporting. The act also required schools to disclose the relationship between campus security and state and local government law enforcement agencies. It required disclosure of the results of disciplinary proceedings to the alleged victim of any crime of violence or nonforcible sex offense.

Violence Against Women Act

The Violence Against Women Act of 1994 (VAWA) was originally part of the Violent Crime Control and Law Enforcement Act. The first comprehensive federal legislation designed to end violence against women, VAWA was developed in response to women's groups that lobbied Congress to protect women on the grounds that the states were not protecting them (Legal Momentum, n.d.).

The law was proposed in 1990 by Senator Joe Biden, then chairman of the Senate Judiciary Committee (Biden, 2014). Prior to this time, violence against a woman who was a voluntary companion was seen as a "family affair" and a lesser crime than one perpetrated against someone by a stranger. Violence against women within a marriage or dating relationship was considered a dark little secret to be dealt with at home. The Judiciary Committee brought in health professionals, advocates, and survivors to testify to Congress about the abuse taking place in American families. Even with this evidence, it took four years to secure sufficient votes to pass the Violence Against Women Act.

Once passed, VAWA provided vast improvements for victims of sexual violence. In its original form, VAWA was designed to strengthen criminal justice responses to domestic violence and sexual assault and increase the availability of services to victims. Specifically, it required a coordinated community response. It strengthened federal penalties for repeat sex offenders and included a federal "rape shield law" intended to prevent sexual offenders from using a victim's past sexual conduct against her or him at trial. VAWA made states enforce protection orders issued by other states. The law made it harder for abusers to use immigration laws to prevent victims from calling authorities. While the law enabled victims to seek civil rights remedies for gender-based crimes, this provision was declared unconstitutional by the US Supreme Court in 2000 (Office on Violence Against Women, 2009).

Congress and women's advocate groups spearheaded three reauthorizations of VAWA, in 2000, 2005, and 2013, that increased the law's scope and its ability to support victims of sexual violence. Each iteration added to programs and funding to support victims and to enhance reporting. The current, and perhaps final, version required higher education institutions to keep more detailed statistics and to provide this information to incoming freshmen. It also clarified when an institution could remove reports of crimes that were unfounded. And it required institutions to develop and provide annual security reports as well as policies on procedures and due process, and to ensure that all individuals conducting these proceedings are appropriately trained.

"Dear Colleague" Letters

A "Dear Colleague" letter (DCL) is a letter sent by a member of a legislative body to all other members, usually to rally support for or opposition to a proposed bill. The letters have a long history. In 1849, Abraham Lincoln sent a DCL to his fellow senators informing them that he planned to introduce a bill abolishing slavery. Congress and many other government departments use this method of communication as a mechanism for informing those concerned about important issues. While these letters may not contain procedures required by law, they do offer strong suggestions that should be taken seriously when attempting to comply with legislation.

Several DCLs have been written related to Title IX. The first was sent in 2006 by the Office for Civil Rights (OCR) of the US Department of Education, with the intent to remind those involved in Title IX oversight of the importance of the issue. This letter also referenced the Revised Sexual Harassment Guidance of 2001 (Office for Civil Rights, 2001) and reminded educational institutions of their responsibility to take immediate steps to prevent sexual harassment and to mitigate its effects when prevention is not possible (Monroe, 2006).

Arguably the most important DCL relating to Title IX was sent by Russlynn Ali, assistant secretary for civil rights, on April 4, 2011. It was a "significant guidance document" intended to provide recipients with information to assist them in meeting their obligations and to provide the public with information about their rights (Ali, 2011). The letter served as a supplement to the 2001 revised guidance published by OCR. It provided practical examples of Title IX compliance as well as proactive efforts schools can take to prevent sexual harassment and violence.

The letter covered a school's obligation to respond to sexual harassment and violence on campus. It stated that if the school knows or reasonably should have known about student-on-student harassment that creates a hostile environment, Title IX requires that the school take immediate action to eliminate the harassment. It also listed the procedural requirements pertaining to sexual harassment and violence that any institution receiving federal financial assistance must follow. Each institution must publish a notice of nondiscrimination, must establish a Title IX coordinator, and must adopt and publish a grievance procedure.

The letter informed schools that the Office for Civil Rights would review all aspects of their grievance policies. Four areas were outlined as needing more explanation, starting with whether the notice of the grievance policy was written in language appropriate for the reader. The second issue was whether the investigation of complaints was adequate, reliable, and impartial. Third, a school's grievance policy should have a designated and prompt time frame. Finally, both parties in a grievance must be notified in writing of the outcome of an investigation.

Additional letters were sent in 2014, 2015, 2016, and 2017, although none had the impact of the letter of 2011, which sent some school administrations into a tailspin, unsure how to comply and feeling overwhelmed. To address these concerns, OCR sent a follow-up letter, "Questions and Answers on Title IX and Sexual Violence" (OCR, 2014), which contained no new regulations or requirements.

In the DCL of 2015, the main focus was to set out guidelines for the selection, responsibilities, and duties of an institution's Title IX coordinator (Lhamon, 2015). In this letter, OCR states that, to avoid conflict of interest, the Title IX coordinator must be independent and must report only to the institution's senior leadership. The coordinator should be full time and have all the necessary training, authority, and time to address all complaints throughout the institution. Where possible and appropriate, multiple coordinators may be appointed. The letter also outlined the responsibilities of the coordinator and stated that he or she must have the full support of the institution.

According to the letter, each coordinator must establish the Title IX email address of TitleIXCoordinator@school.edu. This allows everyone to directly contact the coordinator without use of personal email addresses. The coordinator must be visible to the community through notices of name, title, and contact information and must be trained and knowledgeable in all areas of Title IX compliance.

In the May 13, 2016, DCL, the Office for Civil Rights focused on gender issues (Lhamon and Gupta, 2016). It reminded that Title IX applies to all students regardless of their gender identity and that schools must treat a student's gender identity as his or her "sex" for purposes of administering Title IX. Under this understanding of the law, institutions must not treat transgender students differently than any other student. One of the most important issues of this significant guidance is the requirement that came under the heading of "Sex-Segregated Activities and Facilities." If a school offers sex-segregated activities and facilities, transgender students must be allowed to access facilities and participate in activities consistent with their gender identity.

The final DCL to date was sent February 22, 2017 (Battle and Wheeler, 2017); in this DCL, OCR again addressed transgender issues. This time OCR decided it had gone too far and was withdrawing the guidance reflected in the 2016 letter. The 2017 letter concluded that the guidelines offered in 2016 did not "contain extensive legal analysis or explain how the position was consistent with the expressed language of Title IX, nor did they undergo any formal public process" (p. 1). It added no additional guidance or requirements to the law.

Has Federal Legislation Gone Too Far?

All of these laws would appear to have made the world a much better place for students. However, there are those who say that the federal government has gone too far in its attempt to protect victims of sexual assault, especially on college campuses. Organizations like the Foundation for Individual Rights in Education (FIRE) and the CATO Institute assert that in their attempt to protect women, these laws have limited the rights of others.

These criticisms are not unique; nor have they begun only recently. There have been critics of these laws from the beginning, although in 1972 the original Title IX faced comparatively little controversy. Crafted after the Civil Rights Act of 1964, the law seemed to simply extend the basic civil rights put forth regarding race and sex discrimination (US Government, 1997). It was not until years later that the wisdom of this law was questioned. Many today blame Title IX with limiting sports opportunities for men. The unintended reverse discrimination has caused men's collegiate sports to be decreased or even removed on some campuses in order to achieve or retain equity between men and women. For example, since the law passed in 1972, the number of men's wrestling teams has dropped by more than four hundred and fifty, with only about three hundred schools now having teams (Sommers, 2014).

Much like with Title IX in 1972, few objected to the Clery Act when it passed in 1990. At the time, it was critically needed to bring greater awareness about campus violence and help families and students make informed choices. As amendments were passed, however, the reporting became a challenge for colleges, given the complexity and often conflicting requirements of the reports (McNeal, 2007). In 2002, California state schools reported that even within the state's own system, applying the law was proving difficult (Van Airsdale, 2002), since the schools possess a range of attributes. While the schools differ in traditional areas such as size and location, they also differ in terms of the act's relevant issues such as an independent campus security system or reliance on local police departments.

After the 1998 amendments went into effect, many campus administrators were unclear about their impact and whether the burden of the additional reporting might decrease the amount of money and time available for preventing the crimes (Woodhams, 1999). Other concerns were whether reports given in confidence to counselors should be included (Burd, 1999). At the time, counselors said campus police were rarely satisfied with just the statistical data—they wanted details to help investigate the crime—but the counselors thought this information was considered privileged and not open to being shared.

The Violence Against Women Act has had its critics from the start. In the late 1990s, Chief Justice William Rehnquist and representatives from several other judicial organizations led opposition to passing the law, saying it would bring too many family disputes into federal courts where they did not belong and where they would overwhelm the system. Among judicial organizations, only the National Association of Women Judges supported the civil rights remedy.

This opposition has not diminished over the years. When the 2013 amendments to the law were being considered, 22 Republican senators voted against them. Their objections ranged from questions about whether the money could be better spent to stop violence against women to concerns about granting tribal jurisdiction to prosecute non–Native Americans who commit crimes while on reservations (Ball, 2013).

Compliance with all of the legislation, especially the complexity of the reporting, remains a concern. Another angle that has not been resolved is that much of the reporting is left up to college administrators to interpret. Different colleges may place similar crimes committed on their campuses into different categories, meaning that comparing reports from the colleges is like comparing apples and oranges. Compliance has become so difficult that an entire industry of training organizations has developed. Organizations like the Association of Title IX Administrators (ATIXA), CypherWorx, and Thomas Reuters, to name a few, have started up or have adapted to respond to the increasing need for training. Schools have a range of options, from private onsite training to large, open-to-anyone regional sessions.

Even the 2011 DCL has not gone uncriticized. FIRE has criticized it for several reasons, possibly the most important being the "preponderance of the evidence" standard to determine the guilt of a perpetrator (Creeley, 2012). FIRE believes that given the seriousness of some of these crimes, a higher standard is needed. A jury should be more than 50.01 percent certain that the accused actually committed the crime.

FIRE advocates the more commonly used "beyond a reasonable doubt," the standard that would be used in a court trial for many of the crimes that would be investigated by the school.

In the 2011 letter, OCR established the requirement that if a school allows the accused to appeal the verdict of a university judicial process, it must also allow the accusing student to appeal a verdict. FIRE says this is a serious threat to due process. If the accused has already been found not guilty, this requirement may allow him or her to be retried for the same alleged crimes.

The CATO Institute believed that OCR went too far in the 2013 DCL in limiting due process. The charge from CATO was that pressure from the federal government had become so strong that campus administrators felt the need to react quickly—in some cases too quickly. A well-known example is the *Rolling Stone* magazine story of the gang rape of a University of Virginia student at a Phi Kappa Psi fraternity party (Erdely, 2014).

Within hours of publication of the *Rolling Stone* article, and in response solely to the article, UVA's president had contacted Virginia's governor and the Charlottesville police chief (Quizon, 2015). By the next day, Phi Kappa Psi voluntarily suspended its charter activities, and within a few days the university's president suspended all fraternity and sorority activity for the remainder of the semester. All of this was done without any university verification of the charges made by the supposed victim of the attack. As the facts continued to unfold, the accuracy of the story came into question. Turns out the person named "Jackie" in the article made up the story to gain the attention of a fellow student who had rebuffed her romantic overtures (Shapiro, 2016). The pressure to respond to unsubstantiated allegations was so strong that administrators felt compelled to act rather than be held in violation of Title IX.

In the UVA case and others, the reams of red tape involved in compliance has forced administrators to overlook common sense in conducting investigations. As noted above, even OCR decided it may have gone too far, and it retracted some of the more overreaching issues in its DCL of 2016. While there is dispute whether this change of heart was spurred by a change in presidential administrations, it is quite challenging for institutions that a "Dear Colleague" letter can move them down a difficult and very controversial path only to have the letter's guidance countermanded just eleven months later.

Safe Campus Act and Fair Campus Act

To address concerns about the limitations to due process, two bills were proposed in late 2015. The first, House Resolution 3403, Safe Campus Act, addressed three major issues. The first and most controversial was that it would require schools to report any allegation of sexual violence to local law enforcement after obtaining written consent from the alleged victim. It also would prohibit schools from investigating an allegation until they had received the law enforcement report (Salmon, 2015).

The second issue addressed was due process: the Act would require a formal hearing before students could be disciplined for sexual violence. Schools would be required to give all parties two weeks' notice before any hearing could be held. Both the accused and the alleged victim would have the right to an attorney, access to all evidence, and the right to cross-examine witnesses.

Finally, the bill addressed sexual violence education. It would require schools to educate all adult and student staff on sexual assault and the reporting of incidents. The bill strongly suggested that schools provide sexual assault education to all students.

Many believed that while the proposed law did much to address due process, it went too far in requiring the incident be reported to law enforcement. Critics believed the mandated involvement of the criminal justice system would force even more assaults to go unreported by the victims. To address these concerns, House Resolution 3408, Fair Campus Act, was proposed just five days after House Resolution 3403. The only difference between the resolutions was the removal of the required reporting to law enforcement.

On November 11, 2015, both bills were sent to the House Subcommittee on Higher Education and Workforce Training. As of April 2020 they appeared to be still there. Under the current administration, legislation may be proposed or passed to rein in OCR Title IX oversight. While a reduction in the forward progress of the laws protecting sexual assault victims would be a mistake, simplifying the process would likely benefit institutions and students alike.

Safe Transfer Act of 2016

Another proposed bill currently under review, the Safe Transfer Act (Speier, 2016), came before the House in December 2016. It would require a transcript notation for students who are found responsible for violations of Title IX policies on sexual harassment and assault and who seek to transfer to other institutions. Among the bill's supporters are the National Organization for Women, End Rape on Campus Now, and ATIXA (Hendershott, 2017).

ATIXA came out with a statement supporting the bill only days after it was proposed, stating that transcripts were the easiest place to indicate sexually based behavior that an institution might want to consider when making admission decisions (ATIXA, 2016). Others considered the bill one more step in the breakdown of due process on college campuses. Critics said it violates the Family Education Rights and Privacy Act by failing to ensure that the rights of the accused are protected (Hendershott, 2016).

Those opposing the bill say that more than just a student's due process is at risk. More and more universities are being successfully sued by male students who were dismissed from the school for sexual crimes (New, 2015). Male students are winning large judgments against institutions that have violated their due process. The Safe Transfer Act is just one more step in limiting the rights of the accused and opening the door to more legal filings.

Campus Accountability and Safety Act

The bipartisan Campus Accountability and Safety Act, proposed on April 5, 2017, reintroduces a bill proposed in July 2015. It aims to combat sexual assault on college and university campuses by protecting students, promoting equity, and strengthening accountability and transparency (McCaskill, 2017). It would change the way institutions of higher learning address and report sexual assaults and would safeguard victims and accused students. Key provisions would establish new campus support services and require fairness in all disciplinary processes. The bill would ensure minimum training standards for campus personnel and create new transparency requirements by surveying all American colleges and universities about their experiences with sexual violence. The bill would require institutions to enter into a memorandum of understanding with local law enforcement agencies to delineate responsibilities and share information. It also would implement stiffer penalties for institutions with Clery Act violations.

According to Senator Kirsten Gillibrand, one of the bill's eight coauthors, the proposed bill is designed to reduce the risk to women on college campuses through transparency and accountability and to flip the incentives that currently reward institutions for keeping sexual assault in the shadows. As of April 2020 the bill had not been sent to committee, pending a budget estimate from the Congressional Budget Office.

State and Local Laws

In addition to federal law, colleges and universities must also comply with state and local laws. While these laws may not be in opposition with one another, complying with all of them can be challenging, especially for states that have become victim advocates. These states offer more laws aimed at protecting sexual assault victims than other states do.

A report by NASPA (Student Affairs Administrators in Higher Education) and the Educational Commission of the United States provided insight into what state lawmakers are considering (Morse, Sponsler, and Fulton, 2015). The report categorized bills being proposed in twenty-eight states into four categories: affirmative consent, local law enforcement, transcript notation, and legal counsel.

Between 2013 and 2015, sixteen states attempted to pass laws addressing affirmative consent. Of those states, California, Hawaii, Illinois, and

New York have enacted consent laws. California, Illinois, and New York's laws look to codify what welcomed sexual behavior is and encourages institutions of higher education to do the same. The standard presented by the laws is that a lack of protest or resistance does not constitute consent. In California and New York, consent must also be consciously and knowingly given. All three of these states' laws include a provision stating that a person incapacitated because of the use of drugs or alcohol cannot give consent.

Hawaii took a different path. Its consent law created a task force to make recommendations on the University of Hawaii's policy regarding domestic violence, dating violence, sexual assault, and stalking. The consent law defines the charge of the task force and the composition of the task force, and it requires the task force to consider the campus definition of consent when reviewing the university's policy.

Laws stipulating the role of local law enforcement address the responsibility of postsecondary institutions to inform sexual assault victims of their right to report the crime to law enforcement. California, Minnesota, New York, and Virginia have passed laws in this area, with Minnesota and New York affirming the right of sexual assault victims to decide whether to refer the crime to law enforcement.

California and Virginia established requirements for reporting the crime to law enforcement. California's law requires that postsecondary institutions adopt policies to ensure the reporting of sexual assault, violent crimes, and hate crimes to law enforcement. Virginia law differs in that it requires the crime to be reported to the Title IX coordinator, who then reports it to a committee that has as one of its members a representative of law enforcement. This committee decides whether to disclose the crime to local law enforcement.

Laws in the third category, transcript notification, address whether to make a notation of serious violations of campus codes of conduct on student transcripts. New York and Virginia have enacted laws in this area. In these two states, if a student has been suspended or expelled for a serious violation of the institution's code of conduct, that fact must go on the student's transcript. A notation must also be included if the student withdrew from the institution while under investigation for such a violation. Both laws address the conditions under which the notation should be removed, which typically include that a student's finding of responsibility has been vacated or that the student has served his or her suspension.

Concerning the fourth category, Arkansas, North Carolina, and North Dakota all have laws that address the role of legal counsel in an institution's disciplinary hearing, but they do not articulate a clear definition of the role.

Navigating the Muddy Waters of Title IX Compliance

With the requirement to comply with the Clery Act and Title IX and to investigate every charge filed, how does an institution protect its reputation or have any hope of filling seats in the upcoming academic year?

Take, for example, the book *Missoula*, in which Jon Krakauer exposed the dark side of classic sexual assault cover-ups (2015). Was the University of Montana's Missoula campus the only one in the country that was guilty of such behavior? Of course not. It was just the unlucky campus to be highlighted in Krakauer's book. Reports keep emerging on the measures schools will take to keep the public from knowing all that happens on campus.

It's hard to blame the schools for trying to protect themselves. Universities are always balancing the desire to do the right thing with the desire to create the perfect image for families who are about to send their children there. Schools want to appeal to families who in turn want to be sure that they have done everything possible to ensure the safety of their children.

Informed families and students look for schools with low crime incidence reports. And while high-crime reports might indicate full compliance with the law, consumers may not recognize the difference. To them, higher numbers simply indicate more crime. Thus, schools do everything possible to fill their Clery Act reports with positive numbers (deHahn, 2017). Some schools have delayed filing the reports for years. When the Jerry Sandusky scandal broke in November 2011, Penn State's

Clery Act implementation plan was still in draft form (Franklin, Taylor, and Beytagh, 2017). Twenty-one years after the act was passed, Penn State was still not in compliance.

Higher education institutions are heavily criticized for failing to even consider the conflict of interest that arises over the reporting of campus crimes (Franklin, Taylor, and Beytagh, 2017). There is little self-assessment and there are scant procedures in place to ensure that these conflicts are minimized. Unlike in other professions, no ethical rules of conduct guide individuals making these difficult, conflicted decisions.

A recent study of thirty-one four-year universities of ten thousand or more students (Yung, 2015) showed that reporting noncompliance is a problem that goes well beyond the big cases that reach the media. The study examined the crime reports of these schools before, during, and after a US Department of Education (DOE) audit of Clery Act violations. Findings showed that university reports of sexual assaults rose by approximately 44 percent during the audit period. In light of these findings, the DOE should increase the number of audits done on institutions of higher learning (Yung, 2015). Clearly, the audits drove the schools to do more accurate reporting. Increasing the fines charged to schools that are found in violation of reporting laws might also help resolve any conflict of interest.

As the Sandusky case at Penn State demonstrates, hiding facts can hurt a school's reputation. In 2014, Baylor University in Waco, Texas, was listed as a top school in terms of its Clery Act statistics (New, 2015). Then, just a few months later, news broke that one of its football players was indicted on two counts of sexual assault (Mervosh, 2017). The internal investigation that followed revealed a culture of cover-up by the athletic department. This was followed by an investigation by the Texas Rangers. Student athletes were found guilty of rape, and the Office for Civil Rights announced in late 2016 that it would begin its own investigation (Watkins, 2016).

While compliance with the laws regulating campus safety is critical, it's easy to see why administrators are obsessed with impression management. As long as reporting crimes on campus impacts enrollment goals, colleges will be tempted to present statistics that put the school in the best light possible. It may be best to let families know that no campus is completely safe, that crime will happen, and that taking all forms of sexual assault seriously is a much more important standard in a school than a squeaky-clean appearance.

So how do we create safe campuses? How do administrators balance the needs of students, the needs of the victim, the needs of the accused, and the needs of the institution? We propose a model of prevention that takes all of these stakeholders into account and is designed to provide the best possible environment for everyone.

University Protection, Prevention, and Treatment Model

Legal protections for women provide the context within which universities and individuals function. Both universities and individuals must conduct themselves within this context, responding in ways that we characterize as university protection and individual prevention and treatment. Protection, prevention, and treatment are the core elements of our model. The center stem of the model presents the life history of campus sexual assault. Campus sexual assaults are chronic health problems, not accidents, sometimes even having a contagious dimension.

As with all chronic disorders, with campus sexual assault, understanding its life history is the essential first step upon which university protection and individual prevention programs can be designed. Our model of the campus sexual assault problem along with university protection and individual prevention programs is presented in figure 2.1(which is referred to here and in subsequent chapters). It includes surveillance indicators as well, and is drawn from the public health notions of prevention that are anchored in evidence-based epidemiology (see Quick et al., 2013 for a similar model focused on the chronic problem of organizational stress).

Gretchen Carlson (2017) points out the challenges and limitations of the legal system when it comes to the problem of sexual harassment on campus, in the workplace, and in the military. Campus sexual assault is a leadership challenge for university administrators. These leaders

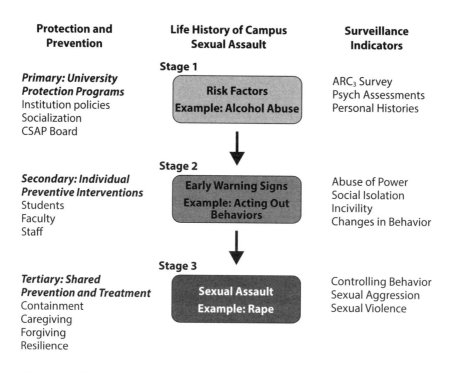

Protection and Prevention	Life History of Campus Sexual Assault	Surveillance Indicators
Stage 1		
Primary: University Protection Programs Institution policies Socialization CSAP Board	**Risk Factors** **Example: Alcohol Abuse**	ARC₃ Survey Psych Assessments Personal Histories
Stage 2		
Secondary: Individual Preventive Interventions Students Faculty Staff	**Early Warning Signs** **Example: Acting Out Behaviors**	Abuse of Power Social Isolation Incivility Changes in Behavior
Stage 3		
Tertiary: Shared Prevention and Treatment Containment Caregiving Forgiving Resilience	**Sexual Assault** **Example: Rape**	Controlling Behavior Sexual Aggression Sexual Violence

Figure 2.1. University Protection, Prevention, and Treatment Model

have a direct responsibility for the health and well-being of all individuals within their domains which is coupled with the personal responsibility of those individuals for their own health and well-being. Ensuring health and well-being is a joint problem of universities and individuals, a community and public health problem. Further, university leaders are not typically expert in campus sexual assault, especially compared to the expertise that is available.

Life History of Campus Sexual Assault

As seen in figure 2.1, campus sexual assaults begin with risk factors. Risk factors do not predetermine that a sexual assault will occur, but they set the conditions that increase the probability. Chapter 3 explores these risk factors, including cultural myths (which are untrue), risky behaviors (such as alcohol and substance abuse), and incomplete brain development in males (not complete until age 25). In Stage 1 of the life history there is not a problem, just the conditions for a problem to arise.

Stage 2 reveals warning signs of more serious issues, from attempted rape to rape and murder. Inappropriate comments and discomfiting language fall in the category of low-intensity sexual assault. Overt but nonverbal behaviors, more early indicators, include acting out and social isolation. Make no mistake, there is a problem at this stage—but the signals can be easily ignored or overlooked. They should not be.

Stage 3 in figure 2.1 accounts for the full dimension of sexual assault, including attempted rape, rape, fondling, and, worst case, fatality. Stage 3 likely will involve a hostile verbal environment with threatening language designed to intimidate and coerce. This environment flashes a red STOP sign; it is a dangerous situation for any person and demands an immediate exit, by force if necessary.

Primary Protection and Prevention: University Protection Programs

The preferred point of intervention from a public health perspective is always primary prevention. Primary prevention aims to eliminate or at least manage the risk. Figure 2.1 indicates three university protection programs: institutional policies, socialization, and a Campus Sexual Assault Prevention (CSAP) Board.

An institutional policy concerning campus sexual assault that lacks clear enforcement mechanisms has no teeth and can be ignored with impunity. Where enforcement mechanisms are in place, individuals know the consequences for failure to comply. While it would be ideal if all university personnel embraced the spirit of a campus sexual assault policy, in reality there will be a small percentage of individuals who will not comply.

In addition to clear policy guidance, universities should have strong newcomer socialization practices that imbue the university's ideals and positive rituals in those who join the community. Embracing university culture helps individuals become aware insiders—contagious agents who spread the word. The socialization process should include plentiful information about university policies and practices regarding sexual assault. Referral agents (members of the community who refer those in need to the professional experts who can help or conduct triage) are an essential component of a healthy campus; while the burden of suffering from this problem has been borne primarily by women, it is not women alone who should have the burden of response.

Campus sexual assaults are not individual problems, and thus a collective response is required. We recommend that this response take the form of a Campus Sexual Assault Prevention Board composed of interdisciplinary professionals (first responders and security forces) and campus community members (athletes and coaches and student-led groups). The Title IX coordinator is in position to be the best leader for the team. Chapter 4 elaborates on the concept of a CSAP Board and how to develop a secure, safe campus culture.

Secondary Protection and Prevention:
Individual Preventive Interventions

Even a strong campus culture and a comprehensive university protection program are never sufficient without individual prevention, at the heart of which lie education and training. Respect for individuals and appreciation of human variance—individual differences and gender differences—are not instinctual skills but acquired skills that develop through structured experience and disciplined practice. Three chapters in the book address these learned skills in the university's major constituencies of students, faculty, and staff.

Chapter 5, which may well be the most important chapter in this book, looks at the educational and training needs of undergraduate and graduate students. Data from a University of Texas System survey of more than two hundred thousand students show meaningful differences between the experiences and vulnerabilities of undergraduate students, on the one hand, and graduate and professional school students, on the other, the mean difference in the ages of these populations being about five years. These are consequential years in the development of young women and men.

Chapter 6 focuses on the education and training of faculty, who have a uniquely vital bearing on a student's college experience. The power differential between faculty and students is consequential as a risk factor. Socializing faculty to use their positions of authority for good is a crucial aspect of acculturating them in a large social system.

Chapter 7 addresses how the role of staff in identifying and preventing campus sexual assault will vary by the staff member's location and function within the university and its myriad departments. Universities are complex systems with variations in norms and patterns of behavior. Anyone can tell that a river runs downstream, but it takes a master of the river to know its backwaters and underwater dangers. Colleges and university staff members need to become masters of their university.

Tertiary Protection and Prevention:
Shared Prevention and Treatment

A university can do everything right, and still bad things happen. The university community must be prepared for the worst. Figure 2.1 includes a third level of preventive response, where the burden is shared by the university and the individuals within it. The eleven to thirteen members of the CSAP Board play the central role in orchestrating tertiary prevention responses. The Title IX coordinator as team leader engages the appropriate members following the report of an incident.

Figure 2.1 depicts a four-step protocol for tertiary prevention and treatment intervention. The first two steps, or phase one, must be rapid. They are (1) containment of the perpetrator and securing the venue of the incident and (2) caregiving for victims and bystanders. Chapter 8 discusses in detail these two steps.

Phase two occurs over an extended time and includes (3) forgiveness for all concerned, not just for those involved in the specific incident, and (4) resilience and recovery for continued healing. Crisis events come with time-lag effects that must not be ignored. Adolf Meyer, the pioneering psychiatrist-in-chief of Johns Hopkins Hospital and distinguished professor at the medical school in the early 1900s, found a marked risk for health disorders from twelve to eighteen months following a major life change. A rape would certainly qualify. Chapter 9 explores the details of this second phase in the process of healing. We discuss three institutional cases in chapter 10.

The burden of suffering costs, both emotional and financial, escalate markedly at Stage 3 in the life history of sexual assaults. The burden of response costs associated with designing and implementing protection and prevention programs at Stages 1 and 2 likely outweigh the burden of suffering costs in those first two stages. However, accepting the burden of response costs up front and making an investment aimed at reducing or eliminating sexual assault incidents can pay significant dividends when Stage 3 issues must be addressed.

The financial costs range from costs for medical, psychological, and security personnel to litigation costs when legal action ensues. The emotional burdens range from pain and suffering for survivors to self-recrimination and guilt on the part of offenders. The moral and humanitarian argument for tertiary prevention and treatment goes beyond the utilitarian cost argument.

Surveillance Indicators: Based on the Evidence

The right-hand column in figure 2.1 features surveillance indicators. These indicators are discussed in chapter 4. To use public health notions of prevention it is essential to pay attention to any evidence of these indicators. Public health is based not on theory but on data. The underlying science for public health is epidemiology, which is the study of disease epidemics. Epidemiologists and public health professionals work from the data and use surveillance mechanisms for screening environments and individuals to ensure they are healthy. The same principles should be applied to the problem of campus sexual assault.

The surveillance indictors in figure 2.1 are among the data-based evidence universities can monitor to identify, ameliorate, and eliminate risks. Identifying the 1 to 3 percent of high-risk individuals who should be monitored over time is a good place to start (Quick, McFadyen, and Nelson, 2014) in activating tertiary prevention and treatment intervention.

Understanding how we begin to create safe campuses is but a first step. We must do all we can to prevent sexual violence on campuses. Understanding how to create a culture of no tolerance through education and training is critical. Also critical is accepting that we will never be able to prevent all violence. With this acceptance comes the responsibility to create programs to support and heal both the victim and the accused.

CHAPTER THREE

Challenges to Protecting Women from Sexual Assault and Its Aftermath

---

THERE ARE MANY CHALLENGES to protecting women from sexual assault and supporting them after it happens. The culture in which we live still, to some degree, accepts rape myths and a mentality of blame the victim. Our culture also creates barriers to reporting assaults and understanding the definition of true consent. For college students, our culture creates some unique situational factors. All of these challenges are discussed in this chapter.

Rape Myths

In attempts to protect women from the abuse of sexual assault and rape, perhaps the biggest challenge has been to convince investigators that the allegations were real. And why would law enforcement personnel, people devoted to protecting, not believe the victims? There are several theories, with the history of rape and sexual assault in the United States providing clues.

The word *rape* comes from the Latin *rapere*, which means to steal, seize, or carry away. The word describes stealing, not violating. The first rape laws upheld that definition of rape—they were established to protect the property of men, not to protect women (Brownmiller, 1975). At the time these laws were established, women were considered property. If a wife was raped, the woman had not been violated; rather, the property of her husband had been stolen. And a daughter being raped devalued the father's property. If a woman did not have the protection of a husband or father, she had virtually no protection against sexual abuse under the law.

Slavery in the United States enhanced the devaluation of women, especially women of color. No laws in the nineteenth century viewed the rape of a black woman to be a crime (Maschke, 1997). And later, when sexual assault laws were enacted, they were written to protect white women from being assaulted by black men, not by their white husbands or acquaintances.

As society continued to develop, sexual assault began to be seen as more than just a violation of men's rights. However, the concept of rape was still limited. Prior to the 1930s, rape was seen only as a sex crime where women were always the victims and men were always the perpetrators. During the next three decades, a shift in perceptions of sexual assault began. Perpetrators of rape and sexual assault were no longer deemed criminal but instead were deemed mentally ill (Maschke, 1997). Men committing these acts were no longer put in jail; instead, they were sent to mental institutions where they could receive treatment as "sexual psychopaths."

In the late 1960s into the 1970s, feminism took on the issue of rape. It was through this movement that the concept of a rape culture came into focus. Feminists found that changing laws was not easy, but changing society's perception of the situation was even more difficult.

The term *rape culture* was coined in the 1970s when feminists applied it to the whole of America (Smith, 2004). It is generally used to define false beliefs used to shift the blame from perpetrators to victims (Suarez and Gadalla, 2010). Feminists worked to bring awareness to the prevalence of rape and dispel the idea that rape, incest, and wife beating rarely happened (Rutherford, 2011). The idea of a rape culture posited that rape was "normal" in the United States as an extreme outgrowth of its misogynistic and sexist society. Society began to perceive rape as a crime of sex rather than a crime of violence, and moved away from seeing it as a mental health issue. The focus was now on male dominance, intimidation, and control (Brownmiller, 1975; Maschke, 1997; Chasteen, 2001). This rape culture manifests itself through the acceptance of rape as an everyday occurrence and even a male prerogative (Parenti, 2005). Reluctance to go against patriarchal norms influences the way police and institutions investigate sexual assault. A rape culture also underpins rape myths.

One of the earliest works that addressed rape myths, Susan Brownmiller's *Against Our Will: Men, Women, and Rape* (1975), counters three dominant myths. The first myth dispelled was that there was a stereotypical rape victim. Brownmiller affirmed that any woman could be a rape victim regardless of age, race, or status. The second was that all rapists were evil or mentally ill men. Finally, Brownmiller posited that rape took many forms and was not just the classic case of a violent forcible assault by a stranger.

These ideas challenged the prevailing concepts that rape victims were always young, careless, beautiful, or sexually promiscuous, and that this profile invited the male, "unable to control himself," who raped them. It also challenged the view that rape was perpetrated by a stranger. Now society was confronted with the idea that all women were subject to being raped and not just by a stranger but by husbands and acquaintances. It was not a mindset change that was welcomed.

Blaming the Victim

Laying responsibility for rape with the victim for reasons such as "she was dressed too sexy," "she should not have been at that party," or even "she didn't really put up a fight" was common before the 1970s (and even later). Men who buy into this myth use it to justify male sexual violence (Lonsway and Fitzgerald, 1994). Women who accept this concept often do so to help deny personal vulnerability.

Two very disruptive outcomes emerge from living in a blame-the-victim environment, beginning with revictimization. When society blames the victim, it is saying that she deserved what she got. This leads many victims to accept responsibility for the assault. So not only is the victim suffering from the assault itself, but her suffering is now compounded with the guilt of feeling responsible that it happened.

Just because a woman wears a sexy dress, she has not asked to be sexually assaulted. But we're not suggesting that we excuse all behaviors of the victims. Everyone, victims of sexual assault included, must examine his or her role in any situation to ensure not being victimized again. Victims should ask themselves what they could have done or should have done. This knowledge will help them to protect themselves in the future.

The second outcome of the blame the victim mentality is it allows perpetrators to deny responsibility for their actions (if we blame the victim, men are not responsible). Before 1994, with the passage of the Violence Against Women Act's federal rape shield laws, the standard practice to defend a man charged with sexual assault was to attack his accuser (Swiss, 2014). Defense attorneys would dig up every aspect of a victim's sexual history and portray her as promiscuous and therefore a willing participant. This defense probably got many men acquitted. By failing to hold men accountable, however, this legal defense let all of society down: women by not protecting them, and men by allowing the rape myths to continue and behaviors to go unpunished.

Acquaintance and Spousal Rape

Rape myths held that rapes were perpetrated by violent strangers or people with mental illness. Anything that happened between a husband and wife, a dating couple, or even friends was consensual. Until these ideas were challenged, women had few options when it came to protecting themselves from the men in their lives. Working under the concept of women as property, society did not see spousal beating as a crime until 1920, and spousal rape was not a crime until the mid-1970s. These ideas were changed through a lot of hard work by early feminist researchers, feminist organizations, and the actions of women who brought the issue of rape to light after a sexual assault crisis in their own lives.

Yvonne Wonrow, Inez Garcia, and Joann Little each brought attention to the concept of resisting rape when she killed either her sexual assailant or her child's sexual assailant and went to prison for defending herself or her child (Thuma, 2015). The cases were embraced by feminist groups and civil rights activists to bring the issues of spousal abuse and sexual assault to the front of societal awareness.

The attention raised by these cases along with continued work by feminist groups led to the first rape crisis centers opening in 1972. Out of this awareness campaign also came groundbreaking research showing that most rapes were committed not by violent strangers but by spouses, boyfriends, family members, and acquaintances (Estrich, 1987).

Law Enforcement and Rape

While society's understanding of sexual assault issues has come a long way since the 1970s, we have not eliminated the rape myth biases. The persistence of these biases can be a major issue in the very beginning of any sexual assault investigation. This is the time when others' recognition that an offense has been committed is critical and a belief in rape myths could limit an investigation. Do the police investigators think the case "unfounded"? Do they believe the victim's story (Spohn and Tellis, 2012)? Police who believe rape myths can be led to label a case as unfounded if the victim knows the perpetrator, there is no physical injury, use of alcohol or drugs, or a history of mental illness (Kerstetter, 1990). Acceptance of rape myths is particularly challenging for investigations of sexual assault on college campuses, because most charges of sexual misconduct will be against someone the victim knows. Investigators who are biased by rape myths will compromise the investigation.

Over the past few decades, existing laws have been refined and new laws created to protect women and put perpetrators in jail. Even so, the percentage of reported rapes has changed very little since the mid-1990s (US Department of Justice, 2016). In 1995 only 29 percent of rapes and sexual assaults were reported to police. Reporting reached a high of 59 percent in 2003, but seven years later only 32 percent of rapes and sexual assaults were reported to police. In 2016, according to the US Department of Justice (2017), only 230 of every 1,000 sexual assaults are reported to police. Of these 230 reported cases, only 46 arrests will be made and only 9 will be referred to the prosecutor (Federal Bureau of Investigation, 2017; Office of Justice Programs, 2017). Only 5 cases will have a felony conviction. Only 4.6 people will be incarcerated (FBI, 2017; Office of Justice Programs, 2017).

This low reporting, trial, and conviction rate has several causes. Women choose not to report for reasons that have been well documented and are beyond the scope of this book. (See Jones et al., 2009, and Spencer, Stith, Durtschi, and Toews, 2017, for a discussion of why college women do not report.) For reported sexual assaults, the roadblock of the investigating law enforcement is one of the main reasons so few reports result in trials and convictions. Many male (and fewer female) police officers still buy into aspects of the rape myth (Rich and Seffrin, 2012). And their acceptance of these myths influences their attitude toward rape victims and about whether a report is "real."

The number of false rape allegations is estimated to be between 4 and 8 percent of all reported rapes (Lonsway, Srchabault, and Lisak, 2009). Yet, as noted above, law enforcement continues to arrest only a small percent of subjects for every 1,000 reported rapes (FBI, 2017; Office of Justice Programs, 2017) and many reported sexual assault cases are determined by police to be unfounded (Yung, 2017).

According to the FBI's Uniform Crime Reporting Program, crimes should only be classified as unfounded if after investigation the case is determined to be false or baseless—in other words, if it is determined that no crime was committed (Uniform Crime Reporting / FBI, 2013). Uninvestigated cases of sexual assault are regularly reported as unfounded, however (Yung, 2014).

Politics, personal factors, and the culture influence law enforcement to call a case unfounded (Yung, 2014). Police are pressured by the public and its fear of crime. They also feel pressure to reduce crime rates, because crime statistics often are used to determine officers' raises and promotions. Finally, law enforcement officers are subject to cultural forces. According to Yung, these forces function in subtle ways. While manipulating data for political reasons is clear and intentional, the cultural forces "operate within a larger cultural framework that is hostile to the stories of rape victims" (Yung, 2014, p. 1218). Police offices, as members of society, follow that cultural norm, buy into the rape myths, and do not believe the victims.

One way to mitigate the effects of the acceptance of rape myths is to include more women in the interview process. Although some women still believe rape myths and continue to blame the victim, significantly more men than women do (Suarez and Gadalla, 2010; Hockett, Smith, Klausing, and Saucier, 2016). Female officers have lower rape myth acceptance than do their male counterparts (Rich and Seffirn, 2012). While there are male officers who can be unbiased and whose strong interview skills produce valid outcomes, on average female officers will be more effective investigating a rape claim. But there is a problem, in that there are few women in law enforcement.

In 2018, approximately 12.6 percent of all federal law enforcement officers were women (Federal Bureau of Investigation, 2018). The number for local law enforcement is even more dismal. In 2013, women accounted for approximately 13 percent of local law enforcement (Crooke, 2013). The percentages of women are even lower in the upper ranks of most police departments. Which means that, more often than not, it's men who conduct the investigations.

This challenge also affects investigations conducted on college campuses. Campus security officers have the same rape myth acceptance problem, and they are mostly male, even at predominantly female schools (Oehme, Stern, and Mennicke, 2014). As noted above, about 30 percent of those in the general population who are sexually assaulted report it to the authorities. But only about 20 percent of college students report an assault (Office of Justice Programs, 2014). Low reporting figures mean that creating a more comfortable reporting environment is critical—especially on college campuses.

Barriers to Reporting

Accurate reporting of sexual assault and sexual violence is essential for three reasons:

1. determining the extent of the public health problem through public health surveillance,
2. protecting victims and reducing risk to others within the community, and
3. identifying possible serial or repeat offenders.

But victims face both personal and societal barriers to reporting. Removing the barriers involves a two-step process. First, identifying the underlying psychosocial forces that keep these barriers in place (what supports the status quo?), then removing the barriers. The barriers to reporting include denial (unacknowledged rape), emotional vulnerability, social threat, fear of consequences, structural ambiguities, process ambiguities, and social stigma.

Denial

Wilson and Miller (2016) found that many sexual violence survivors do not label their experiences as rape. Rather, they use more benign labels, such as "bad sex" or "miscommunication." Relabeling is a form of denial about what really happened. If a survivor does not tell himself or herself the truth, then it is not reasonable to expect the survivor to "report" something that "did not happen." To estimate the mean prevalence of unacknowledged rape, Wilson and Miller (2016) conducted a meta-analysis using PsycINFO, PubMED, and PILOT data that reported percentage of unacknowledged rape that occurred since age 14 of female survivors. The moderator variables were mean participant age, recruitment source, rape definition, and unacknowledged rape definition. The researchers found twenty-eight studies with thirty independent samples that contained 5,917 female rape survivors. The results yielded an overall weighted mean of 60.4 percent unacknowledged rapes, with a significantly higher prevalence among college students than among noncollege survivors. Well over half of all female rape survivors do not acknowledge that they have been raped. In interviewing survivors, researchers recommend using behaviorally descriptive items about sexual contact rather than terms such as *rape* that may allow for individual interpretation and open the door to denial.

Emotional Vulnerability

While Taylor and her colleagues (2013) established that women have a stronger system for tending and befriending in the face of danger, stress, and trauma, some individuals will not open up or allow themselves to be vulnerable given the pain and suffering already experienced. The victim may withdraw from reliving the incident, which reporting requires a person to do. Establishing an empathetic connection and creating a psychologically and emotionally safe context in which to report can increase a victim's willingness to report. Confidentiality underscores this process.

Social Threat

Offenders who commit sexual violence will not want these acts known, especially where they meet the threshold of criminal acts. Bazelon (2017) and Krakauer (2015) explored cases where male offenders directed social threats at female victims which were designed to discourage reporting. Social threats go to the heart of the power and control dynamic of the sexual assault problem. Rather than being primarily a sexual problem, sexual assault is a problem of power, control, and manipulation. Social threats are a form of coercive power that are effective only when the offender can control the social environment. Restraining offenders and incapacitating their power to threaten is one response but can only be effective when the potential threat is known. The alternative is for victims to have, or be offered, social support so they are not as susceptible to these threats. Social attachments provide both strength and defense against the offender. Thus the reporting of sexual assaults becomes a powerful tool to use as a shield against offenders. Factual reporting of events is not itself an aggressive response to the wrong.

Other Barriers

In addition to these barriers to reporting, there are at least four others to consider. One is the fear of consequences associated with reporting a sexual assault. Offenders are unlikely to report what they have done due to the fear of criminal or other punitive consequences. This fear incentivizes the offender not to report. From the victim's perspective, there may also be fear of consequences: for example, subsequent attack from the offender. Another barrier is the structural ambiguity that may exist, including in a university, as to how and to whom one should report a sexual assault. Process ambiguities are still another barrier, where there are no clear markers for what happens after reporting the event. Process ambiguities can present a barrier for the victim and also for a third party. Finally, social stigma can be a barrier that incentivizes both the victim and the offender to keep the incident private. This barrier is especially prevalent among student athletes.

Consent

One of the most confusing aspects of managing sexual assault anywhere including on college campuses is understanding sexual consent. This challenge exists for students, faculty, staff, police, and administrators. Consent used to be understood as a person not saying no. Today what constitutes consent is hotly debated.

Most people agree that affirmative acknowledgement of agreement or confirmative consent is needed, but everyone understanding and agreeing what constitutes confirmative consent is much more difficult. And in many situations affirmative consent can be unclear because is it not clear whether the person is able to give that agreement or would be considered incapacitated and unable to give consent.

According to the Rape, Abuse & Incest National Network (RAINN), consent is really about communication (n.d., What consent looks like). Giving consent one time for one thing does not indicate agreement to do it again at another time. Any time the type of sex or the degree of sexual activity changes, a partner should reaffirm consent by asking, "Is this OK?" RAINN also suggests that partners use physical cues to let the other person know when they are uncomfortable taking things to the next level.

Role of Alcohol and Drugs in Consent

When under the influence of drugs or alcohol, an individual cannot give legal consent to have sex. In 2012 the Department of Justice updated its definition of consent to recognize that a victim may be incapacitated and therefore unable to give consent. Any sexual encounter with a person who is intoxicated could by definition be considered sexual assault.

Statistics clearly illustrate the role of alcohol and drug use in sexual assaults on college campuses. An estimated one in six college freshmen will be sexually assaulted while incapacitated by alcohol (Carey, Durney, Shepardson, and Carey, 2015). Research has found that of the women who said they had been sexually assaulted while in college, 71 to 82 percent were intoxicated when the incident occurred (Lisak and Miller, 2002; Mohler-Kuo, Dowdall, Koss, and Wechsler, 2004).

Even though the use of mind-altering substances increases the vulnerability of young people, the cultural push to engage in drinking is strong. A survey conducted by the Core Institute at the Southern Illinois University Carbondale Student Health Center (2014) found that students engaged in drinking and drug use because it was an icebreaker; drinking made women feel sexier and facilitated female bonding. Like young men, young women, especially freshmen, want to fit into their new environment, and one way to do that is to drink. This desire is so strong that they may be willing be make themselves vulnerable through intoxication in order to be part of their new social group. Some of these women become intoxicated as a result of someone else's premeditated, predatory plan (Lisak and Miller, 2002). Some students become predators and seek out those who could be vulnerable. They are adept at identifying victims and testing their boundaries. They groom their victims and isolate them. Most unsettling is that they seem to share the same predatory characteristics as convicted serial rapists (Lisak and Miller, 2002).

State Consent Laws

Many states are creating their own definitions of what constitutes consent. State laws do not attempt to alter or contradict the Department of

Justice definition, but they do offer guidance to bring consistency to the affirmative consent policies of institutions of higher education in their state. In recent years, all changes in the consent definitions and laws have moved in the direction of making sure that sexual encounters are wanted by both parties. The laws have tried to enhance communication between the parties and encourage acknowledgment of willing participation. Recent considerations of an old ruling in North Carolina may have taken consent a few steps backward, however.

A 1979 North Carolina Supreme Court ruling, still on the books, is challenging new affirmative consent laws. In this ruling, the court ruled that once a woman gives consent, she cannot withdraw it. Two cases have recently been reviewed under this law (Redden, 2017). In the first case, a woman agreed to have sex with her estranged husband to stop his escalating anger. But when he became violent during sex, she begged him to stop. Because his wife had initially agreed, he was charged not with rape but with misdemeanor assault. In a similar case, a young woman consented to have sex with a man at a party. When the sex turned violent, she withdrew consent, but the man did not stop. Even with video evidence, the perpetrator cannot be charged because the woman willingly entered into the encounter.

Lawmakers in North Carolina put forth a bill that would close this loophole. It is in committee, with no sign it will be brought to a vote any time soon.

Tea and Consent

A unique way to communicate consent to college-age students is via a 2015 video produced in England called *Tea and Consent* (see Consent Tea, n.d., for a link to a censored version). The three-minute video, created by Blue Seat Studios with text by blogger Rockstar Dinosaur Pirate Princess, was developed as part of the Thames Valley Police Department and Thames Valley Sexual Violence Prevention Group's #ConsentIs Everything public service campaign.

The video compares offering someone a cup of tea to sexual consent. It takes the viewer through the process of offering, making, and giving a cup of tea to someone who initially wants it, then does not. Throughout, the video relates how the person changing her mind about the tea is like changing her mind about sexual consent.

Potential High-Risk Situations

Extracurricular activities are integral to the college experience. While students are in college primarily for an education, the social life that accompanies academics is just as important for full development. There is no guarantee of protection from sexual assault in any aspect of college, no matter what a student or the institution does, but there are behaviors that can put a student at greater risk of becoming a victim.

Seemingly innocent events can lead to an increased risk of being assaulted. And while we are not attempting to blame the victims by saying they should not engage in activities or behaviors known to involve higher risk, we are saying that students engaging in these activities should use precautions and always be aware of their situation. The use of drugs and alcohol is one behavior that carries a higher risk of sexual assault; others are participating in Greek life and athletics, hooking up, and study abroad.

Greek Life

In early 1987, when activists were first trying to bring awareness to sexual assault on campuses in general and the dangers of fraternities in particular, female students visited the provost of Princeton University. The provost told the women that sexual assault was not a problem at Princeton and that "Princeton men don't assault women. Princeton men are gentlemen" (Kitchener, 2014). Not long after, on April 27, the first march of Take Back the Night on Princeton's campus was held. During the march, about three hundred participants encountered a group of thirty men waiting for them in front of the eating clubs, Princeton's version of fraternity houses.

The men shouted at the marchers. One of them held a sign that said "We can rape whoever we want." One young man pulled down his pants, saying, "You can suck my dick!" Others yelled threats and insults, including "Get raped!" "Fucking beat them up!" and "Take back the dykes!" The incident was videotaped, and administrators quickly got involved.

This behavior is not unique to that time or to Princeton. In 2015, members of Yale's chapter of Delta Kappa Epsilon's pledge class marched past freshman housing in Yale's Old Campus chanting, "No means yes, and yes means anal" (Clark-Flory, 2010). And in 2013 an email with the subject line "Luring your Rapebait" was posted on the TotalFratMove website http://totalfratmove.com/ (Kingkade, 2013). The email had been circulating about Georgia Tech fraternity Phi Kappa Tau. It explained to members how they could get sex at the next party.

While these examples are bad enough, what research on this subject reveals is even more shocking. Two studies found that fraternity members are three times more likely to commit sexual assault than other college men (Foubert, Newberry, and Tatum, 2007; Loh, Gidycz, Lobo, and Luthra, 2005). And the dangers of Greek life do not stop with fraternities. Women who belong to sororities are 74 percent more likely to experience sexual assault than other college women (Minow and Einolf, 2009), and those who live in sorority houses are three times as likely to experience rape (Mohler-Kuo, Dowdall, Koss, and Weschler, 2004).

Not all fraternities are problematic, of course. For example, research shows that the behaviors described above happen almost exclusively in white fraternities. Minority organizations, Black and Latinx, do not have an alcohol culture; nor, typically, do they own fraternity houses in which to host these types of events (Eberhardt, Rice, and Smith, 2003).

Athletics

Arguably no aspect of campus sexual assault has gotten more media coverage than its link to college athletic departments. Observers assert that these unacceptable situations are ignored because sports are such large parts of the campus scene and are vital income generators. The incidents at Penn State and Baylor (described in chapter 2) show the behaviors some athletic staff and teams engage in. Often these behaviors are "handled" within the athletic department. Rape culture attitudes—and money—are most definitely at play.

In 2015, 231 NCAA Division I schools generated $9.15 billion in revenue (Gains, 2016). While no amount of money justifies condoning sexual assaults and the cover-ups that follow, and while in our view institutions of higher education should not be in the sports business, the funds generated are not something from which most schools can easily walk away. These funds fill the gap left after tuition and state and federal funding. This is one reason stopping sexual assaults is difficult.

In 2015 Texas A&M sports generated $194.4 million in revenue and added over $57 million to the university's bottom line (Gains, 2016). This is a major financial resource that could be threatened by revealing criminal behavior within the ranks. The financial gain from athletics does not justify schools condoning sexual assault, but they may feel an overwhelming need to deal with it quietly, to protect the school from backlash.

Regardless of the reasons, institutions cannot continue to protect athletic staff or athletes. The number of sexual assault violations attributed to these members of campus is just too great. In 1996, shortly after research on campus sexual assaults began, research on schools with NCAA Division I teams found that while athletes composed only 3.3 percent of the male student body, 19 percent of the male sexual assault reports were attributed to athlete perpetrators (Crossett, Ptacek, McDonald, and Benedict, 1996). In a more recent study, researchers found that the attitudes about women and sexual assault held by athletes were significantly different from those held by nonathletes. Specifically, athletes were more accepting of rape myths and traditional gender roles. These attitudes lead to sexually coercive behaviors. In 2016, 54.3 percent of athletes admitted to such behaviors, in most cases meeting the legal definition of rape (Young, Desmarais, Baldwin, and Chandler, 2016).

Hooking Up

A new sociocultural norm regarding sex has taken hold. A *hookup* is described as a quick sexual encounter between individuals who are uncommitted—not romantic or even dating. Researchers have posited that a shift to casual sex from the traditional courting rules seen in romantic relationships has been evolving for sixty years (Bogle, 2007, 2008). In one study, undergraduates reported twice as many hookups as first dates (Bradshaw, Kahn, and Saville, 2010). This study included both male and female respondents, who demonstrated a willingness to freely discuss their acceptance of the norm (Garcia, Reiber, Massey, and Merriwether, 2012).

Hooking up activities include kissing, oral sex, and penetrative intercourse (Garcia, Reiber, Massey, and Merriweather, 2012). Hooking up venues include parties (67 percent of survey participants), dorms or fraternity houses (57 percent), bars and clubs (10 percent), cars (4 percent), and any convenient available place (35 percent) (Paul and Hayes, 2002).

A specific concern regarding hookups arises in combination with substance abuse, and whether a student who is inebriated has consented to hookup sex. Fielder and Carey (2010) found that, from a sample of female college students in their first college semester, 64 percent engaged in hookups following alcohol use. Lewis, Granato, Blayney, Lostutter, and Kilmer (2011) found that 61 percent of college students consumed alcohol prior to or during their most recent uncommitted sexual encounter. Heavy alcohol consumption was linked to penetrative sexual activity, lighter alcohol consumption to nonpenetrative sexual activity, and minimal alcohol consumption to no sexual activity (Owen, Fincham, and Moore, 2011).

Research at a large urban university found that in almost half of the 1,160 women who had suffered a sexual assault, alcohol was a factor (Abbey, Ross, McDuffie, and McAuslan, 1996). In another study, respondents who engaged in penetrative hookups reported their level of intoxication as highly intoxicated (35 percent), moderately intoxicated (27 percent), nonintoxicated (27 percent), and maximum intoxication (9 percent) (Fisher, Worth, Garcia, and Meredith, 2012).

One concern associated with alcohol consumption and hookups is an enhanced opportunity for sexual assault. Flack, Hansen, Hopper, Bryant,

Lang, Massa, and Whalen found that female college students who experience greater levels of alcohol consumption coupled with higher levels of hookup activity were somewhat more inclined to be victims of sexual assault. Their study of 373 female undergraduates indicated that the riskiest hookups leading to campus sexual assault occurred with acquaintances and former partners (Flack et al., 2016).

Study Abroad Programs

American students study abroad in ever-increasing numbers. In 2007 the estimate was more than 250,000 students going abroad for a semester or more. In 2010 the number was more than 270,000 students. It is expected that the numbers likely will continue to increase.

Students, like all travelers, may face challenges while traveling abroad. A risk for women traveling abroad may be a higher risk of sexual assault. Such risk stems from decreased supervision and support, cultural differences, and easy access to alcohol (Buddie and Testa, 2005; Hummer, Pederson, Mirza, and LaBrie, 2010; Parks, Romosz, Bradizza, and Hseih, 2008; Kimble, Flack, and Burbridge, 2013).

Research findings indicate that students face increased risk when traveling abroad, especially in non-English-speaking countries. It is very important for institutions to recognize and address the availability, or lack, of support and resources for sexual assault victims in study abroad programs (Kimble, Flack, and Burbridge, 2013).

Managing Risky Situations

It would be simple to tell students to just stay away from these increased-risk situations, but millions of students engage in these behaviors with no problems. Clearly, all students should know where the danger zones lurk. Knowledge is power. The solution is not to eliminate parties, sporting events, or studying abroad but to stress education and training for all students—men and women—with particular attention given to members of fraternities and athletic teams.

Men Can Be Victims, Too—of Sexual Assault and False Accusations

In a 2015 survey, 11.2 percent of all students said they experienced rape or sexual assault while in college (Cantor et al., 2015). In this same report, 23.1 percent of all women and 5.4 percent of men reported being a victim of sexual assault. The probability that a woman will be sexually assaulted is somewhat lower (by 20 percent) on a college campus than in the general population (DOJ, 2014a). However, for men the probability is significantly higher. A male college student is 78 percent more likely to be sexually assaulted than a male the same age in the general population (DOJ, 2014a).

We are as concerned about men who are being assaulted as we are about women who suffer the same fate. Male student victims will be equally helped by our recommendations. There is no evidence that any special programs are needed to protect male sexual assault victims.

What we are most concerned about in terms of male students is accusations made falsely against them. As already discussed, the number of false accusations is small, but even if it is only one person, it is a problem that cannot be ignored. In 2015 the US Department of Education's Campus Safety and Security website indicated there were over 7,000 reports of domestic and dating violence (US Department of Education, 2015). If an estimated 4 to 8 percent of rape claims are false (Lonsway, Srchabault, and Lisak, 2009), that means there were between 280 and 560 false claims against innocent men.

Life-Altering Events

Take the case of Drew Sterrett, a freshman at the University of Michigan (Yoffe, 2014). In March 2012, CB, a member of Sterrett's group of friends and a sophomore, came and asked him if she could stay the night in his dorm room, because her roommate had family staying in her room. Before this day, Sterrett and CB had engaged in kissing but nothing more. After visiting for a while, CB crawled into Sterrett's bed and they started kissing. When things began to progress, CB asked Sterrett about a condom. He got up and retrieved one from his dresser drawer.

The encounter lasted so long and was so loud that Sterrett's roommate, who was in another room, sent him a message at 3:00 a.m. saying there would be payback the next day.

In the morning, everything seemed fine. CB asked Sterrett to please not mention the encounter to anyone. Sterrett agreed, figuring CB was embarrassed. The semester ended and Sterrett left to go home to New York for the summer break.

Over the summer, Sterrett was contacted by Heather Cowan, program manager for the university's Office of Student Conflict Resolution. She gave no reasons but asked him to be available for a Skype interview. Once the interview started, Sterrett realized that CB must have told Cowan about their encounter.

Sterrett asked Cowan if he should consult an attorney. Cowan told him that if he ended the interview to consult an attorney, her report would reflect that fact and the investigation would continue on without him. Sterrett continued the interview and told Cowan that the encounter with CB had been consensual and that his roommate was just a few feet away the entire time.

Cowan told Sterrett during the interview that restrictions would be placed on him in the fall when he returned to campus. The previous year, Sterrett and CB had been in a program called the Michigan Research Community and lived in the same residence hall. He was informed that he would be removed and sent to anther dorm. He was also told that he was not to be in the vicinity of CB, which meant that he could not enter the dorm where his friends lived.

At the end of the interview, Sterrett was told the matter was completely confidential and that he should not discuss it with any other student, especially not anyone who could potentially be a witness for him. At this point, Sterrett still had not been informed what charges had been filed against him.

The university learned of the encounter between Sterrett and CB because during the summer, CB's mother found her diary and questioned her about it. Then CB's mother called the university to report that CB would be filing a complaint against Sterrett. CB's mother drove her to the campus and CB met with Heather Cowan.

In an affidavit sworn on Sterrett's behalf, CB's sophomore-year roommate, LC, said she received a call in July 2012 from a very upset CB, who said her mother had found her diary. LC remembered that CB kept detailed descriptions of her sexual encounters, drinking, and drug use. CB asked LC if she remembered CB mentioning her night with Sterrett, but LC said she never mentioned it. CB told LC, "I said No, No, and then I gave in." LC said CB's mother repeatedly called her during the summer, asking her to not speak to anyone about the incident and to please take CB's side during the proceedings. LC said she never saw any change in CB from the time of the alleged incident until the end of school, but she did see a significant difference after CB's mother found her diary.

On November 9, 2012, Sterrett was given a one-page document entitled "Summary of Witness Testimony and Other Evidence." The document contained statements from two anonymous witnesses saying that CB told them she had tried to push Sterrett off her. But CB said she did not know who these witnesses were and even confirmed that she never claimed this in her original statement. The document also said Sterrett confessed to his roommate that he had nonconsensual sex with CB. Sterrett's roommate, who was never told the purpose of the investigation, said he told Cowan that Sterrett had told him he regretted the encounter with CB. The roommate assumed Sterrett's regret was because CB was a member of their group of friends, not because he had done something wrong. Cowan interpreted it as a confession.

The final report concluded that Sterrett had engaged in sexual intercourse with CB without her consent and that the incident was sufficiently severe to create a hostile environment. He was suspended from the university until July 2016. He filed an appeal stating that the affidavits from classmates included statements that had been misconstrued or even falsified. Still the university stood by its findings of guilty, but changed the reason. Cowan issued an addendum stating that Sterrett's behavior was deemed to be sexual misconduct because CB was too drunk to give consent, even though CB said that, while she had been drinking, she was not incapacitated.

Sterrett was required to leave the university. However, he had already decided to leave, because the restrictions put in place so he wouldn't run into CB made it impossible for him to function at school. He filed an appeal to Michigan's University Appeals Board. In July 2013 the board upheld the decision but agreed to put him on disciplinary probation instead of suspension.

In April 2014, Sterrett filed a federal lawsuit against the university, saying it had violated his Fourteenth Amendment rights to due process. The university asked the courts to dismiss the case, but the motion was denied. The denial mandated that the university and Sterrett go into mediation. The result was that Michigan vacated all charges against Sterrett, a rare occurrence in these types of cases (Yoffe, 2015).

While Sterrett's case is extreme, there are numerous other examples of a male student being denied his constitutional rights by a school. Institutions of higher education are "running scared" trying to protect victims of sexual assault. We applaud their diligence but not their actions if they make innocent people victims.

In the last five years, 70 men who had been found responsible for sexual misconduct have filed lawsuits against colleges and universities claiming that their treatment was so biased as to constitute sex discrimination (Yoffe, 2015). In our haste to protect women who have not been protected for so long, we cannot create another group of victims.

An institution of higher education has a moral obligation to create programs that protect all of its students. Men and women must be protected from becoming victims of sexual assault, but it is just as important that men be protected from becoming victims of the system.

Laws can be passed, Title IX coordinators educated and trained, and law enforcement put in place, but until everyone embraces gender equality, we will never solve the problem of sexual assaults on campus. Creating a culture of inclusion is critical to truly tackling this.

Making everyone aware of the problem is a great first step, and the college campus is the right place to begin the process. If we can successfully combat the problem there, may we produce graduates one day who will transform the world.

CHAPTER FOUR

Building a Strong, Secure Campus Culture

THE UNIVERSITY PROTECTION and individual prevention model we presented in chapter 2 shows protection to be primary prevention for campus sexual assault. Primary prevention is always the preferred point of initial intervention when managing chronic problems. University protection is the process of identifying and mitigating the risk factors for sexual assaults before an incident occurs. Primary prevention is where the right conditions are set to eliminate problems before they arise. Failure to prevent can be devastating, as it was for athletes and the university in the landmark Michigan State University case of a $500 million settlement paid into a survivor fund and an additional $4.5 million fine paid to the U.S Department of Education after Dr. Larry Nassar abused hundreds of women gymnasts at the university.

Our model (see the figure in chapter 2) identifies three principal protection mechanisms for the university to implement: institutional policies, procedures, and enforcement mechanisms; university socialization practices and rituals; and a Campus Sexual Assault Prevention (CSAP) Board of interdisciplinary professionals led by the Title IX coordinator. These mechanisms must be set in the context of a campus culture that has zero tolerance for abuse of persons. In addition, the university needs to consider investing resources in protection and prevention to reduce the direct human resources costs of turnover, absences, investigations, litigation, and compensatory awards associated with sexual violence on campus (Cascio and Boudreau, 2011). The failure to commit personnel and funds to protection and prevention risks significant human and financial costs.

The market research firm Laufer Green Isaac's three-in-one framework for intervention with high-risk drinking offers a comprehensive social ecological model for placing interventions in context and can be applied to the sexual assault problem (Laufer Green Isaac Marketing Consultants, n.d.). Specifically, the social ecological model has the individual at the center, in the context of the campus and campus living arrangements: dorm, fraternity or sorority house, or other student housing unit. The campus, in turn, resides within the context of the surrounding community. Boundaries and buffers of varying degree exist between the various levels of analysis, but consideration should be given at all levels. Cass (2007) does this in her analysis considering individual- and school-level factors in routine activities and sexual assaults. The principal focus in this chapter is on the university campus level of analysis. The campus constituencies of individual students, faculty, and staff are addressed at the end of the chapter and set the stage for chapters 5, 6, and 7.

University protection should set the conditions that create a safe, supportive learning environment in which faculty can teach young men and women to grow to their full potential. Teasdale and McKeown (1994) offer a model that can be adapted to the university context for campus sexual assault. It treats casualties (caregiving) as the first response, followed by detection of additional casualties or incidents. Sexual assault must be legitimized as an important problem from the most senior levels of the university. That is precisely what Chancellor William H. McRaven (2017) did within the University of Texas System (discussed below). The message from the top is essential to setting the tone for the university and the basis for action to address sexual assaults. The last three steps in Teasdale and McKeown's (1994) model are to increase awareness, teach skills, and improve organizational culture. Crafting a strong culture is the major issue in setting forth the right conditions for success, in preventing systemic abuse of power (Linder, 2018), and in empowering individuals and groups throughout the university campus (Harris and Linder, 2017).

Once the right tone is set, there needs to be alignment throughout the university from top to bottom. The battle will be won in the trenches, not in the president's suite, although that is the place for issuing the call to action. Eradicating campus sexual assaults begins with strong, articulate leadership—the president must make the issue a priority—but driving campus incidents to zero can only occur on the campus grounds. The University of Texas has set *zero* as the goal—that is, no sexual assaults within the university system (Rossi, 2016). While a goal of zero is challenging and aspirational, any worthy human effort begins with a clear, specific, and difficult goal to achieve.

As McDonald (2012) notes, power dynamics are at the heart of sexual harassment and sexual assault. There's a power struggle going on which is often but not always between genders. Same-gender power struggles play into sexual assaults as well, as in the Missoula case written about by Krakauer (2015), where one woman was the lure for another who was subsequently drugged and raped by a group of males. Such power struggles are the ugly underbelly of a campus culture gone wrong. Setting the cultural conditions that significantly reduce the risk of such an event is job number one for the administration. Linder (2018) advocates for paying greater attention to identifying any systemic abuse of power; to embedding restraining mechanisms to prevent power abuse; and to empowering those who may be disenfranchised.

If power dynamics are at the root of the sexual assault problem, then an understanding of power, its use and abuse, is critical to solving the problem. Physical power clearly plays a role in sexual assault incidents. Self-control and self-discipline are admirable forms of transcendent power but are insufficient for addressing the problem. The university culture and mechanisms for control and discipline must supplement where the individual's capacity for self-control falls short.

To reach zero, the campus culture must be laser-sharp responsive to early warning indicators. Snyder, Fisher, Scherer, and Daigle (2012) report high levels of sexual victimization at the three US military academies (60 percent of total academies' population; 86 percent of female and 42 percent of male). The data show that early indicators—unwanted sexual attention, offensive remarks, offensive gestures—are included in the survey items. A culture that tolerates nonviolent sexually offensive behaviors moves the standards of interpersonal conduct toward sexual violence, and thus toward sexual coercion and rape. Castro, Kintzle, Schuyler, Lucas, and Warner (2015) suggest that the military culture may unintentionally contribute to sexual assault and that examining root causes and numerous myths offers the potential for reform. The long-term goal is to build a campus culture that offers safety and security for all of its members as well as mechanisms for justice. Positive campus cultures set a high standard of interpersonal behavior and embrace enforcement mechanisms to keep faculty, staff, and students on the high road. Reliance on personal integrity alone is inadequate and unacceptable.

Colleges and universities that go beyond legal definitions of sexual harassment and sexual assault run the risk of violating the law and constructing alternative realities (Braceras, 2016). Staying with the evidence is essential from a public health and safety perspective as well as a legal one. One good way of staying with the evidence is through university policy discussion groups that focus on the implications of the university's policies, such as teaching students about concern (Borges, Banyard, and Moynihan, 2008).

Campus Culture

Schein (2017) sets out three levels as the basic structure of any organizational culture, from least visible to most visible:

1. basic assumptions (about, for example, human nature, relationships, and activity);
2. values (both espoused and enacted); and
3. artifacts (personal enactments, ceremonies and rites, stories, rituals, symbols).

Basic assumptions are the deepest level of a culture and may be unconscious as well as invisible. Three basic assumptions relevant to the university are the nature of human nature, the nature of human activity, and the nature of human relationships. A deep dive into a culture is required to fully appreciate this least visible level of the culture's structure.

There is often much greater awareness of values than of basic assumptions. Values are often embedded in the university mission statement. Such statements are the *espoused* values of the university, however, and will vary to some degree from the enacted values. The first element in the University of Texas System's mission statement is to "improve the human condition." That is a powerful, positive espoused value, and it's about people. It is important to examine the alignment of that espoused value with the system's enacted values. Schein recognizes the important distinction between any organization's formal and official elements, on the one hand, and informal and unofficial elements, on the other.

The most visible level of a university culture is its artifacts, although they may be difficult to interpret or fully grasp in context. One of the most important artifacts of an abuse-intolerant culture is the campus sexual assault policy. Then there are the stories about what happens to the perpetrators of sexual assaults and to the survivors. How are they treated? Is justice served? We address this in more detail in the next section of the chapter.

Even in the best universities, the occurrence of sexual assault should evoke a reexamination of the university culture. The questions to consider at this juncture start with the artifacts:

Are there any ceremonies or rites that might open the door to a
  sexual assault?
Are there any stories that send the wrong message about respect of
  women and men?
Are there symbols of any kind that communicate an unintended
  message?

While the surface elements of culture send powerful messages, the important issues of values should be challenged in the aftermath of a sexual assault. This is not the time to complete and file a sexual assault incident report under the letter S and be done. It is the time to ask questions that can pave the way for improving the university's culture:

Are we enacting our espoused values well? How do we all act better?

Do our espoused values bring out the best in our students, staff, and faculty?

Do we have the right enforcement mechanisms to achieve value compliance?

Sexual harassment, assault, and rape cases are single events that must be addressed by the campus community if it is simultaneously to demonstrate compassion, resilience, and intolerance for harm to any of its members.

Campus Leadership

Schein (2017) finds organizational cultures and leadership integrally bound. Campus leaders transmit the university culture in a number of ways. The process begins, as we have noted, with the university president. The president's messages and position on campus sexual assault are central but not sufficient for establishing the secure campus culture. The message of intolerance for sexual assault must be accompanied by several embedding mechanisms.

First among these is appointing the Title IX coordinator and other members of the Campus Sexual Assault Prevention Board. The stature as well as function of these individuals sends a crucial message throughout the campus community. The significance of selection does not end there, however. In choosing its senior campus leaders, the university should weigh the candidates' attitudes and any previous behaviors concerning campus sexual assault incidents. Embedding gender and sexual equality issues in annual performance evaluations for these campus leaders then follows through on the selections made. A key component of these appointments is making sure that the office of the Title

IX coordinator is adequately staffed and financed—the budget matters. Titles and policies that lack funding and enforcement mechanisms are meaningless. In addition, workload consideration for CSAP Board members is consequential and sends a message.

A second essential culture embedding element concerns the policies, procedures, and enforcement mechanisms that ensure organizational justice within the university. A key aspect of a just system is having fair and just procedures and processes that are not corruptible. Consistency in enforcing policies and procedures is critical; thus, the official, stated university culture and the way it really works should be precisely aligned. Consistent treatment means recognizing developmental differences among the various constituencies, such as between entering first-year students and the university's doctoral and graduate professional students. This means treating all freshmen alike and all graduate students alike but not treating freshmen the same way graduate students are treated.

A third aspect of embedding a secure campus culture measures the campus leadership's response to incidents of sexual assault. The university president's main role is to set the conditions for adjudicating these incidents and choosing the right individuals to enact the enforcement mechanisms, starting with the Title IX coordinator. Rather than concentrating power in one or two senior administrators, the university should craft a monitoring (surveillance) plan around protection, prevention, and treatment mechanisms that are robust and systemic in nature.

Assessing Campus Culture

Schein (2017) assesses culture through deciphering, diagnosis, and dialogic mechanisms. Assessing a culture is a precondition to any planned change initiatives. Campus sexual assaults are serious problems for all concerned, and developing a healthy campus climate is valuable for all concerned. The ARC_3 (Administrator-Researcher Campus Climate Collaborative) Survey can be useful in this regard as a screening device. Developed by twenty-three psychologists, social workers, and behavioral science collaborators from leading US institutions, the survey is included in figure 2.1 as a key surveillance indicator at the university level. Nineteen modules cover twelve issues: alcohol use, peer norms, perceptions of campus climate, sexual harassment, stalking, dating violence, sexual violence, institutional responses, peer responses, consent, bystander intervention, and campus safety. The survey makes distinctions between faculty or staff and students. A campus-wide ARC_3 Survey offers the potential to identify colleges, schools, institutes, departments, and units having potential issues or concerns requiring attention. Protection surveillance is designed to identify risks before they manifest as full-blown problems.

Socialization

While it might be assumed that those at high risk of committing a sexual assault will be identified in the selection processes of the college or university, that's generally not the case. Quick, McFadyen, and Nelson (2014) concluded that screening out potentially dangerous employees was especially challenging and had low probability of success. This is not to suggest that all university students, faculty, and staff should bypass the screening process; the primary purpose of screening remains valid: to ensure the right people are selected to enroll and to fill employment positions.

Quick, McFadyen, and Nelson (2014) recommend the organizational process of socialization as a way to more deeply embed institutional norms. The university's rituals and socializing mechanisms offer the opportunity to reinforce values about a wide range of issues relevant to a strong, single culture that at the same time embraces diversity and variations within appropriate limits. A strong culture is not necessarily a rigid culture but rather is one that is supple enough to accommodate individual differences while at the same time being intolerant of damaging behaviors such as campus sexual assault.

The University in Context: Federal, State, Community, and Criminal Justice Interfaces

A positive campus culture is valuable protection against the problem of sexual assault. The Laufer Green Isaac (n.d.) three-in-one framework and comprehensive social ecological model draw attention to the university in its larger context. While the internal leadership, policy, and procedural structures of the university are essential on their own, their interface with the federal and criminal justice system is key to managing sexual assault. Ensuring effective boundary-spanning functions with these elements of the university task environment, which includes local police departments, courts of justice, and local attorneys, is critical for the university's well-being.

Four components of a university environment need monitoring: federal and state governments, the local community, and the criminal justice system. Each university will have a unique set of these constituents. The Title IX coordinator needs a system for understanding all of the laws and guidance on the campus sexual assault issues as well as a system for monitoring changes that may occur in any of the four arenas. Our focus in this chapter is primarily on the internal university elements essential to protecting students, faculty, and staff. External constituencies like federal, state, and local governments are discussed throughout the book.

Institutional Policies, Procedures, and Enforcement Mechanisms

The quality and online availability of university policies and procedures concerning sexual harassment and sexual assault vary markedly by institution. Fusilier and Penrod (2015) found that only 23 percent of for-profit universities made their policies publicly available on their websites, while 99 percent of state universities made their policies publicly available. However, 70 percent of available university harassment policies or websites were deficient on one or more of the following characteristics:

1. mandatory supervisory reporting of harassment;
2. availability of informal and formal complaint procedures; and
3. availability of multiple reporting options to ensure that harassing supervisors can be bypassed.

Policies and Procedures

The formal culture of a university is charted in the policies and procedures in place for a range of behaviors. These are key cultural artifacts that need to align with the informal behaviors and actions within the university. That is why enforcement mechanisms for policy and procedural violations are essential. The CSAP Board can ensure the existence of clear, unambiguous policies and procedures and that appropriate enforcement actions and sanctions are applied. Green, Potts, Treichler, and Levy (2013) note that because definitions of various acts and their status differ widely by state, institution, and even by research study, universities are encouraged to determine the terms and conditions applicable in their community. This is one critical aspect of the university's interface with its community. Green and her colleagues also note that broad changes in the campus culture, as we advocate in this chapter, aid in the effective management of campus sexual assault. However, the researchers do not argue for a specific set of policies and procedures.

Vigorous policies and procedures are needed not only for campus sexual assault but for high-risk drinking. The comorbidity of these two problems argues for an aggressive campus assault on both problems, but not necessarily under the authority of the Title IX coordinator and CSAP Board. Campus leadership should name a second authority to address high-risk drinking. Concerted actions on both fronts can be beneficial in addressing each problem.

Green and her colleagues (2013) offer twelve principles for the university's policies and procedures:

1. University leaders, students, faculty, and staff all share responsibility for and should be represented in the policy-development process.

2. The university should determine the rules, definitions, laws, reporting requirements, and penalties that pertain to sexual assault in the community's criminal justice system.
3. The university's policies and procedures should be clear, readable, and accurate as well as widely disseminated and easily accessible.
4. Clear and explicit guidelines for reporting a sexual assault should state the name, title, and contact information of the reporting authority.
5. Sexual assault reporting is essential for accurate record keeping, public health surveillance, and the prevention of repeat offenses.
6. There should be a single responsible official or office; we recommend that the Title IX coordinator and the CSAP Board hold these positions.
7. Campus policies and procedures should be publicized through a multitude of media channels.
8. Prevention programs should be proactive and include primary, secondary, and tertiary prevention (as noted in figure 2.1).
9. Physical and electronic security measures throughout the campus should be clearly visible wherever possible.
10. Education and prevention efforts should be tailored to those at risk (primarily women) and those most likely to be offenders (primarily men).
11. Bystander interventions aimed at peers and peer groups show promise for engaging a wider spectrum of the campus community.
12. Campus sexual assault policy should address all four campus constituencies, not just students.

The National Institute of Justice (NIJ) calls for university policies to first and foremost state the institution's commitment to the recognition and management of sexual assault (McMahon, 2008). While Green and her colleagues (2013) signal the importance of attending to the local criminal justice system, McMahon (2008) presents a template for compliance with federal policy. The caution on federal policy, and even state and local justice processes, is that it is subject to change based on the administration in office. Statutory laws, on the other hand, are not subject to change based on the administration.

With that caveat noted, McMahon (2008) offers six NIJ recommendations to help build a positive campus culture vis-à-vis sexual assault. University policy should:

1. Affirm the emotional trauma a victim experiences, with services available to reduce the distress.
2. Provide for the victim's safety needs by coordinating services, both on and off campus.
3. Demonstrate a legal system that is sympathetic to the victim through written law enforcement protocols.
4. Offer essential medical and psychological services.
5. Educate the entire campus on the needs of a victim of sexual assault in student orientation and prevention programs directed at Greek organizations and athletics.
6. Assure confidentiality for the victim.

Investigating sexual assaults and punishing perpetrators is an essential component of university policy. There should be set procedures for investigations, rather than an ad hoc process established after an incident has occurred, that specify who is involved in the investigation, how each party engages, and possible punishment. Arbitrary and unfair schemes, as famously used in the English Star Chamber, are not only unacceptable in terms of treating victims and perpetrators but leave the university open to legal challenge (Braceras, 2016). A balance must be defined that protects the rights of both the victim/survivor and the accused. In addition, implementation of the policy should specify the methods by which dual jurisdiction between the university and the community will be addressed.

While it can help to have a template to start from in specifying sexual assault policy, there is real risk in not carefully tailoring the policy to the specific university, city, and state.

Official and Unofficial, Formal and Informal

The university policy and procedure apparatus is the official, archival architecture of the campus culture, focused on what the university says is important and how the process should work. In addition to the official and formal organization, there exists an unofficial and informal culture. Schein (2017) notes that stories are a powerful artifact of a culture and that the stories within universities can be compelling, and are most often transmitted by word of mouth and oral tradition. Therefore, it is important for the campus to work for consistency between the written policies and the ways in which they are implemented. If policies and procedures are only for show, they will have no impact.

Compelled disclosure, mandated reporting. Internal boundaries created by legislative actions aimed at helping solve the problem are an aspect of the campus culture that demands sensitivity. For example, the Clery Act and mandatory reporting by campus reporting authorities have created a potential roadblock for campus security authorities (CSAs). Specifically, if a student comes to a faculty member for counsel about a possible sexual assault, a CSA must inform the student that any discussion between them may have to be reported. The CSA may not have the discretion to have an informal conversation with the student or colleague. Holland, Cortina, and Freyd (2018) have called this situation into question. While they found that the vast majority of universities included most of their employees in their compelled disclosure policies, they found both supportive and conflicting evidence concerning the benefits of such policies.

Survivor-centered reforms. Holland, Cortina, and Freyd (2018) suggest four alternatives that do not compel survivors to enter into the official, formal procedural system:

1. Ascertain and respect survivors' wishes (empower survivors).
2. Create a restricted reporting option (survivors get care but are not required to launch an official investigation).
3. Make use of a third-party reporting system (a possible technological alternative).

4. Reform compelled disclosure procedures (voluntary reporting is the most survivor-centered alternative to compelled disclosure).

Reporting to trained confidential advocates or university ombudspersons, and even to a trustworthy source outside the university, can provide a buffer. The critical issues here are empowering survivors, offering them support in confidential ways as requested, and enhancing the discretionary latitude that survivors have.

Counterpoint. The counterpoint concern is the risk that a dangerous person within the university goes unidentified and may strike again (Quick, McFadyen, and Nelson, 2014). While compelled disclosure is intended to convert unreported incidents into documented incidents, the question is whether the higher bar for reporting may discourage students and others from having any informal counseling with trusted faculty who are also CSAs. The healthy university will have good communication between the formal and informal elements of the culture. What campus leaders do not know can in fact be truly harmful to individuals and the entire campus community.

Compliance and Reporting Channels

Requiring annual compliance training for all faculty and staff makes all faculty and staff essential participants in identifying and acting on sexual assaults, or even as early warning reporters of potential problems. The university should aim not only to stamp out hostile elements but promote positive campus culture.

Those who feel victimized need multiple safe channels for talking about their experience with the option of filing a complaint and pressing charges. Research shows that victims/survivors of sexual assault tell a friend before telling anyone else (McMahon, 2008). The National Institute of Justice finds that victims are more likely to get adequate assistance if the initial contact person is familiar with the problem and the reporting channels available. Victims/survivors want to know the confidentiality practices of the university. The system must pass the test of public scrutiny. The absence of multiple channels leads to a risk that the single channel can be compromised and blocked. The system needs to be sufficiently open to ensure its integrity while not so open that it leaves vulnerable individuals exposed.

Ethics, Integrity, and Reporting

Managing sexual assaults demands the best of all parties involved in terms of ethics, personal integrity, and truth telling. Ethics and morality are most often embedded in university codes of conduct and ethical standards. As noted, artifacts are the most visible elements of the campus culture; an honor code that is anchored in the values can be a powerful artifact (Schein, 2017). The code of conduct must come alive with personal implementation, however, such as panels of Title IX–certified investigators and certified judges which act on sexual assault complaints, as well as stories about the outcomes of those important university processes.

University honor codes resonate with the effort to build a positive campus culture. One of the most renowned is the West Point honor code: *A cadet will not lie, cheat, steal, or tolerate those who do.* But West Point has experienced painful failures of the code, as in the 1970s when nearly one hundred and fifty cadets were dismissed for lying, cheating, or stealing, or for violating the toleration clause (Lynch, 2013; Quick and Goolsby, 2013). Our premise for the positive campus culture is that it should not tolerate sexual assault and that penalties should be clearly specified. The campus honor code should specify the best in what is expected of all campus constituencies, the highest standard of respect and interaction within the community. Setting high standards shapes personal behavior. The evidence on goal setting is remarkably robust and suggests that when people set challenging, specific goals, their performance is better.

An honor code that sets out what is expected in a clear and challenging way will never guarantee that failure does not occur, but it will alter the probabilities in favor of the good. Falling short of the mark (and even abject failure) is more dramatic and clear cut. Even failure can help in telling stories of positive campus cultures, because failures become the basis for "You know what happened to so-and-so for doing such-and-such."

Ethical and Moral Standards

Personal ethical and moral standards need to anchor campus leaders (Solomon, 1992). However, character and virtue have their limitations because of human fallibility, a lack of common understanding among individuals concerning what is right and wrong, and conflicts of interest (Quick and Goolsby, 2013). Therefore, personal accountability and organizational integrity must pick up where character and virtue leave off. When it comes to sexual assault, the best intentions of young men and women whose character would otherwise be considered virtuous may be compromised when under the influence of alcohol or drugs. This does not absolve them of their actions. They are personally accountable for the substance abuse itself, which is why the comorbid problem of high-risk drinking needs to be confronted within the campus culture and judged to be both unacceptable and dangerous on many levels.

Personal accountability should be supported with university enforcement mechanisms that do for the individual and the campus what the individual fails to do for himself or herself. That is why attending to the consequences of behavior is so important. Men and women of good intentions may act badly without particularly disastrous consequences, but avoiding bad consequences does not obviate the need to address bad behaviors.

False Allegations?

One of the myths within the domain of sexual assault is that a substantive percentage of allegations are false. This view is inaccurate, misleading, and too often used to discount the preponderance of legitimate claims. While false allegations do compromise the integrity of the system, each complaint that is filed must be taken seriously and investigated completely. Guarding against false allegations is essential to ensure justice, however. Implicit and gender biases can undercut the process of accepting and investigating charges, which is wrong.

What does the evidence say with regard to false allegations? The evidence suggests that maybe 5 percent of sexual assault allegations are false. In one study, one in seventeen allegations was found to be false in a review of 136 cases reported over ten years (Lisak, Gardinier, Nicksa, and Cote, 2010). Only 8 (5.9 percent) of the 136 cases are coded as false allegations. These results, taken in the context of an examination of previous research by the investigators, indicate that the prevalence of false sexual assault allegations is between 2 percent and 10 percent and more likely on the low side of the range. While this is not an insignificant percentage, it hardly suggests that false allegations are a major concern—rather, quite the contrary. The vast majority of sexual assault claims are found to have merit.

Science can be seductive when attempting to work from the body of knowledge to the individual case. To avoid bias, each case must be taken on its own merit, and even that is not enough. Despite being certified for competence, sexual assault investigators carry bias within themselves of which they may be aware or, more likely, unaware. Hence the advantage of at least two investigators of different genders teaming on every investigation.

Power, Restraint, and Development

Sexual assault and rape are violent acts that rely on force and control. As noted above, the heart of sexual harassment and sexual assault is power, not sex (McDonald, 2012; Quick and McFadyen, 2017). Hence Linder's (2018) advocacy for university mechanisms to prevent abuse that restrain the power of some while empowering those who may be abused. One of the challenges for adolescents is the calibration and restraint of their own power. Many young men lack self-awareness of their strength and knowledge of how to restrain the force within. Arain, Haque, Johal, Mathur, Nel, Rais, Sandhu, and Sharma (2013) report that adolescence is generally accepted to be from age 10 to age 24; thus, many college students and even young graduate students are in the late stages of adolescence. This is especially important with regard to brain development, which is not complete until age 25 (Arain et al., 2013). Lack of complete brain development becomes relevant to the ability to exercise good judgment, decision making, and self-control. Universities require structural mechanisms to assist young men and women in the restraint of their developing power and strength. The ability to exercise good judgment, decision making, and self-control should be encouraged, especially among the athletes. At the same time, there is the demand for clear boundaries for interpersonal behavior, especially when it comes to those who are not as strong.

A developmental challenge for college students is the difference between men and women when it comes to interpreting cues and making decisions related to sexual encounters (Ambrose and Gross, 2016). These cognitive and social information-processing differences bring ambiguity concerning sexual intentions, leading to confusion and miscommunication (that is, the sent message and the received message may not be the same). Women's risk perceptions for sexual assault and their ability to respond to threat influence whether they are victimized or not (Gidycz, McNamara, and Edwards, 2006). In addition to the ambiguity over intentions that can result in sexual abuse, male peer encouragement can be counterproductive and a significant predictor of abuse (de Keseredy and Kelly, 1995). While universities often deal with late adolescent development, what they might not be aware of are a student's history of childhood and adolescent sexual abuse, which is a predictor of engaging in sexually risky behavior (Littleton, Grills, and Drum, 2014).

Restraining Forces

If young men and women lack the brainpower of the fully mature adult, then the university must build restraints to compensate for their limitations and keep them safe. In particular, Linder (2018) advocates for greater restraints on potential perpetrators. Restraining students and preventing them from becoming perpetrators of sexual violence can be a challenge when students cluster in intimate communities such as the

Greek system or on athletic teams whose members form close bonds and are physically proximate (Cass, 2007). While tight-knit student groups or cohorts may pose some risk if they become closed off, they offer opportunities for university leverage in a positive way: older and more mature members of the group help socialize younger, less mature members. There is a "sport protection hypothesis" proposing that athletic participation can protect female athletes from sexual victimization through a range of psychosocial mechanisms such as team membership, physical strength, and self-confidence. There is some evidence to support this hypothesis and no significant gender gap between female and male athletes; however, student athletes are significantly less likely to report sexual victimization than their nonathletic counterparts (Fasting, Brackenridge, Miller, and Sabo, 2008).

Recognizing the individual differences in adolescent development, especially brain development, is valuable. Faculty and staff advisers, especially athletic coaches and those in the division of student affairs, have the opportunity to form strong, secure relationships with students that provide channels for strong, secure influence. Many in student advisory roles will be mandated reporters, or campus security authorities. These mandated roles may shape the amount of informal information and early warning signals available. Educating young men and women about the degree to which these faculty and staff advisers are acting in the long-term best interest of students is crucial. Gidycz, Orchowski, and Berkowitz (2011) found positive effects on social norms around aggression from a bystander intervention program designed specifically for men and evaluated among men only living in first-year dormitories.

Empowered Bystanders

One of the emerging and potentially most powerful actors in the campus sexual assault arena is the bystander. Bystanders who know the individuals engaged in a risky encounter have a perspective others do not and may be in a position to prevent the sexual harassment, assault, or rape. Banyard's (2015) extensive review of bystander helping behavior has a strong focus on prevention of sexual and relationship violence but draws on bystander research and practice beyond that. It can be valuable to translate bystander helping behavior, such as from bystander interventions in occupational contexts (Quick and McFadyen, 2017), into the campus culture. The 2013 Campus Sexual Violence Elimination Act requires universities and colleges to provide bystander-based training to reduce sexual violence. CSVE does not tell universities how to do the bystander-based training, which is good. Universities should take responsibility, as has Colgate University, to design a bystander program suited to their specific context and culture.

One of the challenges for bystanders is knowing when, and when not, to intervene. Sexual harassment is a long-standing problem in universities, and one of the early difficulties in addressing it was the absence of a clear and commonly accepted definition in psychology research (cf. Rubin and Borgers, 1990). While definitions of sexual harassment have become clearer, better articulated, and scientifically grounded (Busch-Armendariz et al., 2017a, 2017b), there remains ambiguity that can leave bystanders hesitant to step in or report (Bowes-Sperry and O'Leary-Kelly, 2005). Snyder, Fisher, Scherer, and Daigle (2012) use the broad term *sexual victimization* to capture a spectrum of verbal and physical actions, from unwanted sexual attention to rape. At what point and for what verbal or physical actions does the bystander intervene?

Coker, Cook-Craig, Williams, Fisher, Clear, Garcia, and Hegge (2011) did a cross-sectional survey of a random sample of 7,945 college undergraduates to evaluate the Green Dot active bystander behavior training. The Green Dot strategy aims to shift campus culture and increase proactive preventive behavior by targeting influential members from across a community with basic education, skill practice, and reactive interventions to high-risk situations. Every choice to be proactive as a bystander is categorized as a "new behavior" and thus a Green Dot; individual decisions (green dots) group together to create larger change. The researchers reported positive outcomes from the active training, including more active bystander behaviors, more observed bystander behaviors, and lower rape myth acceptance scores.

McMahon, Allen, Postmus, McMahon, Peterson, and Hoffman (2014) measured both the attitudes and the behaviors of bystanders in an effort to better understand and capture bystanders' attitudes toward high-risk situations, post-assault support for victims/survivors, post-assault reporting of perpetrators, and proactive opportunities for interventions before, during, and after an assault. The subjects in their research were first-year students ($N = 4{,}054$) at a large public university in the Northeast who completed a survey in 2010 as part of a larger longitudinal study of a sexual violence bystander education intervention program on campus. The research team concluded that the both the Bystander Attitude Scale—Revised (BAS-R) and the Bystander Behavior Scale—Revised (BBS-R) provide reliable measures that can be utilized to evaluate sexual violence bystander programs.

In a longitudinal study of 1,390 first-year students, McMahon, Winter, Palmer, Postmus, Peterson, Zucker, and Koenick (2015) found that one dose of peer education theater bystander intervention had positive impact on both male and female students, but that a three-dose approach yielded better outcomes than the one-dose approach in summer orientation. In addition, female students consistently scored higher on each outcome. The outcomes of interest were bystander intentions, bystander efficacy, perception of friend norms, and bystander behaviors.

The theater approach to bystander education is not the only way to prepare students for active engagement as bystanders. Potter, Moynihan, Stapleton, and Banyard (2009) aimed to empower bystanders through a poster campaign on campus. The campaign used student actors to model appropriate bystander behaviors, and undergraduates were invited to complete a web survey the last week of the campaign. Results suggested that those who saw the campaign were more aware of prosocial bystander behaviors and more willing to intervene in cases of sexual violence.

Salazar, Vivolo-Kantor, Hardin, and Berkowitz (2014) tested a web-based sexual violence bystander intervention in a random sample of 743 male undergraduate students (ages 18 to 24) attending a large urban southeastern university. At the six-month follow-up, it was found that the respondents intervened more often and engaged in less sexual violence perpetration compared to controls. In addition, the web-based intervention participants reported:

- Greater legal knowledge of sexual assault
- Greater knowledge of effective consent
- Fewer rape myths
- Greater empathy for rape victims
- Less negative date rape attitude
- Less hostility toward women
- Greater intentions to intervene
- Less hyper-gender ideology
- Fewer positive outcome expectancies for nonconsensual sex
- More positive outcome expectancies for intervening
- Less comfort with other men's inappropriate behaviors

Bennett, Banyard, and Garnhart (2013) explored perceptions of bystander behaviors among first-semester college students in an effort to understand the facilitators for and barriers to intervention. The intrapersonal variable of prosocial tendencies was found to increase helping behavior. Not all students will be predisposed to bystander intervention, and exploring ways to motivate students who may not be inclined to intervene is important.

Many bystander-based interventions are targeted at the individual level to educate and empower the bystander to intervene when and where appropriate. Sexual assault is a community problem, however—a public health problem. Therefore, adopting a campus-level focus seems important in considering bystander intervention. Coker, Bush, Fisher, Swan, Williams, Clear, and DeGue (2016) conducted one multicollege bystander intervention evaluation for violence prevention from 2010 to 2013. They chose three university campuses, one of which implemented a bystander intervention in 2008. The two comparison campuses had no bystander intervention at baseline. The interpersonal violence victimization rates, measured over the previous academic year, were 17 percent lower among students attending the bystander intervention campus relative to the two comparison campuses. Violence rates were lower on the bystander intervention campus for unwanted sexual victimization, sexual harassment, stalking, and psychological violence, victimization, and perpetration in dating relationships.

Harris and Linder (2017) advocate for an empowerment-based model for diverse groups within the university in addition to empowered bystanders. Such groups include women of color, deaf people, hard-of-hearing people, those along the queer spectrum, and others who may be at elevated risk of sexual violence. Harris and Linder aim is to redress the imbalance of power across constituencies throughout the university, to preclude any one individual or group from gaining undue leverage within the system. Empathy and compassion are emotional competency skills that can be especially useful in power dynamic dialogues.

Socialization of Campus Constituents: Administrators, Students, Faculty, Staff

All constituents play a vital role in addressing the threat posed by sexual violence to the well-being of the community. This section addresses the responsibilities of administrators, students, faculty, and staff, including campus security staff, health clinic and counseling staff, psychological service providers, and chaplains. The socialization of each constituency, with attendant rituals, is a primary protective factor for the institution (figure 2.1). Socialization takes newcomers from neophytes to masters of the organization's culture and ethics (Nelson and Quick, 2013).

Administrators

The administration should be aligned to support campus leadership and, most importantly, to service a triage function to ensure that those faculty and students needing either care or channels of reporting get to the right points of contact. Because of the control and power coaches have over athletes, athletic administrators in particular must be aware of the potential for sexual harassment and the federal requirements for Title IX (Wolohan, 1995).

Students

As the discussion above about student interventions illustrates, student roles in sexual assaults are varied—both good and bad (Cass, 2007). Students who are motivated offenders may not appear so. Rather, they may present themselves as trusted allies, only to be foxes aiming to identify a target. For this reason alone, it is crucial for students to work on mastery of their own intuitions and "gut feel" (de Becker, 1997). Having a sense of fear and discomfort in another's presence may be the most valuable signal that something, or someone, is not right. Rather than ignore that sense, de Becker (1997) encourages students and others to listen to their deeper sense, which may appear neither logical nor reasonable. In her study of eleven institutions of higher education, Cass (2007) confirmed earlier research that campus programs aimed at reducing motivated offenders and suitable targets while increasing capable guardians (good men and women) do not seem to reduce sexual assaults on campus. This may be because universities are prone to aim prevention strategies at nighttime attacks by strangers rather than at the more frequent date or acquaintance sexual assaults. These latter incidents are where intuition may be most valuable in keeping a potential victim out of harm's way.

All groups within the university, to include administrators, students, faculty, and employees, are at risk of having a deviant or even dangerous member emerge within the group. These dangerous individuals in an organization frequently do not start out that way, and efforts to identify them in order to screen them out are frequently not productive (Quick, McFadyen, and Nelson, 2014). Cass (2007) found that individual-level factors rather than school-level factors (all of which were insignificant) were most statistically significant for predicting the probability of a sexual assault. Drug use, marital status, and being female were statistically significant risk factors. We discussed the important role of the bystander, which is a powerful positive role for a student to play, earlier in this chapter. Chapter 5 explores student education and training for prevention more extensively.

Faculty

The role of the faculty in protecting student rights and freedoms is distinctive in higher education (Green, Potts, Triechler, and Levy, 2013). Because faculty are among the most trusted adults in a student's life through their multiple roles as teacher, mentor, and adviser, they also may be among the first to whom a student reports a sexual assault. If the faculty member is a campus security authority, it is crucial for the integrity of the exchange for the student to have this information and to understand the obligation the faculty member has to report a sexual assault. Most faculty members will not be CSAs and therefore will not be obligated to report in accordance with the Clery Act. The implication is that most faculty will be neither trained investigators nor mandated reporters of sexual assault incidents.

Green, Potts, Triechler, and Levy (2013) suggest that faculty may offer important support in at least five ways:

1. They can listen to a student's disclosure and then make referral to the campus authorities or service providers best equipped to help.
2. They can take the disclosure seriously and help the student clarify his or her own confusion or doubts.
3. They can consider the need for immediate medical or psychological care.
4. They can clarify campus policy, procedures, and reporting; support the student in filing a report; and accompany the student in taking action.
5. They can help the student clarify her or his own thoughts about immediate or more long-term options.

Some see faculty in the role of capable guardian for students who come to them at a vulnerable time (Cass, 2007). Others see faculty as advocates, advisers, even comforters. But faculty members are not their students' parents. Framing the faculty role can be crucial. A particularly awkward possibility is for a student offender to confide in a trusted faculty member. Supporting a student to act courageously and do the right thing after committing a wrong is not easy.

While faculty are best cast in one or more of the positive roles just noted, they may be forced into the victim role, too. Especially women faculty are at risk of victimization (Dey, Korn, and Sax, 1996). The evidence shows a clear pattern of negative consequences for those who have been sexually harassed, which sadly is not surprising. Educating and training the faculty is addressed more extensively in chapter 6.

Staff

Staff can play a constructive role in addressing sexual assault. Campus security, safety, and police are instrumental in screening and monitoring the campus, a critical public health function. In addition, they apprehend suspects and take reports. Self-defense and resistance training, especially for young women students, can be an integral mission of the campus police force (Balemba and Beauregard, 2012; Gidycz and Dardis, 2014). Rape-resistance strategies have been documented to be effective, so it is surprising that feminist self-defense training has not gained more traction.

Caregiving is another staff function crucial with sexual assaults, including medical and psychological services as well as counseling and chaplain services. Time to presentation is an important variable to consider in these incidents, with delay resulting in adverse consequences for the survivor. Most women who present for exam following sexual assault do so expeditiously; McCall-Hosenfeld, Freund, and Liebschutz (2009), however, found that when the assailant is a family member or date, a woman is more likely to delay post-assault care. This may have particular relevance on a campus, where victims/survivors and offenders know each other. While their primary role is to provide after-incident support for anyone harmed, staff can be scripted into valuable preventive and educational roles as well. Their training and sensitivity to sexual assault is an essential ingredient in a comprehensive university system for a safe learning environment. Early intervention is always preferred. Chapter 7 explores staff training and education in greater depth.

Staff, faculty, students—all need to know how, where, and to whom to report a sexual assault. This should be determined by the university in its federal, state, community, and criminal justice context. The normative expectations of members within each of these four key constituencies may be in conflict with or may even silence what the university considers important and essential issues. In the worst cases, individuals or small groups within the university may hide or cover up wrongdoing for a range of misguided reasons, such as protecting a friend who is "a good person" and would be ruined by one bad incident report.

Campus Sexual Assault Prevention Board

The third institutional primary protective factor identified in figure 2.1, the Campus Sexual Assault Prevention Board, should include within it a smaller Sexual Assault Response Team (SART) with security and caregiving expertise that addresses incidents as they occur. The SART is composed of the first responders. (The origins of the SART model are discussed in chapter 7; we discuss our concept of a SART in chapter 8.) The CSAP Board should address the full range of sexual harassment issues (see Borowski, 2012, for the full continuum) and should be led by the Title IX coordinator. An additional eleven stakeholder groups have a vested interest in ensuring a secure educational experience:

1. Administrators and deans
2. Residential affairs and residential life personnel, to include student residential advisers
3. Students and student leaders
4. Human resource and personnel staff
5. Faculty
6. Student health services staff, to include both medical and psychological expertise
7. Athletic directors and coaches
8. Student organizations
9. Campus security

10. Legal services

11. Facilities personnel and managers (library, dining facilities, gyms)

While a CSAP Board of eleven to thirteen may seem large, the significant risk of sexual assault warrants a systemic commitment of resources. The budget matters when investing in people, protection, and prevention. The risks associated with sexual violence include both economic costs and burden of suffering costs for each campus sexual assault. Financial costs range from personnel costs for medical, psychological, and security forces to litigation costs when legal action ensues (see Cascio and Boudreau, 2011, for a thorough discussion of the financial impact of human resource initiatives). Burden of suffering costs range from pain and suffering for victims/survivors to guilt on the part of offenders who have caused harm. The moral and humanitarian argument for tertiary prevention and treatment is in addition to the utilitarian cost argument.

Universities underresource the office of the Title IX coordinator and CSAP Board at their own risk. Weick and Sutcliffe (2015) suggest that a key principle in dealing with unexpected events is deference to expertise. The concept of deference to expertise is critical with a campus sexual assault. There is a need for diverse stakeholder representation but also for core expertise in legal, medical, and psychological issues, and in campus security. The SART should be a first responder subset of the CSAP Board, the latter being a standing unit of the university engaged with surveillance, oversight, and monitoring of preventive interventions. The SART is a smaller, more nimble force under direction of the Title IX coordinator and aimed at immediate tertiary prevention with specific concern to avert death and long-term disability in worst-case incidents.

The CSAP Board concept is an extension of the organizational health center (OHC) model developed in the US Air Force (Adkins, 1999; Adkins, Quick, and Moe, 2000; Quick, Tetrick, Adkins, and Klunder, 2003). An OHC represents a comprehensive, integrated, cross-functional organizational health approach that addresses the full scope of protection and prevention in the occupational setting. Its mission is to keep people healthy and safe while advancing organizational performance and productivity. These goals are achieved by focusing on workplace stressors, organizational and individual forms of distress, and managerial as well as individual strategies for preventive stress management. The OHC seeks to combine organizational protection and individual prevention into a single function that reports to the senior leader in the organization. This reporting chain provides the executive team with a single point of entry into the health of the organization and its employees. In the case of one 13,000-person industrial complex, Quick and Klunder (2000) reported a $33 million cost savings from the protection and prevention program, as estimated by the human resource office. This model is adaptable to universities and colleges with primary focus on campus sexual assault problem.

The CSAP Board relies on a similar comprehensive, integrated, cross-functional approach to the specific worst-case risk of sexual assault. The board's preferred point of preventive intervention should be primary prevention, which emphasizes the risks and contextual factors that can set the conditions for sexual assault. While the ultimate goal would be to drive the incident rate to zero, the first-order goal should be to markedly lower the incident rate while impacting the low-intensity problems that may be precursors to worst-case outcomes. While the CSAP Board is best led by a senior university administrator, that person should collaborate with a psychologist, medical officer, or social worker with specialized knowledge in campus sexual assault or domestic violence.

The CSAP Board should have established, published, and well-advertised active early warning systems that seek equally to identify potential offenders and members of the community at risk of being sexually assaulted. Monitoring both categories of individuals is critical; monitoring for potential offenders or at-risk victims alone is insufficient. It also is important to identify employees at risk for physical, psychological, emotional, or behavioral distress.

Because of the scope and complexity of the operations, implementation of an OHC requires collaboration among a range of university functions concerned with human resources and relies on public health notions of surveillance that offer early warnings before disaster strikes. Once surveillance indicators are triggered, a range of preventive interventions can strengthen individuals and the university. Weick and Sutcliffe's (2015) emphasis on deference to expertise in high-reliability organizations translates to ensuring that the full range of expertise is represented in the CSAP Board.

Collaboration to Protect People

While a chief psychological officer in a university might be an ideal CSAP Board leader, so, too, might a social worker or a public health professional. The leader's role is to ensure a fully integrated body of expertise involving the human resources professional, health services staff, occupational safety personnel, security, legal advisers, athletic and fitness staff, university chaplains, student affairs, international office, and even financial aid, in partnership with representatives from students and faculty. The team approach brings a synergy to the work, reduces conflict among various subgroups, and can provide a source of social support to fellow team members, reducing the stress often associated with the emotional side of service provision.

This range of experts is also critical to establishing a monitoring system for people within the university. A cross-functional team approach reduces gaps and redundancies in services, enables better targeting of risk factors, and leverages resources to address those factors. A clear picture of who's healthy and who's at risk only emerges when all of the experts with responsibility for people and their well-being pool information. This collaboration is central to the protection of everyone in the university.

A strong, secure campus culture serves a protective function for the university and is a form of primary prevention for the problem of sexual assault and violence on campus. Within public health, the preferred point of intervention is always primary prevention. Primary prevention and campus culture set the conditions for ensuring success and safety within the campus community. Figure 2.1 identifies three key protective factors for universities: institutional policies and procedures; socialization and rituals; and a CSAP Board. Given the chronic nature of sexual assault, however, there is no reasonable expectation that primary prevention will solve the problem. Therefore, there is a need for secondary prevention (chapters 5, 6, and 7) as well as tertiary treatment (chapters 8 and 9).

While rape and attempted rape are infrequent events on most college campuses, they are of course significant. Lower levels of sexual assault and violence are more prevalent. The seriousness of a public health problem is determined by its pervasiveness, its rate of progression, and the intensity of its impact. That is why surveillance and screening are essential to monitoring for safety and security. Personal vigilance can pick up where campus surveillance systems reach their limits. Strong and committed campus leadership is essential to drive sexual assaults on campuses toward zero.

CHAPTER FIVE

Student Education and Training Programs

EDUCATING STUDENTS ABOUT sexual assault is one of the most important things any college or university can do. This education should start with first-year orientation and continue through graduation. This chapter is devoted to describing the types of education and training programs that have proven effective in developing the safest campus possible and includes case studies that illustrate what students should do to prevent sexual assault.

The Differing Benefits of Education and Training
Education

The *Oxford English Dictionary* defines *education* as the giving of systematic instruction. The instruction in this chapter encompasses the body of information known as Title IX plus supplemental information related to it.

Education should be a never-ending activity, because information is ever increasing and understanding of information is always changing. Laws will change over time, and how they are applied will change. Changing sociocultural norms may affect student behavior. How institutions of higher education address Title IX will evolve, too. So we must develop systems that are prepared for a never-ending process of information collection and dissemination.

Training

The *Oxford English Dictionary* defines *training* as activities that develop skills and behaviors and enable the learner to become more effective at applying knowledge. Students need to develop effective skills in, for example, identifying potential sexual assault perpetrators. Sitting through meetings and hearing a speaker describe Title IX will not help someone develop proficient skills in the way that ongoing training, especially with experiential exercises, will.

Ongoing training is needed due to continually changing laws and regulations, new cases, new employees, new faculty members and, of course, new students every year. The commitment to create safe campuses requires adequate resources for education, training, supervision, and administration of the processes and programs. A safe campus must be the highest priority, and it begins with commitment from the top levels of the institution and every level below.

For an example of the importance of ongoing education and training, consider military personnel. Soldiers are very aware of how fear impacts a person's ability to reason and react. In battle a soldier must rely on effective habits to survive. Combat training is both rigorous and repetitive for a reason: ingrained habits take over when mental reasoning disappears. During sexual assaults, fear can overcome the victim. Without effective habit learning, the victim may react passively or incomprehensibly. These behaviors and reactions are likely to confound investigators, witnesses, responders, and authorities (Hopper, 2015; Hopper, 2015, June 23).

Recommendations on Student Education and Training from the US Office for Civil Rights

In general, students should be the main focus of the institution's efforts to provide a safe environment. The US Office for Civil Rights recommends that students receive education and training at regular intervals throughout their college experience. The OCR also recommends that education and training should, at a minimum, cover the following topics (Office for Civil Rights, 2014).

1. What is Title IX?
2. Definitions of sexual harassment, sexual assault, sexual violence, same-sex sexual violence.
3. The institution's policies regarding Title IX.
4. The institution's definition of affirmative consent related to sexual activity, with examples.
5. How the institution determines unwelcome conduct related to Title IX.
6. How the institution determines the link between unwelcome sexual activity and creation of a hostile environment.
7. A student's options on making a formal or informal report, options regarding confidential disclosures, and the institution's reporting time frames.
8. The institution's grievance procedures related to sexual assault complaints.
9. The institution's disciplinary code related to sexual assault and related consequences.
10. Sexual assault trauma and possible neurobiological effects.
11. The link between alcohol and drugs and sexual assault cases, and how perpetrators use alcohol and drugs in sexual assaults.
12. Bystander intervention skills.
13. Instructions on how to report sexual assaults on campus and, if desired, to local law officials, and the option to pursue both campus and criminal proceedings simultaneously.
14. What protections against retaliation are provided by Title IX.

Additionally, we believe that students will be well served to receive education and training on the topics of students' rights with regard to Title IX; rape myths; and the hookup culture. Students also ought to receive education and training in identifying high-risk people and situations, assertiveness skills, and steps to take following an assault.

Understanding the Law on Sexual Assault

Administrators, faculty, security and other staff, and students all need to know the state's statutes regarding sexual assault. It is important not to make assumptions or speak from ignorance on such an important topic.

DeMatteo, Galloway, Arnold, and Patel (2015) conducted a review of the sexual assault statutes in all 50 states, and their findings revealed notable inconsistencies. First, while all states have laws on the books, some states have only one provision, while other states have considerably more (Massachusetts and Wisconsin, for example, have one provision; New York has twenty-six). Second, only 7 states provided an explicit explanation of consent, and only 14 states specified a definition of acting without the victim's consent. In the case of inability to consent due to alcohol or drugs, 24 states explicitly defined the matter within the statute; however, only 11 states addressed intoxication, and only 7 discussed voluntary intoxication (DeMatteo, Galloway, Arnold, and Patel, 2015).

Other notable differences between the states' statutes:

- In defining the offense, 18 states included the definition of *sexual assault*, 17 states included the definition of *rape*, and 11 states included the definition of *sodomy*.
- In 28 states, the statutes defined the requirements for *sexual conduct*, but only 14 states provided the requirements for *illegal sex act*. In 15 states, sexual assault charges can be altered depending on the specific sexual act. For instance, vaginal intercourse may result in criminal charges different from criminal charges for anal intercourse.
- In 19 states, sexual assaults among married couples were dealt with using a different legal standard, which may result in lower penalties following conviction. Another requirement may be the need to show physical force for conviction regardless of the statutory definitions for sexual assault or rape.
- In rape cases outside of marriage, 21 states had a "use of force" requirement and 17 states specifically identified the elements of "force."

- Most states used gender-neutral wording in their statutes. However, three states established that the victim must be female, while two states indicated that perpetrators must be male.

One of the challenges facing college administrators is aligning the statutory regulations with the sexual assault offenses committed on campus. In other words, do the state's laws have relevance for sexual assault victims on the state's college campuses? At the least, the statutes provide a legal avenue through the criminal justice system for victims of campus sexual assault. However, many state statutes do not specifically address the issues found in many campus sexual assault cases. One such area involves alcohol and drugs. Another area is where states require the perpetrator to have known the victim's capacity for alcohol and drugs at the time of the assault. Proving prior knowledge of incapacity can be a difficult hurdle to overcome at trial.

Sexual Assault Assertiveness Training

Assertiveness training, in particular situation-specific sexual assertiveness, can be helpful in preventing sexual assaults, especially in cases where prior sexual assault has occurred (Livingston, Testa, and Van Zile-Tamsen, 2007). Messman-Moore, Ward, and Walker (2007) identified four types of assertiveness that might be helpful in preventing sexual assault: relational assertiveness, sexual agency, sexual standards, and sex-related negative affect. Relational assertiveness describes sexual assertiveness in the context of a relationship or partner. Sexual agency is concerned with confidence in the level of sexual communication skills of the individual. Sexual standards describe the individual's ability to set limits and boundaries. Sex-related negative affect describes negative emotions connected with sexual activity.

The challenge for women who have been sexually assaulted is to overcome the difficulty of being sexually assertive in future sexual activities. The difficulty may stem from a lack of confidence that she has the right to refuse sexual advances or that her wishes will be respected

(Livingston, Testa, and VanZile-Tamsen, 2007). The ability to respond assertively to unwelcome sexual advances may also be affected by cognitive and emotional issues (Norris, Nurius, and Dimeff, 1996). Focusing too heavily on having a good time might prevent a woman from being aware of a potentially dangerous or vulnerable situation (Norris, Nurius, and Dimeff, 1996). Likewise, fear of being injured, of becoming self-conscious, or of losing a relationship may prevent a woman from responding assertively. If she responds assertively in a harmless situation, she might feel embarrassed or, worse, rejected (Nurius and Norris, 1996). The fear of "making a scene" or overreacting, or calling unwanted attention to herself, may prevent her from being assertive in sexual situations.

Sexual assertiveness is also dependent on a person's level of self-confidence in carrying out the resistance behaviors (Walsh and Foshee, 1998). A decrease in sexual resistance self-efficacy has been linked to increased sexual victimization, especially among young women (Kearns and Calhoun, 2010; Walsh and Foshee, 1998). Research suggests that in order to act in a sexually assertive manner, women must have strong assertiveness skills, be confident in their ability to act, and believe the benefits outweigh the costs.

Defining Affirmative Consent

Students must understand what constitutes consent so they won't be caught off guard after the fact. In general, it is expected that consent must be clearly expressed, voluntary, and understood. Incapacitated persons cannot grant consent. Persons under the influence of any drug cannot grant consent. Consent cannot be granted under the condition of coercion, force, or threat. Consent can be withdrawn at any time (OCR, 2014).

In many states, a person's age can prevent the granting of consent. In California, anyone under the age of 18 is legally unable to give consent. Consent cannot be granted if the person lacks the mental capacity to do so and such incapacity is obvious and understood by the perpetrator.

Affirmative consent includes:

- Checking with your partner before you advance from one activity to another. Example: When you move from kissing to touching or caressing intimate areas, you ask, "Is this okay with you?"
- Verbalizing your agreement by saying "Yes" or "I am okay with that for now."
- Signaling your agreement by nodding yes or guiding your partner to the next level. In other words, if you want your partner to caress you, you put his hand where you want to be caressed.

Affirmative consent differs by state. In New York, the state university system has developed the following guidelines (State University of New York, n.d.):

Affirmative consent is a knowing, voluntary, and mutual decision among all participants to engage in sexual activity. Consent can be given by words or actions, as long as those words or actions create clear permission regarding willingness to engage in the sexual activity. Silence or lack of resistance, in and of itself, does not demonstrate consent. The definition of consent does not vary based upon a participant's sex, sexual orientation, gender identity, or gender expression. . . .

- Consent to any sexual act or prior consensual sexual activity between or with any party does not necessarily constitute consent to any other sexual act.
- Consent is required regardless of whether the person initiating the act is under the influence of drugs and/or alcohol.
- Consent may be initially given but withdrawn at any time.
- Consent cannot be given when a person is incapacitated, which occurs when an individual lacks the ability to knowingly choose to participate in sexual activity. Incapacitation may be caused by the lack of consciousness or being asleep, being involuntarily restrained, or if an individual otherwise cannot consent. Depending on the degree of intoxication, someone who is under the influence

of alcohol, drugs, or other intoxicants may be incapacitated and therefore unable to consent.

- Consent cannot be given when it is the result of any coercion, intimidation, force, or threat of harm.
- When consent is withdrawn or can no longer be given, sexual activity must stop.

Misperception of Consent

One of the most common and significant problems with consent is a *perception of consent* versus explicit consent. Signals may be misperceived as consent. Some behaviors or body language that may be accepted as consent but are not include a lack of negative consent or simply not saying no; neutral consent or lack of resistance; accepting drinks; accepting a meal; going to an isolated spot; going to an apartment; flirting; suggestive talk; touching, especially private touching or heavy petting (Warshaw, 1988).

Misperception of sexual intent is enhanced by alcohol consumption (Abbey, McAuslan, and Ross, 1998). Men frequently perceive a woman's drinking as a signal of availability (Abbey, McAuslan, and Ross, 1998). A number of studies have supported this finding (Abbey and Harnish, 1995; Corcoran and Thomas, 1991; George et al., 1995).

Alcohol affects higher-order cognitive brain functions such as abstraction, conceptualization, and complex stimuli interpretation (Leonard, 1989; Steele and Southwick, 1985). When these brain functions are altered, cues can be misinterpreted. Men can easily misconstrue or misinterpret the simplest of cues when consuming alcohol. Women under the influence of alcohol may send signals that are difficult to interpret.

Rapist Profile

One of the keys to promoting personal safety and preventing sexual assaults is to educate and train people to recognize high-risk people and situations. People who commit sexual assaults have certain behaviors that can help identify them. The following list of chartacteristics and behaviors may help students identify a potential rapist (Warshaw, 1988; Malamuth, Sockloskie, Koss, and Tanaka, 1991). A rapist may

1. Try to demean you emotionally or attempt to control or abuse you emotionally.
2. Try to control you in different ways, such as controlling how you dress, use makeup, or style your hair, and controlling who you spend time with, including family or friends (try to isolate you).
3. Speak disparagingly about women; tell demeaning jokes and stories about women.
4. Get jealous without apparent provocation.
5. Frequently abuse drugs or alcohol and pressure you to join in.
6. Verbally pressure you to get drunk, use drugs, have sex, or go to isolated locations.
7. Refuse to let you share dating expenses or get angry if you offer to share.
8. Become physically violent.
9. Attempt to intimidate you, verbally or physically.
10. Be unable to cope with sexual or emotional frustration.
11. Act mentally, physically, or socially superior.
12. Be preoccupied with weapons.
13. Take pleasure in hurting animals or children or in bullying weaker people.
14. Frequently blame you for his shortcomings (see himself as never being wrong).
15. Objectify women (see women as sexual objects); make comments indicating an intense focus on body parts.
16. Verbalize attitudes of women as property or conquests; show a lack of respect toward women.

A less ominous indicator of a potential sexual predator is his dating history. A number of studies have indicated that frequent dating and sexual activities at an early age portend a higher level of sexual assaults and violence (Malamuth, Sockloskie, Koss, and Tanaka, 1991; Koss,

Leonard, Beezley, and Oros, 1985; Malamuth et al., 1995). These characteristics may or may not be accompanied by the behaviors listed above.

Students should be trained to see patterns of behaviors and the frequency with which they occur. A one-time observance of one behavior may not be a reliable indicator of a potential rapist. On the other hand, frequent demonstrations of multiple behaviors should be cause for alarm, or at least great caution. Someone who demonstrates a lack of respect for others may not be a good person to be alone with in a risky situation.

Bystander Research and Training

Another key component of reducing sexual assaults on campuses is a bystander program. The bystander phenomenon was conceptualized following the 1964 stabbing of a young woman in Queens, New York. According to a front-page *New York Times* article published soon after the incident, nearly forty people watched a man stalk and murder 28-year-old Kitty Genovese. During the thirty-five-minute attack, not one person reported the crime. Although many elements of the *Times* report have subsequently been debunked, including the assertion that no witnesses attempted to intervene, this tragedy sparked research efforts that continue to this day (Merry, 2016).

Researchers have suggested that in deciding whether to intervene, bystanders consider the relationship between the victim and perpetrator (Banyard, 2011). If the perpetrator was a stranger, it was highly probable that he or she would flee in the event of an intervention. If the victim and the perpetrator knew each other—if they were spouses, for example—it was highly probable that the perpetrator would stand and fight with the intervening bystander. In the first situation, the threat of personal injury to the bystander would be considered low. In the second instance, the threat of personal injury would be high, possibly very high (Shotland and Straw, 1976). Even so, the researchers found that even when the threat of injury to the victim and the bystander was high, bystanders were still likely to intervene (Fischer, Greitemeyer, Pollozek, and Frey, 2006). When bystanders are in a group they are less likely to intervene than when they are alone (Latane and Darley, 1970). In a group of friends or when the victim is known, however, bystanders are more willing to intervene (Levine and Crowther, 2008).

Bennett and Banyard's 2016 study found that having a relationship with the victim makes the bystander more willing to intervene. Thus bystander intervention training on preventing sexual assaults must encourage participants to imagine that they know the victim. Another finding from the study: when the bystander knew the perpetrator, intervening was less likely. To encourage bystanders to take action, institutions should craft policies that offer bystanders a safety net (Bennett and Banyard, 2016).

Bystander prevention education and training generally address sexual assault education, building empathy for the victim, and how to safely intervene (Palm Reed, Hines, Armstrong, and Cameron, 2015). Researchers have suggested that utilizing students in the training process promotes more open communication and less defensiveness (Palm Reed, Hines, Armstrong, and Cameron, 2015). In a typical campus sexual violence prevention education program, the focus tends to be two-fold: perpetrator penalties and victimization prevention skills (Kleinsasser, Jouriles, McDonald, and Rosenfeld, 2015). Researchers hold that such education programs may fail to fully engage the students due to their inability to identify as either the perpetrator or the victim (Kleinsasser, Jouriles, McDonald, and Rosenfeld, 2015; Foubert, Langhinrichsen-Rohling, Brasfield, and Hill, 2010). One step toward engagement is to add bystander intervention training to the sexual violence prevention program. Such a move makes everyone a potential actor in creating safe campuses (Kleinsasser, Jouriles, McDonald, and Rosenfeld, 2015).

Negatives related to conducting sexual violence prevention programs include the amount of time it takes to train thousands of students in small groups and the resources needed, such as a fully trained and experienced staff. Additionally, some students might be uncomfortable talking about sexual violence in a mixed-group setting. To address these concerns, one approach, called Take Care, was developed as an online presentation. Because the course is just twenty minutes long, its developers were forced to focus on one outcome and one process. The outcome was bystander intervention among friends, and the process was to increase an individual's willingness to intervene.

The Take Care online video training program has been evaluated using an experimental method. Ninety-three students were randomly assigned to either Take Care or a control group that viewed an online study skills program. Participants were measured on their beliefs and ability to execute bystander behaviors. Respondents in the intervention group reported higher levels of efficacy for performing bystander behaviors at the post-test measurement as well as two months later, compared to those in the control group. As noted above, friends are more likely to help a friend than to help a stranger. Since many sexual assaults occur in the victim's campus residence, typical bystanders are likely to be roommates or friends. Participants in the treatment group reported performing increased bystander behaviors for friends at the two-month follow-up assessment. The researchers assert that the results indicate the program can increase bystander behavior toward friends (Kleinsasser, Jouriles, McDonald, and Rosenfeld, 2015).

Bringing in the Bystander, a sexual assault prevention program that focuses on bystander intervention, was created at the University of New Hampshire (Senn and Forrest, 2016). Among undergraduate students, it has shown positive results in bystander self-efficacy, attitudes, and behaviors. Additionally, students indicated increases in knowledge about rape, changes in attitude toward rape, and readiness to change (Banyard, Moynihan, and Plante, 2007; Banyard, Eckstein, and Moynihan, 2010; Senn and Forrest, 2016).

The University of Windsor added a novel implementation plan to the Bringing in the Bystander program by embedding Bringing in the Bystander into undergraduate courses. Two undergraduate courses trained facilitators who then went out to other courses to instruct more students. The facilitators were students who worked in male-female pairs under the supervision of a faculty member. One course focused on sexual violence theory and research and bystander intervention theory and research. The second course focused on additional sexual violence content and group facilitation skills (Senn and Forrest, 2016). The facilitators provided the three-hour workshop to first-year students, and it proved effective in improving bystander efficacy and increasing bystander intervention readiness, intent, and proactive behavior (Senn and Forrest, 2016).

A male-focused bystander program, the Men's Project, is facilitated by graduate students who are introduced to the participants as sexual assault and gender experts (Stewart, 2014). It is conducted over eleven weeks with two-hour sessions each week. The first three weeks explore masculinity, socialization, and male privilege, then five weeks are devoted to all aspects of sexual assault. The last three weeks focus on bystander intervention strategies.

Week 1: Explore gender and multiple qualities of masculinity

Weeks 2 and 3: Analyze gender socialization, male privilege and power, male sexuality, homophobia, and prejudice

Weeks 4, 5, and 6: Thoroughly analyze sexual assault

Weeks 7 and 8: Develop victim empathy by engaging with assault survivors

Weeks 9, 10, and 11: Conduct training in bystander intervention and sexual assault prevention

The Men's Project has demonstrated increases in participants' bystander efficacy, bystander intervention, and feminist activism. Participants indicated reductions in sexism, rape myth acceptance, and the use of gender-biased language (Stewart, 2014).

Preserving Evidence

Following a sexual assault, correctly preserving evidence is very important if a formal complaint is to be made either to the institution or to law enforcement. While sexual assault victims may choose not to report the assault to the police or to the university, collecting evidence is vital to keeping the options open. (Note that in some jurisdictions, underage assaults must be reported to authorities.)

Even when a student victim is not yet sure whether she or he wants to have a sexual assault forensic examination (also called a rape kit) performed, it is strongly recommended that the victim *not* do any of the following:

- Wash any part of the body
- Use the bathroom
- Remove or wash articles of clothing (if any clothing is removed, *do* use a paper bag to protect it)
- Comb hair or brush teeth
- Clean the area of the room, building, or elsewhere where the assault occurred
- Eat or drink anything

Usable DNA can perhaps be collected as long as 120 hours after the assault (Office of Justice Programs, 2017). However, going immediately to the clinic or hospital to have an exam done provides the best chance of collecting and preserving the evidence. Other things to consider within five days of an assault are pregnancy prevention and sexually transmitted diseases treatment as well as toxicology testing. Toxicology testing may be recommended within 96 hours if the victim has an awareness of lost time, unconsciousness, or periods of confusion (Office of Justice Programs, 2017). This testing is also indicated if the victim has motor control problems or memory loss or is suspicious of having been drugged.

Students Helping Students following an Assault

Students should be trained on how to help a friend who becomes a victim of sexual assault. They should let their friend know that they believe him or her. Students should also show their friend support by doing the following (Bohmer and Parrot, 1993):

- Listen carefully without interrupting
- If your friend just wants to sit quietly, just sit quietly
- Acknowledge your friend's feelings
- Ask what you can do to help
- Offer to go to the hospital or to the police with your friend, if she or he wants to go

- Offer to go to the Title IX coordinator with your friend
- Remind your friend that the perpetrator is at fault, not the victim
- Offer to stay with your friend if she or he does not want to be alone
- Help your friend recognize rape trauma signs
- Avoid saying anything that might be construed as blaming the victim
- Recognize that your friend might not want to be touched or hugged
- Respect your friend's privacy, and keep all details confidential
- Help your friend examine the options following the assault

Working with Established Programs
White Ribbon Campaign

The White Ribbon Campaign offers five workshops based on social learning theory, social norms theory, belief system theory, and bystander theory. The first workshop, Building Ally-ship Together with Women and Girls to End Gender-Based Violence, runs 1½ hours and costs $250 and up for schools and nonprofit organizations. It discusses the causes of gender-based violence and preventions for gender-based violence, and it shows participants how to understand their own emotions; bystander interventions; consent; and healthy masculine qualities.

The second workshop, Building Ally-ship and Unpacking "Bro-Culture," runs 2½ hours, costs $350, and extends the material to white male privilege, rape culture, and the bro-culture prevalent in the media and on social media. Participants also explore ways to promote gender equality and healthy masculine qualities. The third workshop also runs 2½ hours, costs $350 and up, and focuses on consent and speaking out against violence. The workshop consists of discussions, role-play, and skills development.

The fourth workshop, Building Ally-ship and Exploring My Own Role and Commitment to Ending Gender-Based Violence, runs 4 hours, starts at $500, and expands the previous content to include educating participants on how to become change agents in their communities. Experiential learning activities are used to develop skills in survivor support, addressing gender norms, developing empathy, listening, and affirmative consent.

The fifth workshop is titled Building Ally-ship through Storytelling and Action Planning. This workshop lasts 6½ hours, costs $750 for educational institutions and nonprofit organizations, and combines the materials from the first four programs with action planning to end gender-based violence in communities. Participants brainstorm, prioritize objectives, and create a plan. They also learn how to tell their own story and connect with others.

White Ribbon claims to be the world's largest movement that engages men to end violence against women and promote gender equality in building healthy relationships. The organization began in Toronto in 1991 and is active in sixty countries. No quantitative studies have been made gauging its effectiveness.

The Men's Workshop

The Men's Workshop is presented to male undergraduates over two sessions: a prevention program lasting 1½ hours and, four months later, a 1-hour follow-up. The program is designed to create empathy, correct misunderstandings about what is "normal," define consent, and explore bystander intervention. The workshop follows an integrated model that suggests that the willingness to commit or justify a sexual assault is influenced by the person's attitudes, beliefs, socialization, and peers. The program seeks to dispel rape myths and improve attitudes toward women; improve peer group attitudes and behaviors toward sexual assault; instill appropriate sexual behavior norms; improve willingness to intervene and support a sexual assault victim; better understand what constitutes consent; and reduce sexual aggression.

Participants discuss their dating frustrations and after completing the prevention program are more receptive, it is hoped, to discussions of masculinity, rape myths, bystander interventions, empathy, consent, and sexual aggression. In the follow-up booster session, the participants review affirmative consent and bystander intervention behaviors. They also engage in small group discussions about their experiences using content from the first workshop.

One study using an experimental model indicated that compared to the control group, the participants showed less motivation to engage in sexually aggressive behaviors, fewer interactions with peers who exhibit sexually aggressive tendencies, and fewer sexually explicit media experiences (Gidycz, Orchowski, and Berkowitz, 2011).

The Men's Program

The Men's Program: Ending Rape through Peer Education is designed as a rape prevention workshop based on a peer-to-peer format with male peers delivering the content to college-age males. The objectives are to help the audience understand what a rape victim experiences (victim empathy), how to help a rape victim recover, bystander intervention, and rape prevention. A DVD and a manual facilitate an interactive dialogue between the presenters and the audience. The materials are freely available on the website https://cultureofrespect.org/program/mens-program/.

The theoretical foundation for this program follows belief system theory and the elaboration likelihood model. Belief system theory indicates that interventions must take into account a person's existing self-concept in order to effect attitude and behavioral changes (Grube, Mayton, and Ball-Rokeach, 1994). Consistent with this theory, the Men's Program relates to the audience as people who know sexual assaults are wrong and would not commit them, instead of treating the audience members as potential perpetrators. The elaboration likelihood model of persuasion indicates that there are two paths we use to make decisions and become persuaded. People who are motivated and engaged are able to make logical, conscious decisions. This process can produce permanent changes in attitudes and behaviors. The second path, the peripheral route, is characterized as being swayed by surface factors such as liking the speaker. Attitude and behavior change are likely to occur but only on a temporary basis (Petty and Cacioppo, 1986b).

The Men's Program begins with the 37-minute video that describes the rape of a male by another male. The video wants to show how a rape survivor feels following the assault. Then the program presenters connect the male survivor experience to the female survivor experience, to elicit empathy toward all survivors. Next the audience is shown how to support a sexual assault survivor. Presenters help the audience understand affirmative consent and role-play bystander intervention techniques. Finally, the audience members learn how to confront a peer when they hear inappropriate and demeaning jokes about women or sexual assault or when peers boast about abusing women (Foubert, 2011).

Research on the effectiveness of the Men's Program indicates a significant increase in self-reported willingness to intervene when witnessing a sexual assault and perceived efficacy to engage in bystander techniques. Some research has shown significant decreases in rape myth acceptance based on self-reports as compared to a comparison group. Researchers have also suggested that after attending the program, participants who might be at high risk to perpetrate sexual assault are less likely to do so (Foubert, Tatum, and Donahue, 2006; Langhinrichsen-Rohling et al., 2011).

Green Dot

Dr. Dorothy J. Edwards created the Green Dot bystander intervention program in 2007. Following a 50-minute motivational speech, intensive bystander training begins and can last up to 6 hours. The speech, provided by the Green Dot staff, motivates students to engage in sexual assault prevention. The bystander training is provided for groups of twenty to twenty-five students and focuses on using intervention techniques safely and effectively. The speech is presented to large groups of students; the bystander training is usually voluntary.

Green Dot utilizes peer opinion leaders to train a select number of students who in turn spread the bystander techniques to the larger campus population. The peer opinion leaders are nominated for the bystander training by faculty, staff, students, and resident assistants.

Typical peer opinion leaders are student organization officers, athletes, high academic achievers, and student government leaders. Faculty and administrators also can become Green Dot facilitators by attending a 4-day train-the-trainer program.

The theoretical basis supporting the Green Dot program includes diffusion of innovation theory, bystander intervention literature, and literature related to how victims are targeted (Coker et al., 2011). A study in 2014 compared one Green Dot campus with two other campuses that lacked bystander intervention programs. The campus with the Green Dot program indicated significantly lower violent victimizations. Violent perpetrations were also lower among men who participated in the Green Dot program (Coker et al., 2011).

In the Coker, Cook-Craig, Williams, Fisher, Clear, Garcia, and Hegge 2011 study, Green Dot participants indicated significantly lower rape myth acceptance scores than nonparticipating students; participants also reported significant increases in bystander behaviors in themselves and others. Students who attended the training reported more active bystander behaviors than students who only attended the speech.

The Green Dot organization invites institutions to contact it directly to discuss using its programs. Programs are developed to meet specific needs of an institution, with fees calculated case by case.

Ohio University Sexual Assault Risk Reduction Project

In Ohio University's Sexual Assault Risk Reduction Project, the social learning model focused on awareness of high-risk situations and coping by implementing role-play exercises and modeling techniques (Gidycz et al., 2001). The researchers also drew from the elaboration likelihood model and the health belief model (Petty and Cacioppo, 1986a; Gidycz et al., 2001). In keeping with the former, the program focused on maximizing central route reprocessing by making the message more relevant to the attendees, which increased motivation to actively participate in the workshop. Central route processing is posited to contribute to increased stable attitude and behavior change. The health belief model suggests that a change in beliefs precedes a change in behavior.

That is, when facing a perceived threat coupled with a perceived vulnerability, people are more likely to take action when they believe the threat can be overcome (Gidycz et al., 2001).

The program was presented in one session to undergraduate women only and lasted 3 hours. Goals were to increase awareness of the risk of sexual assault, learn defensive behaviors focusing on assertiveness techniques, reduce victim blaming, boost victim support, and reduce both victimization and revictimization. Two videos were shown ("I Thought It Could Never Happen to Me" and "Sexual Assault Risk Factors: A Training Video"), and role-plays and interactive discussions were used in both large and small group settings.

Seven hundred sixty-two women were randomly assigned to either a treatment group or control group. The most important finding was that women in the treatment group who experienced sexual assault between the workshop and the two-month follow-up were less likely to be revictimized at the six-month follow-up (Gidycz et al., 2001).

Assess, Acknowledge, Act Resistance Training

Assess, Acknowledge, Act (AAA) was developed as a training program for resisting acquaintance sexual assault (Rozee and Koss, 2001; Senn, 2013). It helps young women at the high school and university levels and is delivered in three 3-hour courses, adaptable to 90 minutes.

To prepare women to resist acquaintance rape, research identified the need to develop risk perception skills (Gray, Lesser, Quinn, and Brounds, 1990). AAA increases the perception of acquaintance sexual assault risk. Heightened perceptions are expected to generate much quicker danger assessments in dealing with acquaintance rape (Senn, 2013; Nurius and Norris, 1996).

The program also increases participants' belief in their ability to defend themselves from sexual assault. This idea contrasts with the often held ideas that women fear getting hurt or angering the perpetrator if they resist, and that women are unlikely to resist verbally or physically because their efforts are believed to be ineffective. Sexual assault myth resistance and the most effective resistance tactics, which

AAA addresses, have been shown to increase a participant's belief in successful resistance (Senn, 2013; Ullman, 1997).

AAA also reduces acceptance of rape myths, leading to reduced self-blame. The myths countered include "uncontrollable" male sexual urges and female provocations as causes of sexual assaults.

Assess, Acknowledge, Act Curriculum. In the first of the three AAA courses, topics include learning the difference between resistance and prevention, debunking rape myths, identifying social and environmental risks and their connection to personal safety, linking dating practices to women's safety, and identifying male behavioral cues leading to sexual assaults. In the second course, topics include defining personal sexual boundaries, identifying the effects following a sexual assault, analyzing obstacles to acquaintance sexual assault resistance, developing resistance skills against verbal attacks, and overcoming miscommunication. In the third course, students learn sexual assault resistance tactics, how to overcome resistance obstacles, acquaintance resistance tactics, self-defense (martial arts) training, how to overcome surprise attacks, and effective attitudes toward responsibility and blame (Senn, 2013).

The three courses utilize "information providing games, many lectures, facilitated discussion, brainstorming, large and small group activities, application practice with DVD and audio clips, written scenarios and role-plays" (Senn et al., 2013). For course details contact Dr. Charlene Y. Senn at the University of Windsor.

Using Experiential Learning in Student Training

It is clear that effectively training students is the first and arguably most important step in creating safe campuses. Getting students to buy into the process is easier said than done, however. All the same reasons they feel invulnerable in general can lead them to feel the training is unnecessary. For these reasons, it is critical to find ways to train students which will not only be effective but hold their attention.

We believe the best way to do this is with experiential training and case scenario discussion. Research shows this type of learning to be effective

(Gosen and Washbush, 2004). Students are motivated and therefore can reasonably be expected to stay engaged (Ambrose et al., 2010). Research on the outcome of experiential sexual assault training showed that it increased the students' knowledge and insight (Jozkowski and Ekbia, 2015).

The following three scenarios could be part of student training.

Case One

It was the first week of the fall semester, and the largest fraternity on campus was having a party. An open invitation went out to all students. Susie, a first year, and her dorm mates Joy, Amanda, and Cindy decided to go as a group and stick together since they did not know many people on campus yet.

And they did stay together the first hour. They also began accepting drinks from the fraternity brothers. It wasn't just being polite to accept the alcohol, it was a way to overcome their shyness. Susie in particular was happy to drink quickly to reduce her anxiety about being in a new place.

A couple of hours and many drinks later, the four dorm friends were obviously drunk." The fraternity leader announced that all the women were required to "run the gauntlet." Twenty fraternity brothers lined up against each wall along the second-floor hallway. As the women proceeded down the hall, the fraternity brothers were touching, grabbing, and undressing the girls. By the time the women reached the end of the hall, their breasts and genital areas had been fondled by multiple fraternity members.

After the gauntlet, the dorm mates immediately left. The girls were disgusted but did not discuss the experience back at the dorm. The next day, over breakfast, two of the girls could not remember much about the night but felt very uncomfortable. The other two girls remembered the gauntlet and were distraught. They wanted to report it to the resident director. The first two girls argued against this for fear of being branded snitches and being ostracized, especially by the popular fraternity brothers. After much back and forth, the girls decided not to report the incident.

1. Describe and discuss the dorm mates' actions prior to the gauntlet.
2. What actions might have helped the dorm mates during the experience?
3. Do you agree with the decision not to report the incident?
4. Should the dorm mates preserve evidence in case they decide to make a formal report?
5. Should the dorm mates tell their friends about their experience at the party?

Case Two

Antonio was the All-America captain of the basketball team. Sylvia was a sophomore and a big basketball fan. Sylvia met Antonio at a party after the second home game of the season. Antonio was the high scorer that night and was having a few beers to celebrate. Sylvia was taken with Antonio's personality. Antonio invited Sylvia to the next home game with a front-row ticket. Sylvia was thrilled.

After the game, Antonio invited Sylvia to his apartment to have a drink. Sylvia, knowing that Antonio lived with four other guys, was not overly concerned about being alone with him. At the apartment, Antonio pulled a bottle of wine from the refrigerator and poured Sylvia a glass. Antonio invited Sylvia to his bedroom, and she went without hesitation. After half a glass, Sylvia began to feel drowsy. She tried to leave and opened the door, then fell onto Antonio's bed. One of Antonio's roommates noticed Sylvia's attempt to leave and saw her falling backward into the room.

The roommate went to the door just as Antonio pushed it closed. The roommate opened the door and saw Sylvia apparently unconscious on the bed and Antonio attempting to remove her clothes. The roommate asked Antonio if Sylvia was passed out. Antonio just laughed.

Antonio proceeded to have sex with Sylvia. When he was finished, he turned over and fell asleep. A few hours later, Sylvia stumbled out of the room and asked the roommate who had witnessed the unconscious Sylvia for a ride home. The roommate took Sylvia back to her dorm without saying a word.

The next morning Sylvia was confused and fearful. She could not remember anything from the night before except, vaguely, someone coming into the bedroom saying Antonio should stop. Her pelvic area was very sore, and she thought she might be bleeding. She removed her underwear and noticed blood and semen on it. One of her breasts had what appeared to be bite marks. She didn't know if she should call the police, go to the hospital, or report the incident to the university administration.

1. Describe and discuss Sylvia's actions.
2. Describe and discuss Antonio's actions.
3. Critical moments? Decisions? Results?
4. Should Sylvia preserve the evidence?
5. Should Sylvia go to the hospital or contact the Title IX coordinator?
6. Should Sylvia speak to Antonio's roommate to find out what happened?
7. Should she report the incident to campus security?
8. Should she make a complaint to the police?

Case Three

The four women and four men were all seniors at college but had been friends since elementary school. During high school and college they had casually dated each other, and they knew each other well. Every spring, they would go on weekend bike trips. The mountains near campus provided a wonderful escape from the stress of classes and exams. The trips would begin Friday evening and conclude Sunday night. For the two nights on the road, they would sleep in tents. The sleeping arrangements were pretty casual. Dating couples would sleep together. Everyone else would pair up and pick a tent. Everyone felt safe.

On Saturday night of their most recent trip, Olivia and Billy ended up in a tent together. In the middle of the night, Olivia awoke with a sharp pain in her pelvic area. Billy had slid her panties down and inserted his penis into her vagina from behind. Olivia was shocked and afraid. She lay there motionless, pretending to be asleep. She feared that if she said anything, Billy might harm her. When they had been dating she had rebuffed his advances many times. Although he would make his frustration clear, she hadn't felt threatened by him. Now she was afraid that he was having sex with her without her consent.

When Billy ejaculated, he pulled her panties up and rolled over and went to sleep. Olivia got up and went to the tent where the other women were sleeping and asked to stay with them. Without asking for an explanation, two of the other women agreed.

In the morning, after everyone was up, Olivia confronted Billy, demanding to know why he had raped her the night before. Billy stammered that he thought Olivia was okay with the sex because she didn't protest. He apologized for committing the act without her consent. Olivia announced that she could not finish the trip. She and two of the other women headed back to campus.

1. Describe and discuss Olivia's behavior before, during, and after the incident.
2. Describe and discuss Billy's behavior during and after the incident.
3. Can you explain Olivia's response after the incident?
4. Should Olivia preserve the evidence?
5. Should Olivia make a formal complaint to the Title IX coordinator or campus security?
6. Should Olivia make a formal complaint to local law enforcement?

This chapter on student education and training may be the most important in the book. On a college campus, students are the largest and most vulnerable population, so efforts to create safe campuses should focus on them. The truly committed institution must consider sexual assault education and training to be as important as obtaining a degree. Providing ample resources for all aspects of creating a safe place to live and learn is one important measure of that commitment. The goal is to create a campus free of sexual violence and assault.

CHAPTER SIX

Faculty Education and Training

FACULTY MEMBERS PLAY an integral role in the lives of college students and have a unique relationship with them. The faculty give instruction in the classroom and provide advising to help students select classes and navigate their curriculum choices. They support student clubs and sports teams as academic advisers and accompany students who travel abroad. Due to their involvement with students on many levels, faculty members may be contacted by students who wish to report incidents of sexual assault.

Faculty members have an opportunity to be a catalyst for change when it comes to sexual assaults. They can take on the challenge of educating and training students, faculty, and staff, and the outreach of these efforts can extend to the community and to high schools and elementary schools. Faculty can encourage students to initiate proven programs, such as Take Back the Night, and can act as advisers for these programs. Faculty members can embed sexual assault training within their courses, or create new courses, to help students continually appreciate the importance of this topic.

Interested faculty can engage in related research, take a role in developing institutional policy and grievance procedures, and participate as hearing board members. They can engage in campus-wide programs to increase awareness.

To be effective, faculty members need extensive education and training in all areas of sexual violence and sexual assault. The Office for Civil Rights of the US Department of Health and Human Services recommends that faculty members have training in:

- Federal and state laws on Title IX and Title IV
- The institution's policies on Title IX and Title IV
- Definitions of sexual harassment, sexual violence, sexual assault, and dating violence
- The institution's jurisdiction and responsibilities both on and off campus
- Procedures for a complainant to report a violation
- Identifying a potential or actual Title IX or Title IV allegation or complaint
- Who to contact (for example, security, the Title IX coordinator) and telephone, email, and office location information for the contact
- How students may file a criminal complaint and their rights to do so
- What to do if a student reports a Title IX or Title IV allegation
- How to respond
- How to preserve evidence
- How to effectively communicate without discouraging a complainant from reporting incidents
- How to accept and process a Title IX allegation
- State and federal definitions of consent, rape, sexual assault, dating violence, stalking, and sexual harassment
- Institutional policies and procedures related to sexual assault, dating violence, stalking, and sexual harassment
- Consequences following Title IX allegations

Additionally, faculty members should know:

- How to appropriately interact with sexual victims to avoid further trauma

- How criminal investigations differ from institutional Title IX investigations
- When and how to share information with Title IX institutional investigators
- The consequences of providing false information during a Title IX investigation
- How to cooperate with criminal investigations and proceedings
- How to encourage victim and witness cooperation during investigation
- The complainant's and the alleged perpetrator's rights during investigations, hearings, and appeals
- Remedies for the complainant following Title IX allegations
- The difference between "preponderance of evidence," "clear and convincing evidence," and "beyond a reasonable doubt"

Responsible Employees and Mandated Reporters

The US Department of Education defines a "responsible employee" as "any employee who has the authority to take action to redress the harassment, who has a duty to report to appropriate school officials sexual harassment or any other misconduct by students or employees, or an individual who a student could reasonably believe has this authority or responsibility" (Office for Civil Rights, 2001). It is the responsibility of the institution to clearly identify and notify employees considered to be responsible employees. It is also incumbent on the institution to train responsible employees how to respond to sexual assault victims and how to report according to the institution's policies.

"Mandated reporters" are those institution members who are governed by law to report incidents of child abuse. Abuse is usually defined as physical abuse, sexual abuse, or emotional abuse. Mandatory reporting laws differ from state to state. Certain states require that specific professions must report child abuse to the appropriate authority, whereas in other states, anyone who suspects that a child has been abused is required to report (Child Welfare Information Gateway, n.d.).

While most states designate which professionals are considered mandated reporters of child abuse (social workers, teachers, school administrators, and other school employees; doctors, nurses, and other health care personnel; mental health counselors and therapists; child care providers; law enforcement personnel), there are state-by-state distinctions about which further occupations or professions are designated as mandated reporters. Commercial film or photo processors are required to report in twelve states, computer technicians are in six states, and day camp, youth center, and recreation facility employees and volunteers are in thirteen states. In eleven states faculty members, administrators, athletic personnel, and employees and volunteers in colleges, universities, and vocational schools are designated mandated reporters (Child Welfare Information Gateway, n.d.).

Institutions of higher education are required by Title IX to state which employees are designated as responsible employees or mandated reporters for all incidents of sexual violence and sexual assault. Institutions also must publicize which employees are responsible employees, so a student can make an informed decision whether to report a sexual assault to an employee thus designated. A responsible employee is required to report all sexual assault incidents to the Title IX coordinator and other appropriate institution officials. A responsible employee is also required to inform sexual assault complainants of his or her reporting obligations (OCR, 2014). Roles that are designated as "responsible employee" or "mandated reporter" vary among institutions.

A faculty member who is not a responsible employee or mandated reporter is not required to immediately report a sexual assault to the Title IX coordinator or other appropriate officials (OCR, 2014). These faculty members can decide for themselves how they will handle the reporting of such incidents. All institutions should explicitly designate their "responsible employees" as required by the Office for Civil Rights (2014).

All institutions need to review the laws in their jurisdiction to comply with the mandated reporter requirements. It is strongly recommended that institutions take a proactive approach to ensure that all parties are informed and trained on their responsibilities.

Faculty Members as First Responder

A faculty member may become a first responder to a sexual assault victim in multiple ways. One is when the student approaches the faculty member and reports an incident. A second is when the faculty member recognizes one or more of the warning signs of assault and approaches the student. The third way a faculty member may become a first responder is when another party notifies a faculty member about an assault.

A Student Reports an Incident

In the case of the faculty member being directly approached by the student, the faculty member should first ask if medical attention is needed. If it is, the faculty member should help the student get to the proper medical facility. Faculty members should know in advance where students should go for medical attention in the event of a sexual assault (American Association of University Professors, 2012).

If the student does not need immediate medical attention and the faculty member is a mandated reporter, the faculty member should state his or her status as a responsible employee who is required by the institution to report the details of all sexual assaults. Then if the student would rather speak to someone who can maintain confidentiality, the faculty member should provide the student with a list of names and contact information that he or she should have on hand, ready to share (OCR, 2014).

If the student still wants to report the incident to the faculty member, then the faculty member should listen carefully as the student relates the details. When the student stops talking, the faculty member may ask some open-ended questions (Cole, Hustoles, and McClain, 2006). The faculty member's objective is to provide a sympathetic ear. The faculty member is not required or expected to make a determination whether a crime has been committed. It is especially important that the faculty member avoid further trauma to the student, so the faculty member must avoid judgmental or biased comments or questioning (OCR, 2014).

Once the student has finished describing incident details, the faculty member should assist with the next steps. First, the student should be encouraged to make a formal complaint. The student should be advised that a supportive adviser can accompany the student during the filing meeting. Then if the student chooses, a complaint can be made, with a request of confidentiality, to the Title IX coordinator (OCR, 2014).

A Faculty Member Observes Warning Signs

In the second scenario, the faculty member notices a change in a student's behavior or grades or mood, or notices an unusual interaction between students, and approaches the student. The faculty member should be prepared for any response. The student may say that something is bothering her and agree to talk about it. The faculty member should then arrange a meeting to discuss the matter. It is important to conduct the meeting in a quiet, comfortable place soon after approaching the student.

If the student says that something is bothering her but does not want to discuss it, the faculty member should respect the student's wishes. The student still needs to speak with someone, however, so the faculty member may suggest that she speak with the Title IX coordinator (if the faculty member suspects the student is a sexual assault victim). Or the student could speak with a campus counselor who will maintain the student's confidentiality (OCR, 2014). Or the faculty member may suggest that the student speak to another faculty member with whom the student feels more comfortable.

The student may say that nothing is bothering her and she has no need to speak further. If he or she has exhibited signs of possible sexual assault but adamantly denies that anything is wrong, the faculty member may suggest a future meeting if the student ever wishes to discuss anything. The faculty member may remind the student of the confidential counselors available on campus as well as the help available from the Title IX coordinator (OCR, 2014). All faculty members should be able to provide names and contact information in case any student needs to discuss a problem now or in the future.

It is strongly recommended that all of the institution's employees be trained on the warning signs of sexual assault victims. Faculty members in particular can identify and assist students who may be victims. The warning signs are many (Rape Crisis, 2017).

Physical warning signs include:

- Sobbing or other signs of being emotionally upset for no apparent reason
- Unable to focus or concentrate
- Staring off into space or other signs of not being mentally present
- On edge, restless
- Lethargic, sluggish, sleepy
- Self-absorbed, unwilling to socialize
- Unwilling to be alone
- Unable to communicate clearly; may stammer or speak in a hesitant manner
- Easily startled, jumpy
- Heightened sense of alertness; hypervigilant
- Easily agitated
- Reveals relationship problems with friends and family members
- No longer want to be intimate
- Unexplained lifestyle changes (such as residence changes, physical appearance)
- Drug and alcohol abuse
- Changes in personal hygiene (increased or decreased bathing)
- Self-destructive behaviors: suicide attempts, cutting, high-risk acts (like walking on a window ledge)
- Changes in grades, attendance

Psychological warning signs include:

- Heightened anxiousness and anxiety; worried
- Feeling guilt, self-blame, unworthy, worthless, undeserving
- Self-loathing or extreme disgust with self (turning inward)
- Feeling helpless, hopeless
- Feeling humiliated, ashamed, embarrassed

- Has low self-esteem, low self-worth
- Feeling dirty, unclean, soiled
- Angry
- Aloneness (excluded from others, isolated)
- Numbness (shocked, unable to think or feel)
- Confused
- Memory loss
- Mentally replays the assault over and over
- Flashbacks
- Nightmares and night tremors
- Depression
- Suicidal

A faculty member may observe unusual behavior between students that may indicate a problem. For example, while exiting a classroom, the faculty member witnesses a heated conversation. A male student is speaking sternly to a female student, who appears to be very emotional. The male student is pointing his index finger in the female student's face. What should the faculty member do if he or she suspects that the female student is the victim of sexual assault?

The faculty member may intervene and invite either student back to the office for a brief discussion. The faculty member may then ask about the hallway conversation. Or the faculty member may note the students' names and choose to speak with either or both later, to ask if something more serious is going on. Finally, the faculty member may choose to monitor both students to see if a later conversation is warranted. Of course, the faculty member may report the incident to the administrator over student affairs.

It is very important for faculty members to handle students' reports of sexual assaults effectively. Unless the faculty member is trained in counseling assault victims, the interaction needs to remain at the reporting level only. The objective is to avoid extending the trauma during the reporting of the event.

Faculty members should see themselves as a sounding board during the report. The goal should be to let the student just tell the story without interrupting. The faculty member should not do or say anything that might have a negative impact. There should be no attempt to make light of the situation; nor should there be judgmental language or victim blaming.

The faculty member should probably not press the student for details or make any determination regarding the event. During the initial report, if a student says he or she was assaulted or touched inappropriately, the faculty member should use the same language. The faculty member should be empathetic and, if asked, express belief in the account.

The faculty member should encourage the student to make a full formal complaint to the Title IX coordinator. If the victim wishes not to or wants to speak confidentially, the faculty member should know people on campus who can help: mental health counselors, pastoral counselors, social workers, psychologists, health center employees, employees with a professional license requiring confidentiality (OCR, 2014).

If appropriate, the faculty member may advise the student of the need to preserve evidence. If the assault has just occurred, the student should go to the nearest hospital to have a sexual assault examination performed. If the sexual assault happened within the previous 120 hours, a sexual assault examination can collect valuable evidence (US Department of Justice, 2017).

If the student chooses to do nothing, the faculty member should encourage the student to at least report the incident to the Title IX coordinator or one of the confidential reporting personnel. Before listening to a student's sexual assault report, a faculty member who is a responsible employee should state that any information revealed must be reported by the faculty member to the Title IX coordinator or other designated institution official. The faculty member is required to report the names of the alleged perpetrator and victim, as well as relevant details, including date, time, and location of the incident. The faculty member should inform the student of the option to ask the school to maintain confidentiality. The faculty member should let the student know that information can be shared confidentially with the institution's counseling, advocacy, health, mental health, or sexual assault–related services.

Faculty members should be knowledgeable about the trauma resulting from sexual assault, which may affect whether the victim can accurately remember details. Where details cannot be remembered, the faculty member should reassure the victim that memory loss is okay and that memories may return at a later time. The faculty member should not pressure the victim to remember details of the assault (Hopper, 2015).

A Faculty Member Is Approached by a Third-Party Student

In the third scenario, the faculty member is approached by a student claiming to have knowledge of a sexual assault. The faculty member might ask if the third-party student witnessed the assault, was told of the assault directly by the survivor, or overheard other students talking about it? If the third-party student has direct knowledge of the survivor, then the faculty member should encourage the survivor, through the third-party student, to report the incident to the Title IX coordinator. If the third-party student witnessed the assault, then the faculty member should encourage that student to make a report of the incident to the Title IX coordinator.

The faculty member should remind the third-party student that the Title IX coordinator is ready to assist the survivor. Also, there are trained counselors available who can maintain the survivor's confidentiality, if requested. What is paramount is to encourage the survivor to utilize the many resources available to sexual assault survivors.

Catalyst for Cultural Change

Given their unique position within the institution and their specialized skills, faculty members can have a significant impact on all members of the campus community. They have direct and frequent interaction with the student population. Points of contact begin in the classroom, and in many institutions the faculty play advisory roles with campus organizations in addition to advising on academic issues. The faculty can design and conduct training for students and staff and conduct research in all areas of sexual assault to expand understanding of the causes and prevention techniques. Finally, pedagogical research is needed to improve our ability to relate the information to others. In specific ways faculty members can become catalysts for cultural change on campus.

Safe Campus Week

Safe Campus Week (Bohmer and Parrot, 1993) is a highly visible example of an institution's commitment to the cause. A faculty member should be appointed to lead the effort and may appoint a committee to help develop the activities. Other faculty, students, staff, and administrators should get involved, and planning should continue throughout the year.

The main guest speaker—whose presentation is the focal point of the week—should be someone who can competently and appropriately address sexual assault and dating violence, perhaps a representative of Rape, Abuse & Incest National Network or Take Back the Night, a sexual assault survivor, or a community leader who counsels in this area. The speaker event should of course be heavily advertised and held when the greatest number of students can attend.

Faculty members can devote a few minutes during class lectures to show support for Safe Campus Week and inform students how they can participate. Likewise, faculty can inform students about Title IX resources on campus and how to access them. Faculty can show students their support for the whole idea surrounding safe campuses—and thereby facilitate cultural change.

Faculty members can facilitate workshops to present research and train other faculty members, especially new faculty members. The faculty might also hold workshops for students to examine topics of interest.

With faculty guidance, students can present research findings and poster sessions or workshops (American Association of University

Professors, 2012) to educate other students. Male students could lead focus groups on male-oriented topics. Survivors could tell their stories. Trained students could lead small-group sessions on specific issues and do bystander training.

Safe Campus Week activities might utilize students to facilitate programs like Take Back the Night and Heart One. The idea is to involve students as much as possible, to get increased commitment from all of the students to support the need to create a safer campus. Active participation will have a longer lasting impact than passive involvement. Safe Campus Week might be a great opportunity to conduct campus surveys and discuss results from previous surveys.

As part of Safe Campus Week, local martial arts school personnel might come on campus to do personal safety training (Schewe, 2002) and possibly create demand for additional training. Local police and sexual assault nurse examiners might speak about what happens when a criminal complaint is made. An assistant district attorney could be invited to join the discussion.

To get the most out of Safe Campus Week, top administrators and sports coaches should be recruited. Utilizing these influential officials, especially at the beginning of the week and in a visible way, would do much to solidify the institution's commitment to creating a safe campus.

One question is whether to hold Safe Campus Week every semester or once each academic year. If done once a year, the fall semester is preferable so the majority of incoming students will be instructed. Safe Campus Week might also best be conducted during the first month of the semester, before students are distracted with exams or papers and activities.

Course Development

Faculty members have skills that can be used to positively impact an institution's culture. Faculty can develop courses on many of the topics that flow from sexual violence. The list of topics is extensive: affirmative consent, the influence of alcohol and drugs, bystander training, revictimization, effective support for victims, legal issues, avoiding high-risk situations, preventing violence, and many more.

One-credit courses could explore almost any topic and be taught on a rotating schedule basis for flexibility in student scheduling. A one-credit class would not impact pursuit of a degree. A first-year seminar (three credits) might involve a subject matter and format outside the course catalog. In one institution, with a simple approval process faculty can choose to teach any topic that would interest the students. Three-credit courses could be developed around a sexual violence theme and allow for in-depth discussion and analysis.

Sexual Assault Prevention Workshops

Faculty members can use their skills to provide workshops for diverse audiences (AAUP, 2012). The Office for Civil Rights has recognized that all members of the campus community need education and training on sexual violence and sexual assault. Workshops should address all topics surrounding this issue. A challenge is securing the resources, as there will be substantial costs to the institution. Nevertheless, the commitment to education and training must be ongoing if the institution wants a safe campus for all students. Training and education programs should become as common as orientation.

Faculty members can extend their reach beyond the campus with workshops for the public. These would be a great way to influence parents about the attitudes they need to instill in their children. A most important population that could benefit are students in high school and elementary school. The earlier we begin educating and training, the more we can expect appropriate behaviors entering the college years. There also is a case to be made for educating local law enforcement on biases, rape myths, and rape trauma syndrome. Recent research indicates that even in the second decade of the twenty-first century many students are further traumatized once they make a formal criminal complaint (Smith and Freyd, 2014; Shaw, Campbell, Cain, and Feeney, 2017).

Sexual Assault Research

Potential faculty research areas include bystander effects, victim trauma, sexual assault revictimization, and prevention techniques (AAUP, 2012). Promising research areas involve effective education and training programs for men and women on all areas of sexual violence and sexual assault. Two examples are the bystander study at the University of Windsor and the Men's Project at Clark University (Senn and Forrest, 2016; Stewart, 2014). Plenty of opportunities exist to conduct longitudinal studies in changing the culture and bystander efficacy of college-age students.

Student Club Adviser

Faculty members might become faculty advisers to groups like Take Back the Night and Heart One. Many such organizations have resources that institutions can utilize to educate and train. Faculty support and influence could have a profound impact on these programs, raising their credibility and providing continuity from year to year as students graduate and begin their professional lives. The faculty adviser can provide strategic guidance and help resolve conflicts; he or she can recruit students into the clubs and help them gain access to the appropriate administrators if such support is warranted.

The Role of Adjunct Faculty

Institutions need to address the role of adjunct faculty in Title IX compliance. Adjunct faculty who have other career commitments might not be appropriate for responsible employee training, but circumstance may cast them as a first responder needing to assist the student victim of sexual assault. The part-time faculty member needs to know who to refer the student to and should have ready access to all of the Title IX information. While the adjunct faculty member may not be a designated "responsible employee" or a "mandated reporter," it is good practice to report sexual assault incidents to the Title IX coordinator. If the student has just been assaulted, the part-time faculty member needs to know how to get the student immediate emergency medical help. It is important for the institution to establish limits on part-time faculty members' responsibilities, however; in order to properly help students who are victims of sexual assault, full-time faculty need to be involved.

Additional Faculty Involvement

Interested faculty members can assist the administration in developing policies surrounding sexual assault and sexual violence. They can help develop the procedures that govern violations of the code of student conduct. They can serve on hearing boards in the adjudication of sexual assault complaints (AAUP, 2012). All of these contributions require these faculty members to become immersed in Title IX regulations as well as in the many other topics surrounding sexual violence and sexual assault.

The following three scenarios could be part of faculty training.

Case One

Professor Marks has recently noticed changes in one of his best students. Until a couple of weeks ago, Mary excelled in all areas of his course—assignments turned in on time, high scores on exams, always prepared—but lately she seems disengaged during class, often staring out of the window. She seems depressed and tired, like she's not getting enough sleep. Usually one of the best dressed in class, she now appears a bit disheveled. Something is bothering Mary. However, her grades are still good and she likely will do well in the class.

1. Should Professor Marks approach Mary to ask what might be troubling her?
2. How should Professor Marks approach Mary?
3. Should Professor Marks inform the Title IX coordinator or the dean of students about Mary's behavior change?

Case Two

Professor Taylor, who normally takes attendance, just recognized that one of her top students has missed the last three classes. Susan never misses class. Students in Professor Taylor's class know the professor's policy is for students to email before class if they expect to be absent or late. After class, another student, Jill, tells Professor Taylor that Susan was sexually assaulted two weeks ago. Professor Taylor asks if Susan has sought help. Jill says she does not know if Susan has talked to anyone.

1. Should Professor Taylor attempt to contact Susan?
2. If she does contact Susan, exactly what should she say?
3. Should Professor Taylor contact the Title IX coordinator or the dean of students?

Case Three

Professor Rivers has been approached after class by a student who says she was sexually assaulted last night. Professor Rivers's first response is to ask if the incident has been reported. The student says no but wants to ask Professor Rivers for advice on what to do. Professor Rivers asks if the student needs emergency medical treatment. The student says she does not need to go to the emergency room.

The student accompanies Professor Rivers to her office, where Professor Rivers asks about the assault. The student says her date, a male student, took her to a bar, and when they left he said he would drive her home but first needed to retrieve a gift for her from his room. Thinking he was a nice guy, she accompanied him to his room. He invited her to sit on his bed while he pretended to look for the gift. After a few minutes he sat down next to her. He tried to kiss her, and she kissed him back. Without warning, he pushed her back on the bed and held her down with one arm and removed her underwear with his other hand. She tried to free herself but he was too strong. Before she knew it, he was unbuckling his pants and entered her. Within a few minutes, he ejaculated inside her. By the time he finished, she was crying uncontrollably. When he got off of her, she got dressed and left. She ran to her dorm and took a shower. In a daze, she got into bed and went to sleep.

The student tells Professor Rivers that she's not sure she wants to make a formal complaint. She also wants to keep the conversation private, just between them. Professor Rivers agrees.

1. Did Professor Rivers handle the conversation with the student correctly?
2. Should Professor Rivers report the conversation to the Title IX coordinator or the dean of students?
3. Should Professor Rivers report the incident without revealing the student's name?
4. Is there any advice Professor Rivers should have given the student?

In this chapter, the focus has been on the faculty and the education and training they need to be a positive force in dealing with sexual assaults. An important aspect of faculty members' involvement is utilizing their skills to engage both campus and off-campus communities. Faculty members can have a significant impact in changing the culture of all parties.

Chapter 7 focuses on educating and training the institution's employees, especially the Title IX coordinator and campus security. This central group has much responsibility to ensure a safe campus.

CHAPTER SEVEN

Education and Training for Everyone on Campus

ALL MEMBERS OF a college community need education and training on Title IX compliance. Understanding who is at risk for becoming a victim and a perpetrator is a valuable insight for anyone to have. It is also important to know what to do for these at-risk individuals. And everyone on campus needs to know what to do if they become a bystander and observe a potentially dangerous situation.

This chapter will provide guidance for the training and educating needed by all of the college or university's members. We include training suggestions for the Title IX coordinator or coordinators, staff, administrators, security personnel, faculty, and students.

Title IX Coordinator Education and Training

Colleges and universities are responsible for ensuring that their Title IX coordinators are adequately educated and trained in all areas for which they are responsible. These areas include sex discrimination policies and procedures and addressing Title IX complaints (Office for Civil Rights, 2014). Title IX coordinators should be versed on applicable federal and state laws, regulations, and policies related to Title IX.

Colleges and universities must be prepared to provide training to an employee to assume the Title IX coordinator's role. At minimum, the training should cover the different Title IX features, such as regulatory provisions, Office for Civil Rights (OCR) guidance, and the institution's policies and grievance procedures. Institutions should anticipate that federal and state laws and OCR guidance will be updated, leading to continual training for the coordinator and updates in the institution's policies.

The college or university also must provide ongoing education and training for all employees who are responsible for ensuring Title IX compliance. Institutions may seek assistance from the OCR's regional offices, equity assistance centers, state educational agencies and providers, private organizations, advocacy groups, and community colleges. New Title IX coordinators might seek help from more experienced coordinators and collaborate with regional Title IX coordinators (OCR, 2014).

OCR General Guidance on Title IX Coordinators

Educational institutions receiving federal funds must have one or more Title IX coordinators at all times; vacancies are simply not allowed. To avoid potential conflicts of interest, the Title IX coordinator should report directly to the institution's president. This arrangement increases the likelihood that senior leadership is fully apprised of all Title IX issues. Also, a direct reporting relationship indicates to everyone in the institution that the Title IX coordinator has the authority to coordinate Title IX regulation compliance (OCR, 2014).

It is recommended that the Title IX coordinator not have competing job responsibilities. Appointing an employee as a full-time Title IX coordinator minimizes the possibility of role ambiguity. If the university is large, it may need multiple Title IX coordinators. For instance, having a Title IX coordinator for each building, school, or campus would provide those who inhabit those spaces with more direct contact and familiarity with the Title IX coordinator. Multiple Title IX coordinators might also provide improved training for all designated employees. If the institution appoints multiple Title IX coordinators, one should be the lead and have final decision-making responsibility (OCR, 2014).

Responsibilities and Authority of the Title IX Coordinator

Coordinating Title IX compliance includes hearing grievance procedures. The institution is expected to keep the Title IX coordinator informed of all reports and Title IX complaints, regardless of whether the complaint was originally filed by another person or office or whether another individual or office will conduct the investigation (OCR, 2014).

The Title IX coordinator is expected to coordinate the institution's response to all sex discrimination complaints. The Title IX coordinator oversees outcomes, looking for patterns and addressing them, and conducts campus climate assessments. In general, these activities are designed to prevent Title IX violations by halting recurring incidents that may affect the entire campus. Title IX does not define who determines complaint responses or resolutions. The Title IX coordinator may play a role but is not required to do so (OCR, 2014).

In addition to possessing extensive knowledge of an institution's sex discrimination policies and procedures, the Title IX coordinator should participate in both drafting and updating these policies and procedures. If the college or university conducts a sex discrimination survey, the Title IX coordinator should collect and analyze the data (the OCR recommends conducting an annual campus climate survey). To identify and deal with sex discrimination issues proactively, Title IX coordinators should be provided data on athletic participation, school discipline, and gender-based harassment incidents (OCR, 2014).

Title IX regulations make retaliation against individuals, including Title IX coordinators, unlawful when complaints are filed, either during a Title IX investigation or when the Title IX coordinator is advocating for others. Title IX coordinators are protected from discrimination, intimidation, threats, coercion, or any interference in performance of the job.

Title IX regulations require colleges and universities to make the Title IX coordinator's role known to the campus community. Institutions also must post a statement indicating that it does not tolerate sex discrimination and that questions may be directed to its Title IX coordinator or the Office of Civil Rights. The statement must appear in all communications to the institution's stakeholders such as bulletins, announcements, catalogs, applications for admission or employment, and recruitment materials (OCR, 2014). Institutions should encourage the Title IX coordinator to ensure Title IX compliance and gender equity in education (OCR, 2014).

It is essential for the institution to make the Title IX coordinator's contact information widely distributed and easily found, thus signifying commitment to Title IX compliance. The Office for Civil Rights also suggests that each college and university establish a web page, linked to its home page, with Title IX coordinator name and contact information, Title IX policies and grievance procedures, and other relevant resources.

Training Programs
Education and Training Programs for All Employees

All employees who are likely to receive information about sexual assaults should have regular training, and the institution should verify its effectiveness. The institution's employees should know if they are designated "responsible employees" (defined in chapter 6) and whether they are required to report sexual assault incidents. Training for all employees should include (OCR, 2014):

- How to prevent and identify sexual assaults, including same-sex assaults
- Behaviors leading to sexual assaults
- Bystander attitudes
- First responder techniques to avoid further harm
- How to appropriately respond to a potential sexual assault victim
- How to avoid using judgmental language
- Identifying and dealing with victim trauma
- How to report a sexual assault

As noted in chapter 6, employees who are considered to be responsible employees are those employees who have the authority to address sexual assaults and the requirement to report sexual assaults. The OCR guidelines indicate that responsible employees should receive training beyond the training offered to other employees. They should be trained on (OCR, 2014):

- Reporting obligations
- How to respond to a student's confidentiality request
- How to contact the Title IX coordinator
- How to inform the student about responsible employees' reporting obligations; the student's right to request confidentiality; the availability of confidential counseling, reporting, and support services; and the student's right to file a complaint to the school, campus security, and local law enforcement

Employees designated as responsible should know that they are required to report to the Title IX coordinator all relevant details of an incident, including the names of the alleged perpetrator, complainant, and witnesses. The OCR exempts the following employees from mandated reporting without the student's consent: "campus mental health counselors, pastoral counselors, social workers, psychologists, health center employees, or any other person with a professional license requiring confidentiality, or who is supervised by such a person" (OCR, 2014).

The OCR guidelines state that employees involved in implementing the institution's grievance procedures, employees who receive sexual assault complaints, complaint investigators, and hearing adjudicators should receive the following training (OCR, 2014):

- How to handle sexual assault complaints
- The college or university's grievance procedures
- How to work with and interview sexual assault victims
- Identifying sexual violence conduct, including same-sex violence
- Applying the preponderance of the evidence standard

- Consent and the issue of alcohol and drugs on giving consent
- Accountability for sexual assault perpetrators
- Remedial steps for perpetrators, complainants, and the institution's community
- Determining credibility
- Evaluating the evidence
- Conducting investigations
- Maintaining confidentiality
- Victim trauma effects
- Awareness of impact from sexual assault due to cultural influences

Conducting an Effective Investigation

Conducting an investigation that is considerate of both the complainant and the accused is critical. We suggest following the recommendations of ATIXA, the Association of Title IX Administrators (Association of Title IX Administrators, 2013).

Initial Steps

Before beginning any investigation, meet with the Title IX coordinator to discuss the investigation strategy and process. The Title IX coordinator should identify the investigative team, especially the lead investigator, to ensure that the investigation is handled appropriately. A preliminary timeline needs to be created for each step of the investigation; give the timeline to all designated parties. The timeline might include dates for complainant, respondent, and witness interviews. Dates are established for follow-up interviews, evidence testing, any additional research, and the final report. If the investigation is delayed, written communication of the delay should be provided to the complainant and the accused (ATIXA, 2013).

The institution's policies and procedures that apply to the investigation should be identified. If the complaint has not yet been made, an intake officer or other lead investigator should be assigned. An intake officer should be on the investigation team whenever possible.

Conducting the Complainant Interview

The investigative team should make a written record of the complaint or, if the complainant agrees, by video recording or audio recording the interview. We recommend that the interview be conducted by at least a two-person, gender-diverse team, as described in chapter 8. If having the investigator taking notes disturbs the complainant, the team should try to video record or audio record the interview, or bring in a note taker (ATIXA, 2013).

As part of the process to conduct a successful interview, the following procedures should be considered before meeting with the complainant. At the beginning of the interview, the investigators should develop a rapport with him or her. Open-ended questions should be asked to get the interview started, and the complainant should be allowed to tell the story uninterrupted. Clarifying questions should be asked when the complainant finishes the initial narrative. If the narrative is interrupted, investigators can use open-ended question to resume the interview. The use of leading questions or questions that insinuate blame or suggest bias should be avoided.

The team must allow the complainant to have an adviser or other support person present, and must allow the complainant and the support person to communicate as needed. The interview environment should be private, secure, and as comfortable as possible. Interruptions and distractions are to be avoided.

At the start of the interview, the intake officer should begin by discussing the reason for the interview. Then the institutional policy attached to the complaint and the investigation process should be discussed. At this point, the intake officer should ask the complainant to sign a statement acknowledging understanding of the process.

The complainant should be made aware of the college or university's non-retaliation, privacy, and anonymity policies as well as the institution's confidentiality policy. Investigators should make no promises regarding confidentiality that cannot be honored. Without making any commitments, investigators should ask the complainant what he or she would like the outcome of the investigation to be.

When the complaint is completed, if it is in writing, the investigating team should ask the complainant to sign and date the document. If the complaint is written by an investigator or note taker, the complainant should have time to review, edit, and verify before signing it.

At the close of the interview, investigators should ask the complainant not to discuss the complaint, explaining the need to refrain from discussing so as to avoid defamation or risk of retaliation. Then the investigators should request a list of potential witnesses. The complainant should be advised that he or she will be kept informed about the investigation's progress.

Investigators will then thank the complainant for coming forward and ask for a signed consent to discuss the complaint with the accused parties and witnesses. If the investigators have any questions about the complaint's veracity, then they should inform the complainant of the institution's policies regarding false complaints.

The intake officer should be trained on what to do if the complainant either refuses to make a formal complaint or withdraws a previous complaint. First the investigators should describe how the college or university enforces its non-retaliation policy and how failure to pursue the complaint may put another student in jeopardy. Investigators should give the complainant time to reconsider and return later to make a formal complaint. Finally, the investigators should describe opportunities for changing the complainant's circumstances (such as changing class schedules or living arrangements) to ease his or her concerns about reporting (ATIXA, 2013).

The investigators should follow up with the complainant after a short time. If the complainant still refuses to make a formal complaint, the investigators should notify the Title IX coordinator, who may initiate an independent investigation without the complaint. Possible institutional actions include putting in place programs and workshops, or communicating in a general manner to the alleged perpetrator about the alleged behaviors.

If circumstances warrant, the Title IX coordinator may commence a formal complaint. The complainant should be notified of all actions taken by the institution. The complainant, whether a formal complaint is made or not, should be notified when the accused perpetrator is informed of the complaint. Precautions should be instituted, including alerting the complainant's supervisor, residential adviser (RA), or faculty adviser to the possibility of recurrence. The appropriate administrators must be kept informed of the investigation's progress (ATIXA, 2013).

Conducting the Accused Interview

A major part of any investigation is interviewing the accused. This is a delicate matter. It may be advantageous for the investigators to alert the accused of the complaint immediately. Under some circumstances, however, it may be best to conduct witness interviews first, even knowing that witnesses may alert the accused about the complaint. Interviews and complaint notification should be arranged to avoid potential for fabricating events or coordinating versions of events. When interviewing the accused, it is recommended that investigators strategize about whether the complainant and witnesses should be present (ATIXA, 2013).

Investigators must decide if informing the accused on the reason for the meeting will help or hurt the investigation. If the accused asks about the nature of the meeting, then it must be disclosed. Unanticipated interviews may yield more genuine (unguarded) responses but may be viewed as unfair. Anticipated interviews may help build trust and rapport but may result in a rehearsed version of what happened. Unanticipated *witness* interviews *are* appropriate, and unanticipated follow-up interviews can be used to ensure accuracy of the details (ATIXA, 2013).

The interview should begin with a review of the alleged behaviors by each party, in a neutral, nonaccusatory, nonjudgmental manner. Then investigators directly ask if the described behaviors occurred. After the removal of all identifying data and data where permission has not been obtained, a written copy of the complaint is given to the accused. Written copies of relevant institutional policies are provided to the parties.

If an admission is obtained, the conduct should be promptly defined as a violation of the institution's policies. If no admission is obtained, the investigation process and the anticipated timeline are described. The accused is asked for a signed statement acknowledging receipt of the complaint and institutional policies and indicating that the accused understands the process. The accused must be informed of the college or university's obligation to take all sexual assault complaints seriously and to investigate vigorously in a timely manner (ATIXA, 2013).

Then the accused is asked for his or her version of the events. Investigators should make a record of the interview using written notes or an audio recording or video recording of the interview. Investigators then ask for a signed statement from the accused. The accused is asked for a list of witnesses, and documents, recordings, and any other evidence is elicited.

It is strongly recommended that the accused be notified regarding the institution's policies on retaliation or any further contact with the complainant, direct or indirect. The accused should be told about any no-contact orders or other complainant accommodations that may be forthcoming or already in place. The accused is notified that Title IX complaints and investigations are kept confidential by law.

Finally, the accused is asked for written permission to allow the institution to share the accused's statement with the complainant and witnesses during the investigation. If the accused fails to consent, the statement is not shared (ATIXA, 2013).

Conducting Witnesses Interviews

Many witnesses may be friends of the accused, the complainant, or both. They may be biased. Getting to the truth is the goal, but doing so is rarely easy. Understanding this reality prior to the interview is helpful.

Developing strategies for dealing with witnesses is recommended. These strategies include contacting witnesses, conducting witness interviews, and isolating witnesses to avoid collusion. To begin this process, we suggest the following procedures for the investigating team.

The investigators should, first, draw up questions. They should begin the interview by developing a rapport with the witnesses. At the appropriate time, they will ask witnesses to describe specific behaviors or events they observed. As the witnesses are doing so, the investigators refrain from categorizing any behaviors. Investigators ask if the witnesses have had any contact with the accused or complainant after the incident. If yes, investigators ask what exactly was discussed.

Investigators provide witnesses with the college or university's relevant written policies and procedures.

The investigators may isolate the witnesses, if needed, to obtain genuine observations, even separating witnesses in different locations to prevent communication and limit cellphone use. The witnesses' statements are recorded either in writing or, if agreed to by the witnesses, by audio or video. Witnesses are asked to sign and date the statements. Each witness is asked for a witness list.

Those doing the interviewing should share as little as possible regarding the complaint so as not to bias the witnesses. Witnesses are asked to provide any supporting documents, recordings, and other material that support the witnesses' statements (ATIXA, 2013).

Investigators should inform witnesses of the need for privacy, the need not to discuss their interviews or the investigation with anyone, and possible defamation risks. They should also inform witnesses about institutional policies against retaliation. Finally, they should elicit the witnesses' agreement, in writing, to attend the hearing. Following the interview, the investigators should record their impressions of each witness—such as nervousness, credibility, nonverbal behavior, and consistency—as well as contradictions with the witness statement (ATIXA, 2013).

Concluding the Investigation

Making sure there are no loose ends to be resolved is critical. If this does not happen, it will make an accurate conclusion to the claim difficult. It may also cause the investigation to be reopened later.

To conclude the investigation, the investigating team first evaluates the completeness of the investigation, evidence, and leads. In consultation with appropriate experts, they analyze the evidence. They then create a statement of findings, detailing the evidence and its importance (ATIXA, 2013).

Next, the team assesses the credibility of the complainant, the accused, and the witnesses. They review the evidence and draw a conclusion as to whether a policy violation has occurred. Investigators complete their written report, including support of their conclusions. Next, they remit the complaint and findings reports to the appropriate people: Title IX coordinator, dean of students, administrators. The team determines how the final reports will be shared with the complainant and the accused.

Suggestions for Preparing to Conduct a Hearing

If the results of the sexual assault investigation indicate the need for a hearing, the following information can be used to educate and train the hearing members. First there are suggestions for the hearing board members' competencies, then a discussion of hearing models, and, finally, suggestions on weighing the evidence.

Training for Adjudicators

After an investigation is concluded, it will often go to a hearing board. Competent and trained adjudicators and board members are those who are knowledgeable about the most current laws and the institution's policies. Eighteen training competencies for adjudicators and hearing board members should be considered (Association of School Conduct Administration, 2014):

1. Federal and state laws governing sexual harassment and sexual assaults
2. University or college policies and procedures on sexual harassment and Title IX

3. Student handbook and code of conduct
4. Overview of the complaint, investigation, hearing, and appeals processes
5. Difference between campus and criminal processes
6. Goals and outcomes of the hearing process
7. Participant roles (complainant, accused, witnesses, hearing board members, advisers, lawyers)
8. Facilitation process for the hearing
9. Questioning techniques and follow-up questions
10. Techniques for evidence evaluation
11. Techniques for analyzing credibility
12. Techniques for evaluating policy
13. Deliberation techniques to reach resolution
14. Distinguishing between standards of proof
15. How to determine appropriate sanctions
16. Proper application of Family Educational Rights and Privacy Act (FERPA) regulations
17. How cultural differences may be displayed in the investigation or hearing process
18. Frequent problems and remedies in the hearing process

Resolution Models

On many campuses, resolving Title IX complaints involves some type of hearing. Note that there is more than one resolution method and that the Title IX coordinator should utilize the appropriate method for the institution.

Typically, the hearing follows an investigation that ensures that enough information exists to support a hearing and provide a separate and distinct phase of resolving the complaint. The hearing is usually attended in person, but testimony may be submitted by phone, Skype, or other remote communication processes.

There are two types of hearing models, the administrative hearing and the panel hearing. In the administrative hearing, there is usually just one adjudicator trained in resolving complaints. The panel hearing features multiple adjudicators and at least three members. The members may be faculty members, staff or administrative personnel, and possibly students. The Office for Civil Rights discourages including students on panel hearings, but they are not prohibited (ASCA, 2014).

The administrative model has its advantages. Limiting the number of adjudicators limits access to confidential information. Fewer parties are involved, so scheduling is easier. The administrative model offers a great opportunity for consistency from hearing to hearing and is likely to be viewed as a trusted process.

The panel hearing is more difficult in some ways but also brings benefits. The panel members require significant training to achieve consistency on discharging their duties. Confidential information is shared with more people, including students, if they are panel members. Coordinating multiple members' schedules for hearings, training, and other matters is more difficult. An advantage of the panel hearing is that the student body is likely to view this model as highly supportive of the students. It also brings different adjudicator perspectives to the resolution of the claim (ASCA, 2014).

Weighing the Evidence

The institution should specify what standard of proof is required to conclude that reasonable cause exists to support the allegation of sexual assault. Further, the burden of proof to present such evidence rests with the complainant. Most institutions will use the "preponderance of the evidence" standard of proof. The complainant must provide evidence demonstrating that an incident occurred that violates the institution's policies.

In the event of an accusation and no witnesses, investigators must determine whether reasonable cause exists to support the complaint. They should take into account the following (Cole, Hustoles, and McClain, 2006):

- "He said/she said" accounts are not uncommon and must be fully investigated
- Analyzing complainant and accused credibility, including demeanor and nonverbal behaviors, may help determine reasonable cause
- How details from either the complainant or the accused compare with testimony without supporting facts
- Consistency of accounts of events or timelines
- Consistency of any admissions or denials during multiple interviews
- Exploring with the accused the complainant's possible motive or any explanation for the allegation
- Whether the complainant has shared the assault details with anyone, such as a roommate or close friend
- Observations by witnesses on behavioral changes in either the complainant or the accused after the event, and the timing of the changes
- Evidence of previous allegations by either the complainant or the accused

Sexual Assault Response Team: A Model for First Responders

Moylan and Lindhorst (2015) discuss the community-based model of supporting sexual assault victims called SART, or Sexual Assault Response Team. We adapted the model in the context of our broader Campus Sexual Assault Prevention (CSAP) model (see chapter 2), which goes well beyond first response to a sexual assault incident. While the more comprehensive CSAP teams should be focused on primary and secondary prevention, the SART element within a CSAP team is strictly focused on tertiary prevention.

The original SART is a community-based first responder unit that exists to help sexual assault victims. As originally proposed, the team provides health, legal, and emotional support. In chapter 8 we examine adaptations to this original model.

When a sexual assault victim is identified, the community SART is alerted. Team members bring a coordinated effort of law enforcement, prosecutors, nurse examiners, forensic and medical personnel, and rape crisis advocates to support the victim. The objective is to coordinate victim care immediately following the assault. Team members provide medical treatment, evidence collection, crisis counseling, and referrals for support. They initiate a criminal investigation. Beyond working directly with victims, the team members meet regularly to monitor outcomes and effectiveness.

We propose that Title IX coordinators adapt the SART model for the campus environment. For example, once a complaint is made regarding a sexual assault, the Title IX coordinator would notify the college or university's SART for first response, to secure the incident scene, and to provide essential caregiving. The SART could then liaise with an on-campus investigator, someone to assist the student with evidence collection and going to the hospital, a counselor to help with rape trauma syndrome, and others.

The campus expert in evidence collection and hospital examinations would know exactly how to coordinate the appropriate hospital personnel. The hospital expert would know to arrange a sexual assault nurse examiner, if one is available, or to request specific doctors for the examination. The hospital expert would let the victim know his or her rights and make sure the evidence was not mishandled before arriving at the hospital, and would have a change of clothes for the victim in the event that clothing needed to be surrendered during the exam.

The hospital support person could be with the victim during the hospital exam and contact anyone on the victim's behalf. This individual could encourage the victim to make a formal complaint, explain the process that accompanies it, and recommend appropriate support services following the hospital visit.

The Title IX coordinator or a designee should begin notifying the other members of the CSAP Team. If outside services are needed, the Title IX coordinator can advise the student on where to go and who to see. There could be an on-campus SART and a community SART, with the Title IX coordinator monitoring their efforts.

It should be noted that community SARTs often experience tension between the disciplines. Conflicts arise from role definitions, turf issues, and statutory obligations toward victims (Cole, 2011; Cole and Logan, 2008; Crandall and Helitzer, 2003; Littel, 2001). Members may disagree on the definitions of rape, the victim's needs, and courses of action (Cole, 2011; Cole and Logan, 2010). This may also happen with the campus SART. The Title IX coordinator should address any issues.

Creating Training Programs on Sexual Assault Prevention

One of the job responsibilities of the Title IX coordinator is to develop and conduct education and training programs for students, faculty, and employees. In the area of education for students, the following guidelines may help.

Orientation Programs

The Office on Violence Against Women (OVW) suggests creating a mandatory orientation for all new students regarding college or university policies on sexual assaults, stalking, dating violence, and domestic violence; the student code of conduct; campus, local, and national support resources; and hotlines and legal, medical, mental, and any other assistance available. Other information should be included: how to file a complaint on campus and to the police, myths regarding the causes of sexual assault and violence, victim resources, peer support, offender sanctions, and the benefits gained from reporting assaults (Office on Violence Against Women, n.d.).

Challenges to consider:

- Each college or university should develop its own orientation program to address the unique needs of its student population.
- Should the orientation program for sexual assault prevention be incorporated into existing orientations or exist separately?
- How will the college or university enforce a mandatory requirement that all students attend the orientation?

- Should the orientation cover all of the topics related to sexual and dating violence in one session or in multiple sessions?
- How can the program create buy-in from the students?

The OVW outlines a three-stage program for prevention and education orientation for incoming students: pre-orientation/arrival, orientation/arrival, and ongoing. The effort to reach students should involve websites, presentations, online training, social media, courses, and workshops.

The pre-orientation/arrival stage should begin with contacting the students well in advance of campus arrival. Information on the mandatory orientation for sexual assault training should be provided along with where school policies can be accessed. The student handbook (made available online and also possibly in printed form) should cover reporting instructions and support services and clearly define all areas of dating violence, stalking, and sexual assaults. Students should be able to sign up for sexual assault training and orientation before arriving on campus. Peer chat rooms should be constructed to provide immediate feedback and answer questions.

The orientation/arrival stage should attempt to utilize all of the resources on campus to reach all incoming students. When the college or university holds a formal orientation program, all campus departments and community response members should be consulted. Those responsible for the orientation should take into account when the students need orientation throughout the year, such as midyear arrivals or students taking summer courses. They should also consider developing focused orientation programs for specific populations (athletes, foreign students, RAs) using multiple formats (mixed group, male only, female only). The college or university might sponsor mixers for incoming students where sexual assault issues are addressed. If the institution does not have a mandatory orientation, an online quiz could test students' knowledge and provide feedback to students.

The ongoing stage should continue to schedule education and training activities, with training connected to various campus events and on various campus venues. Athletic events, Greek events, and presentations by guest speakers are just a few opportunities to conduct education and training. It is important to provide specific training for residential advisers. Utilize peer theater presentations for large audiences and continue to use social media to keep the topic in front of the students. To provide ongoing training, colleges and universities can partner with organizations described in chapter 5, such as the Rape, Abuse & Incest National Network (RAINN), Green Dot, the White Ribbon Campaign, and the Men's Program: Ending Rape through Peer Education.

Rape Myths

The acceptance of rape myths is frequently used as an icebreaker quiz to begin the conversation about the problem of sexual assault (Schewe, 2002). The exercise can reveal participants' beliefs about sexual assault and sexual violence; then a facilitator can focus on the least understood areas while avoiding repetition on topics on which the students generally have a correct understanding.

Victim Empathy

Victim empathy training has proved effective in helping students identify with the rape victim's experience and the problems that follow the assault (rape trauma syndrome). Victim empathy also plays a role in bystander training. Bystanders who identify with the potential victim's harm are more inclined to assist before the assault occurs (Schewe, 2002).

In victim empathy training, participants hear sexual assault survivors describe their experiences, followed by active discussion. The training may also ask the participants to imagine that the victim is a close friend or family member. Various scenarios are described: female victim, male perpetrator; male victim, male perpetrator; male victim, female perpetrator. It is recommended that an experienced facilitator handle this topic (Schewe, 2002).

Consequences for Perpetrators

Students should know the consequences for committing sexual assault. The steps following a formal complaint should be described in general terms, then the possible outcomes of a college grievance hearing, what a criminal prosecution sentence might entail, and the possibility of a civil prosecution. Typically, civil judgments result in monetary awards (Schewe, 2002).

Sexual Assault Awareness

Awareness programs cover the definitions of sexual assault, sexual violence, dating violence, and sexual harassment. Exactly what is affirmative consent, and how do you know it has been given? Statistics, rapist behaviors and attitudes, rape trauma syndrome, the Title IX coordinator's role, reporting assaults, post-assault resources—all should be covered.

For students to become active participants in curbing and preventing sexual assault, they need to be fully aware of the problem. While the literature suggests that female students benefit from these programs, male students seemingly do not (Schewe and O'Donohue, 1993).

Affirmative Consent

Students need to know the legal definition of consent, the conditions that affect it, and especially how to give and get affirmative consent to avoid being charged with sexual assault. Students also should know the college or university's policies on the consequences of filing a false allegation.

High-Risk Situations

Training students how to recognize high-risk situations may help them limit potentially dangerous behaviors. To avoid giving potential perpetrators ideas, this training should be conducted with women only (Schewe, 2002). Potential high-risk situations include (Schewe, 2002; Garcia, Reiber, Massey, and Merriwether, 2012):

- Using alcohol or drugs
- Leaving drinks unattended at bars or parties
- Fraternity or sorority parties
- Dating in isolated areas
- Unwise use of social media
- Hooking up
- Hitchhiking

Alerting students to potential high-risk situations such as these helps them make informed decisions and may lead them to take precautions. Some students may choose to avoid situations altogether if they recognize the risk. Of course, telling college students not to do something may encourage them to do it. Students need to make their own choices once they know the risks (Schewe, 2002).

Self-Defense Resistance Tactics

One study reported that after participating in a mugging self-defense course, forty-six of forty-eight women who later experienced sexual assault were able to fight back and avoid physical harm (Peri, 1991). Participants experienced heightened self-confidence and belief in their ability to take action when threatened.

Women who used self-defense strategies forcefully against attackers were more likely to avoid sexual assault. Women who yelled forcefully when an assailant brandished a weapon suffered less severe sexual assault. But women who pleaded, cried, or tried to reason with their attacker experienced greater physical injury (Bart and O'Brian, 1984; Ullman and Knight, 1993).

Assertiveness Training

Effective communication has always been a component of affirmative consent and a tactic to avoid the misreading of cues. When men misread signals and the sexual activity increases, however, forceful assertiveness works as a deterrent to sexual assault. One of the benefits of assertiveness training is that it encourages women to set boundaries. The psychological barriers that women have against calling attention to themselves or making a scene pose a big challenge to overcome with this type of training (Kelley, Orchowski, and Gidycz, 2016).

Choosing Facilitators

Choosing the right facilitator for training programs can have immediate impact on reaching students and making a positive impression. Guidelines to follow when choosing facilitators:

- Use expert facilitators whenever possible
- Use coaches to speak to athletes
- Use peers when appropriate
- Use mixed facilitators (male and female) to boost victim empathy
- Use multimedia and multiple methods to get through to students
- Use posters and social media
- Do training every semester, every year
- Fraternity alumni should speak to new members

Make Students Aware of Their Rights

Per Title IX, schools receiving federal funds must comply with federal regulations that prohibit sex discrimination, including sexual violence, in all activities (Department of Education, 2014). The Title IX coordinator should ensure that students know their rights under these regulations. Specific training in this area is strongly recommended. The Office for Civil Rights of the US Department of Education describes students' rights as well as college and university's responsibilities and requirements (DOE, 2014):

1. A student has the right to report the sexual assault to the institution, expect an investigation, and receive a prompt and equitable resolution.
2. A student has the right to report the sexual assault to the university or local law officials. The institution must still respond promptly and effectively.
3. The institution must acquire and publish complaint resolution procedures for sexual discrimination and sexual assaults. The institution may utilize its student disciplinary procedures; however, sexual assault complaints must be resolved promptly and equitably.
4. The institution must educate students of their Title IX rights. Such rights may include victim advocacy, housing reassignment, academic assistance, counseling, and medical and legal services.
5. The institution must select a Title IX coordinator and inform students and employees on contact procedures. Title IX coordinators must be available for communication and meetings.
6. Title IX affords protection to all students regardless of gender, orientation, citizenship, or disability.
7. The institution is required to protect students, even during the investigation of the complaint.
8. Protections must be afforded immediately following the sexual assault report, which may include changing classes, housing, or transportation. The institution should minimize the impact to the student.
9. A student has the right to report retaliatory actions by the institution's employees, students, and the alleged perpetrator. The institution is expected to respond quickly and effectively.
10. The institution must clearly indicate where students can receive confidential communications and services such as

advocacy, counseling, and academic help. Counselors should be available without initiating an investigation.

11. The institution should indicate the reporting requirements of all employees.

12. Reported incidents should be handled in a confidential manner, and the complainant should be consulted regarding his or her safety and privacy.

13. A student has the right to receive notification of the timing of investigatory stages.

14. A student complainant has the right to provide witnesses and evidence.

15. A student complainant has the right to legal representation if the alleged perpetrator has legal representation.

16. The institution is expected to utilize a preponderance of the evidence standard of proof to resolve the complaint.

17. A student has the right to receive written notification regarding the complaint resolution, appeal, and any rulings.

18. If the institution offers an appeal procedure, both parties must have access to it.

19. A student has the right to documented proceedings such as findings of fact and audio recorded and written transcripts.

20. A student has the right to reject mediation with the alleged perpetrator.

21. If the investigation indicates a hostile environment resulting from sexual violence, the institution must take immediate and effective action to stop the violence, eradicate the hostile environment, and keep both from returning.

22. The institution must provide remedies that may include disciplinary action for the perpetrators and helping victims resume the educational track.

23. The institution may offer remedies for the entire student population to avoid future incidents. The remedies may include additional training, services modifications (such as special rooming accommodations, tutors, trauma counseling), and policy changes.

When a Student Seeks Legal Action

Students must know what to do if they or someone they know is assaulted. Training can help students know the steps to take when confronted with this situation.

The federal criminal process has eleven steps: initial investigation and arrest, charges filed, initial hearing or arraignment, discovery, plea bargain, preliminary hearing, pretrial motions, trial, post-trial motions, sentencing, and appeal (US Department of Justice, 2018). In a sexual assault case, the process begins when the student makes a complaint to the police. Depending on the jurisdiction, the student can file a formal complaint or make an incident report without pressing charges. The student should ask if filing the report will automatically initiate an investigation. Many jurisdictions will only investigate a formal complaint.

Reporting the Assault

Students should make a report to the police department in the jurisdiction where the incident occurred. In the student chooses to file a formal complaint, the police will take the report and initiate an investigation. When filing the complaint report with the police, the student should expect to provide graphic details and a complete account. Failing to describe the assault in detail may cause consistency problems later on. Filing the complaint report can be stressful. Students should bring a trusted adviser to the police station for support. Female students should ask that a female officer take the report if that is their preference (New York State Unified Court System, 2018).

After the formal report is completed, the investigation phase begins and the police will likely visit the crime scene, interview witnesses, and search for evidence. During this time, the student may want to seek an order of protection, which can prevent the alleged perpetrator from harassing or attempting to make contact (NYSUCS, 2018).

Role of the District Attorney's Office

If the police believe there is probable cause, they will present the case to the district attorney's office. The district attorney will review the details and determine whether to prosecute (Campbell, Menaker, and King, 2015). If the district attorney decides to proceed, he or she will represent the state in pressing charges and rely on the complainant to be the principal witness if the case goes to trial. The complainant cannot control the charges or the outcome. The district attorney may offer a lesser charge (NYSUCS, 2018).

As principal witness, the complainant has a specific role: to provide a complete and accurate account of what happened as best she or he can recall (Campbell, Menaker, and King, 2015). The complainant may need to recount the assault details a number of times—during the preliminary hearing, grand jury testimony, pretrial hearing, and the trial. The complainant should expect the defendant's lawyer to ask very personal questions, designed to attack the complainant's credibility (DOJ, 2018). The complainant may be distraught following an aggressive cross-examination.

Arrest of the Accused

After arrest, the accused appears in court for an initial hearing. The defendant is given formal notice of charges and notice of rights, and bail is determined. Within a reasonable time, a preliminary hearing will be conducted to establish whether a felony has been committed and probable cause exists that the defendant committed the offense. Defense attorneys may waive the preliminary hearing to avoid damaging testimony going on the record. Defense attorneys also hope that witnesses forget details of the case by the time of the trial (Inciardi, 2009).

Following the preliminary hearing, the evidence goes to a grand jury to determine formal charges and whether to return an indictment. The district attorney must establish that the defendant is responsible for the felony charges. A majority decision by the grand jury results in a "true bill"; failure to reach a majority results in a "no bill" and no indictment.

The defendant is released following a no bill decision. If the defendant is indicted, he or she enters a plea bargain phase and pleads guilty or not guilty. If there is a guilty plea, the next step is sentencing. If there is a not guilty plea, the trial process begins (Inciardi, 2009; DOJ, 2018).

If there is a trial, the district attorney must prove "beyond a reasonable doubt" that the defendant committed the crime. The defendant's lawyers may present evidence and have the defendant testify, but neither is required. The trial may be presided over by a judge alone or by a judge and jury. The defendant can request a jury. The victim will be called to give testimony, and the defendant's attorney will cross-examine. If requested to do so, complainants must testify at trial. Defendants have a constitutional right to face their complainants (DOJ, 2018).

The defendant should expect to be notified when the trial is expected to begin. If the defendant has accepted a plea bargain, the defendant will plead guilty to the original charge or to a lesser charge. The district attorney may offer a lesser charge for a variety of reasons. Perhaps the district attorney is unable to prove the case beyond a reasonable doubt; or the complainant may have decided not to participate in continued prosecution. In the event of a plea bargain, the trial ends and the participation of complainant and defendant ends as well. Even if the complainant is unhappy with the outcome of the trial, only the defendant can appeal the decision (DOJ, 2018).

If the trial results in a guilty verdict, the judge will impose a sentence. To arrive at the sentence, the judge will consult the penal law guidelines, the defendant's criminal history (if one exists), and the district attorney's recommendation. The defendant may have the opportunity to speak at the sentencing (NYSUCS, 2018).

Decision to File a Criminal Complaint

Filing a complaint may put the complainant in the public eye. The investigation and trial process may easily take a year or longer. The complainant's involvement in the criminal proceedings may affect his or her academic progress. The complainant will likely be traumatized by the defense attorney's cross-examination.

Regardless of the status of any criminal prosecution, a complainant can engage an attorney to begin a civil complaint against the perpetrator. Civil cases allow victims to recoup damages, usually in the form of monetary compensation (NYSUCS, 2018).

Establishing Credibility

The complainant must be aware that the police will be assessing her or his credibility during the filing of the complaint report, looking for consistency in reporting the details of the sexual assault and the ability to recall them. During the investigation phase, the police will continue gauging consistency in statements made at the hospital and by witnesses. Consistent details of the assault, from multiple sources, will help establish credibility, as will corroborating evidence, preserving evidence, and going to the hospital following the assault (Campbell, Menaker, and King, 2015).

When decisions are being made about whether to proceed to trial, the district attorney will examine the complainant's moral character and behavior before, during, and immediately after the assault. Victim credibility is questioned under a variety of circumstances, including evidence of criminal history; when the victim fails to reveal possible culpable behavior, such as intoxication (Jordan, 2004); drug or alcohol use prior to the assault; emotional demeanor at the time of reporting the event; presence of mental illness; and if there is a history of prostitution.

The complainant's credibility is an important consideration for police investigators when deciding whether to arrest the accused and present the case to the district attorney for prosecution. The district attorney's decision to prosecute will be influenced by whether investigators found the victim credible (Campbell, Menaker, and King, 2015).

During courtroom trials, prosecutors attack the complainant's credibility. Credibility can be revealed in several ways. First, by consistency—

in the complainant's behavior following the sexual assault, in the complainant's statement over time, and between the complainant's statement and the witnesses' statements (Lievore, 2004).

Second, credibility can be established when the complainant appears natural in terms of actions, verbal communication, and dress. The complainant does not appear to be speaking or dressing in a way that is abnormal for him or her. The complainant's demeanor is neither combative nor argumentative toward the defense attorney during cross-examination (Lievore, 2004).

Third, the complainant may be angry over the assault but not so angry that a judge and jury would question the complainant's motivation to lie, especially when a prior relationship may exist. Also, the complainant may exhibit some distress but not be withdrawn or distracted in recalling the details of the assault (Lievore, 2004).

Fourth, the complainant shows curiosity about the phases of the trial and how to prepare for the cross-examination. The complainant displays good memory and communication skills. The complainant can focus on the details without dwelling on feelings about the accused (Lievore, 2004).

Finally, the complainant's credibility is established by the corroborating evidence. Preserving evidence and going to the hospital following the assault will help credibility.

What to Expect at the Hospital

The following information on what to expect may lessen the trauma and help a victim of sexual assault prepare for the hospital visit. Here is what generally happens at the hospital:

1. Initial questioning (information gathering).
2. If possible, a sexual assault nurse examiner should perform the exam.
3. The exam will likely include gathering specimens from all body parts involved in the assault as well as the victim's fingernails, hair, and mouth.

4. Before the exam begins, the victim will be asked to sign a consent form. Victims have the right to refuse any part of the exam and to obtain a full explanation about the exam before signing the form.
5. There is usually no exam fee, but the hospital may charge for any tests or services beyond the exam.
6. An advocate may be present during the exam. Victims have that right.
7. Photo documentation may be taken.
8. The victim should be prepared to submit clothing worn during the assault. The victim should bring a change of clothing, just in case.
9. The victim should disclose to the nurse any suspicions of being drugged.
10. The victim should be prepared to discuss pregnancy, STDs, and HIV concerns.
11. The exam may take a few hours.

External Resources for Personnel with Title IX Responsibilities

The Title IX coordinator may utilize outside organizations to provide resources to personnel involved with Title IX responsibilities.

The Rape, Abuse & Incest National Network

RAINN says it is the largest anti-sexual violence organization in the world. Since 1994, RAINN claims to have helped more than 2.7 million people. It focuses on four areas—victim services, public education, public policy, and consulting and training—and operates a 24-hour hotline. Over one thousand local sexual assault service providers assist colleges and universities, government agencies, and other organizations. They also conduct training for organizations.

In the service of public education, over fifteen hundred sexual assault survivors volunteer to speak in local communities. RAINN offers student programs to promote sexual assault prevention on campus as well as free online resources designed to help colleges locate the best sexual assault program for their needs.

RAINN provides consulting and training services in sexual assault education, training, and response. Programs are designed to meet the needs of the organization.

The Association of Title IX Administrators

ATIXA provides training and resources for Title IX coordinators. Its members include Title IX coordinators, human resource administrators, equity and diversity officers, athletic and academic administrators, training officers, attorneys, advocates, and activists.

Member resources include educational videos, investigation and training checklists, suggested policies, reporting requirements, state laws, and a comprehensive guidebook for resolving sexual assault allegations on college campuses. ATIXA also conducts online training and annual conferences. Membership runs from under fifty dollars for students to between two and three thousand dollars for full institutional members.

The National Association of College and University Attorneys

NACUA has more than eighteen hundred institutional members (accredited, nonprofit two- and four-year public and private institutions) and forty-five hundred attorney representatives. Member services include legal resources, educational programs, networking events, volunteer activities, workshops throughout the year and an annual conference, webinars, online courses, audio briefings, and workshop and conference recordings. There are affinity groups, group dinners, new member breakfasts, new member orientation lunches, and mentoring programs.

Volunteers serve on programming and governance committees and speak at educational events. Legal resources include summaries of new cases and developments, a members-only listserv and legal resources library, the *Journal of College and University Law*, a higher education compliance website, salary benchmark surveys, and special publications. Membership fees run between approximately a thousand dollars for individuals to about fifteen hundred dollars for institutions.

Providing training and education for the Title IX coordinator, security personnel, and other college and university employees, as well as students, is essential. Training and education must be ever changing, as shifting federal and state regulations require vigilant updating of policies and procedures. Understanding what's involved in reporting and the investigation of an assault, and the legal rights of the complainant and accused, is also essential. Continual training in all of these areas must extend to all of the institution's constituencies. The future brings hope for even more effective training methods.

In chapter 8 the focus turns to how a college or university must respond following a sexual assault. Institutions should be prepared to assist those who have experienced sexual violence. Properly responding to both the assault victim and the offender can pave the way to justice for those who have been harmed.

CHAPTER EIGHT

Responding to Incidents

WHILE WE CONTEND that campus sexual violence is predictable and preventable, failures in even the best primary and secondary prevention occur (McCall, 1993), and that is when tertiary prevention, caregiving, and treatment are essential. The campus must respond with urgency and compassion while at the same time learning from experience.

What is the best, fairest approach to addressing a report of sexual assault? Staying focused on the evidence and due process for all parties is essential legally as well as for public health and safety. McCall (1993) offers competing perspectives on sexual assault prevention: the crime control perspective and the public health perspective. Braceras (2016) criticizes Yale University's scheme for addressing sexual harassment and sexual assault as being more like the secret Star Chamber of sixteenth- and seventeenth-century England than the open system of justice anchored in the American legal tradition (see chapter 9).

Within tertiary prevention, McCall's (1993) perspectives have very different foci. The crime control perspective focuses on the offenders, with attention paid to conviction, treatment, and rehabilitation. The public health perspective focuses on survivors of sexual assault, with attention paid to caregiving, especially long-term care. In the current sexual assault climate on campuses, this dichotomous approach to labeling offenders and survivors may be problematic. (In chapter 9 we offer an educational model.)

The objective of public health prevention is to reduce incidence rates of the problem. As discussed in chapter 4, Chancellor William H. McRaven (2017) wants to drive campus sexual assault to zero within the University of Texas System with its 220,000 undergraduate, graduate, and professional students taught by more than 17,000 academic staff. This is a worthy but decidedly long-term objective; in the meantime, every incident that is prevented is a success. Schein (1999) notes in his model of process consultation that beginning to ask questions is itself an intervention. Hence, the UT system's assessment of student sexual harassment, assault, and violence is a significant step in effecting cultural change.

While we anchor much of our model in the fundamental public health notions of prevention, we respect the institutional context within which campus sexual assault occurs. The majority of incidents may not occur on campus, but they do involve campus actors (faculty, students, administrators). Weick and Sutcliffe (2015) bring attention to high-reliability organizations (HRO) that are very low in accidents, mishaps, failures, and errors despite operating in complex, high-hazard environments. HROs anticipate the unexpected through a variety of team-based processes, one of which is the reluctance to simplify. The reluctance to simplify is especially appropriate in dealing with assault cases, where attitudes and stereotypes about women, men, and sexual behavior, operating below the actors' conscious awareness, intrude on many aspects of the incidents. Therefore, rather than accept an easy, simple, convenient cause for the problem, it is crucial to look more deeply to discover what others may miss as contributing causes for the problem.

For these reasons—reluctance to simplify and implicit bias—we argue for a team response to each reported incident. We suggest a SART (Sexual Assault Response Team) embedded within the CSAP Board, the former being a subset of the more comprehensive Campus Sexual Assault Prevention body. The SART (see chapter 7) should be limited to first responders in both caregiving and security and should include men and women. Its purpose is to secure the incident environment, mitigate harm, and provide aid. The members may do initial incident reporting but are not required to do investigation. However, they may liaise with those who are responsible for the investigative, post-incident process.

This chapter focuses on the containment and caregiving aspects of treatment listed in figure 2.1; they are the first two steps in tertiary prevention and treatment. (Chapter 9 focuses on the second two steps, forgiving and resilience.) We address the investigative process later in the chapter, where we discuss recording and reporting—making a distinction between the two. The investigation that follows the first response should draw on crime control and public health perspectives, then add a learning perspective that resonates with the university culture. Transcending a conflict model for tertiary prevention is both a challenge and an opportunity in advancing the science and practice of addressing campus sexual assault. The bystander may become the instrumental actor who can de-escalate or even neutralize a perpetrator and care for injured parties, but there are risks in early intervention, just as there are risks for police entering a domestic violence arena, where the conflicted individuals often unite against the intervening party.

Caring for the Injured

Containment requires, first, securing the incident scene, neutralizing any perpetrator (especially one who's violent), and caring for the victim. Bystanders may be able to intervene, depending on training and circumstance. The responsibility for securing a sexual assault scene and neutralizing any perpetrator or perpetrators falls to the SART component of the CSAP Board. SARTs should include team members with expertise in campus security and caregiving. The original SART model by Moylan and Lindhorst (2015) proposes initiating criminal investigation. Our SART proposal is to handle the primary functions of securing the venue, safety of those involved, and caregiving for the injured.

Once the venue and perpetrator or perpetrators have been secured, focus turns to the emotional and physical injuries of the survivor or survivors. Any emotional and physical needs of the alleged perpetrator should be addressed as well. Distinguishing the perpetrator from the survivor can prove a complicated judgment. Physical, emotional, and mental health assessments are included in this element of the response. The goal is to aid especially the victim in a healing and recovery process that leads to a position of survivor and victor over trauma, or even champion for the cause of conquering campus sexual harassment and assault. Because someone has been victimized does not mean that he or she is helpless or that the future is hopeless. Therefore, a critical first decision must be made about where to seek help, which has implications for the next course of action. In an evaluation of the National Sexual Assault Online Hotline, only 8 percent of users rated the volunteers low in knowledge and skills—meaning that this hotline can generally be a reliable source of support. Early decisions about actions taken after an assault have long-term consequences. The SART should be well informed about campus policies as well as state and federal laws to ensure that the rights of all concerned are protected.

Key Decision: Where to Turn for Help

Following a campus sexual assault, very different consequences arise depending upon whether help is sought at a campus clinic or a hospital emergency room. If the incident requires medical care, then the decision may be constrained by the health center's capacity. Universities may favor the campus clinic for treatment of minor injuries or to dispense information on sexually transmitted diseases, but few campus clinics are set up to collect or document evidence—they typically do not have rape kits or photograph injuries.

A hospital emergency room, on the other hand, can collect evidence, document it, and save it. Going to a campus clinic does not foreclose a subsequent decision to file a criminal complaint, but it may limit the amount and type of evidence available to prosecute that complaint. These can be difficult decisions to make in the midst of a traumatic event.

SART first responders should be in a position to provide support within and guidance about the potentially conflicting systems that victims face. First responders should also suspend judgment. They are there to create security and render aid, including essential medical and psychological caregiving.

Victimized Does Not Mean Helpless

Because a person is victimized through a sexual assault does not automatically render him or her helpless in the aftermath. The victim may feel helpless in the moment of the assault, but that sense of helplessness does not have to continue, as multiple resources are available to help him or her decide what to do next so as to become a survivor. Social location—as defined by gender, race, social class, age, ability, sexual orientation, and geographic location—and other contextual factors are important in the attainment of effective formal help (Kennedy et al., 2012). Especially with effective help, being a victim can be a transitory role and survivor the longer-term role. Still, what was done cannot be undone; what was seen cannot be unseen. We learn from Viktor Frankl (2006, 1946) that we have a choice about how we respond. Reacting to events is simply stimulus and response.

During a sexual assault, relying on dominant, learned responses for protection and survival can be invaluable. That is the reaction survival response at work, and it may be lifesaving. Kipnis (2017) challenges the female stereotype of the helpless victim. Putting a space between stimulus and response moves a person from reaction to freedom of choice. That freedom of choice opportunity may not come in the moments of the assault but can come in the aftermath.

The first question is basic: What happened? The answer may require reliving the event, which can be painful but a vital step in transformational coping versus regressive coping, which leads to the second question: What are you going to do about it? Here mindful choice and deliberate consideration of decision alternatives are important. We do not always have control over what happens to us. We take control when we begin the process of choosing how we will respond over time, turning a difficult experience into a learning event through which we become transformed. It can take time and support to mobilize ourselves for a response, but active transformational coping with a tragedy like sexual assault offers the potential for growth and positive possibilities.

It is critical that first responders treat those who have been harmed with respect and dignity, to avoid patronizing or placating, and instead engage in the best caregiving while enabling the individual to take responsibility for what he or she will do next. The learning process from tragedy begins at this point. Reinforcing the reality that something traumatic has occurred is important, but reinforcing the stereotype that the injured party is a victim only plays to a person's powerlessness.

Delaying Care Is a Public Health Risk

The injured party choosing to delay care poses a public health risk for two reasons. First is the potential for failure to contain the offender, leaving other individuals at risk. Second is the concern for any negative emotional, behavioral, or cognitive responses for the injured party associated with the attack. One reason a victim may delay care concerns the process of reporting the incident. If the university's approach is to respect the survivor's wishes, survivors have greater control about where and to whom a report is made. Encouraging the recording of information at the time of caregiving is desirable, again leaving control in the hands of the victim. Victims can be offered the option of retaining the recorded data to keep privately or to file a formal report. From a public health standpoint, the caregiving and incident itself should be part of the public database for epidemiological purposes, but victims should be given a choice whether to mask their identity.

Any connection made between caregiving and formal incident reporting becomes coercive in nature. These should be separate processes dominantly influenced by the discretionary latitude of the survivor or survivors. Holland, Cortina, and Freyd (2018) see an urgent need for survivor-centered reforms of the mandatory reporting requirements in most universities to create alternative and innovative policies and practices. According to the American Psychological Association's Ethics Code, the principle of *beneficence and nonmaleficence* dictates that a psychologist carefully assess that benefits outweigh costs and that harm is avoided before an intervention begins. SART members and first responders should be especially alert to survivor wishes for confidentiality and restraint in recording or reporting while being mindful of the public health requirement for surveillance data and incident reports aimed at protecting the community. We explore this sensitive boundary next.

Recording and Reporting Incidents

The recording and reporting of sexual harassment and sexual assault incidents is critical to the well-being of individuals, the institution, and the community (Cooper and Quick, 2017). In their examination of mandatory reporting in universities, Holland, Cortina, and Freyd (2018) raise a survivor-centered reform of creating a restricted reporting option. We view this alternative to mandated reporting as a worthy innovation to fully explore. In this option, the survivor can make an initial report but choose not to launch an (immediate) official investigation. Thus, the survivor has *recorded* the incident but has not officially *reported* it. Capturing accurate and reliable data as close to the incident in time as possible is critical from several perspectives. Carlson (2017) strongly encourages the documentation of incidents, even video recording or audio recording interactions where possible. Documentation has both pros and cons but should aim for an accurate record of the incident from all involved. The hallmark of this phase in the post-incident process should be the capturing of primary source data—the *facts* insofar as they can be obtained—and perceptions while suspending judgments and not entering into interpretation. Interpretations and judgments come into play during the post-incident investigative phase, which we discuss in the next section.

Data are essential to public health surveillance systems, which in turn are crucial for subsequent preventive intervention. Public health practices, preventive medicine, and preventive management are not grounded in theory or hypotheses. The science of epidemiology demands concrete data as the basis of action. Conjecture or guesswork are too low a standard of evidence in this domain. Ultimately, the aim is to follow the causal chain of events to the original sources. The further away from an incident individuals move in time, the more they must rely on recall. Shaw (2018) has explored false memory as well as the area of high-stakes lies (Shaw, Porter, and ten Brinke, 2013). Her encouragement of the use of apps to begin capturing data about an incident in near-real time is a step toward ensuring accuracy of reporting. While multiple reports would seem to improve the accuracy of incident data, this is not necessarily so. Krakauer (2015) reports a case where multiple high-stakes lies and collusion appear to be in play on the part of those who victimized a young woman in Missoula, Montana (see chapter 10).

We challenge the idea that any incident can be fully reconstructed, given the biases, perceptual distortions, and sensory limitations inherent in human nature. However, we adhere to the absolute standard of accuracy. With good primary self-report data, third-party evidentiary data, and archival records from the scene, a fairly accurate 360-degree account is certainly possible.

Every case of inter-gender or same-gender conflict is a case of sexual harassment or sexual assault. The college or university needs well-trained individuals with good discernment to know what to report and what not to report. From the individual's perspective, it is essential to have more than one reporting channel to consider in filing a formal complaint. A potential problem in incident reporting and investigating is barriers to reporting (Krakauer, 2015). Two questions emerge: What to report—"When in doubt, speak up!"—and who to report to. The formal and informal elements of the university must be navigated in working through the recording and reporting processes (Levinson, 2002).

Guidelines and Protocols

Colleges and universities need clear and explicit protocols for reporting incidents of sexual assault. These should eliminate the ambiguity attendant to the reporting process, lower the threshold that a person may encounter in reporting, and enhance the safety, security, and confidentiality of the process. Details in the guidelines should include when and where to go to report the incident along with a relevant authority's name, title, and contact information. The institution should provide multiple points of contact so the individual can exercise choice in the gender of the person who takes the report as well as the channel for reporting. When a university has a multidisciplinary (in terms of professional expertise and university function) and diverse (in terms of age and gender) CSAP Board, the person who wants to explore making a complaint has latitude beginning the conversation. The team members should include fully certified Title IX investigators and judges, and the guidelines should spell out the institutional links with police, medical facilities, and psychological referral sources. Transparency here is critical. Institutional boundaries should exist between the parties involved in the reporting of, intervention in, and treatment of sexual assaults, but the person reporting is entitled to visibility over the entire system of concern and care.

Complete, Accurate Data

Recording and reporting of sexual assaults is essential for senior university authorities to monitor the health and well-being of the institution. First-person reporting, even self-reporting, should be encouraged. Individuals are entitled to understand the consequences of reporting as well. The university's reporting system should help individuals developmentally and educationally rather than being principally punitive. Third-party reporting should have clear rules of how and to whom that should be done. A reporting system that is fair to all concerned and supports procedural, distributive, and interactive justice will be a system that gathers more complete and accurate data.

Weick and Sutcliffe (2015) caution against simplifying by quickly accepting an easy, convenient causal explanation for unexpected events. Instead, in the recording and reporting of incidents, emphasis should be on enhancing the captured data from everyone involved. Suspending judgments can facilitate the flow of information. The data likely will be conflicting, confusing, and even disconfirming, so the objective should be inclusion, not exclusion or filtering, of information. Being alert to dissonant or inconsistent data can enrich the total pool of data available.

That said, Freyd (2016) was among the first to flag the problem with "required reporting" that can violate the autonomy and integrity of the individual, compelling decisions that he or she does not choose. That is why the innovative alternative Freyd proposes with her colleagues respects the integrity of the survivor while potentially opening a door for informal reporting of general incident data for the university to use for public health purposes (Holland, Cortina, and Freyd, 2018).

Tracking Risks and Dangerous Individuals

Complete and accurate reporting of sexual assaults makes it easier to track risks and reveal potentially dangerous people (Quick, McFadyen, and Nelson, 2014). Dangerous individuals typically compose a very small part of the campus population, maybe 1 to 3 percent, but they should be identified early and engaged before bad—or worse—things happen. A review of the literature suggests that screening out potentially dangerous individuals is not feasible, because their behavior may emerge only after they have become part of the institution. That is, an individual may start down a path of acting out in dangerous ways because of a triggering event (such as binge drinking or peer behavior) at the university or college.

Multiple Channels

Colleges and universities need multiple channels for reporting incidents so no one channel can be used to block the process. While there does need to be a centralized mechanism for consolidating and reporting sexual assaults, a wider scope is required for the data collection process. The risk in having only one or two reporting channels is that they can become compromised and the message never reaches senior authorities in the university.

The Clery Act and Campus Security Authority

The Jeanne Clery Disclosure of Campus Security Policy and Campus Crime Statistics Act (discussed in chapters 2 and 4), which is a federal law, requires universities to report statistics concerning the occurrence of certain criminal offenses that are reported to a CSA—a campus security authority (Bosman, 2017). A campus security authority is defined as:

- A campus police department or campus security department.
- Any individual who has responsibility for campus security but who does not constitute a campus police department.
- An individual or department specified in campus security policy as appropriate to hear a report of crimes.
- An official with significant responsibility for student and campus activities. This includes faculty advisers for student organizations.

While universities typically have their own security forces, a student who is the victim of a crime may be more inclined to report it to someone other than the campus authorities. For this reason, the Clery Act requires all institutions of higher education to collect crime reports from a variety of individuals and organizations that the law considers to be CSAs. This reporting must include offenses that occur on campus, in residence facilities, on non-campus property, and on public property.

The criminal offenses that are required to be reported are murder/nonnegligent manslaughter, negligent manslaughter, sex offenses (rape, fondling, statutory rape, incest), robbery, aggravated assault, burglary, motor vehicle theft, domestic violence, dating violence, stalking, arson, liquor law violations, drug violations, and illegal weapons possession. In addition, the act requires universities to report statistics for hate (bias) crimes for murder/nonnegligent manslaughter, sex offenses (rape, fondling, statutory rape, incest), robbery, aggravated assault, burglary, motor vehicle theft, arson, larceny, vandalism, intimidation, simple assault, stalking, dating violence, and domestic violence.

Universities should have standardized data collection forms that CSAs can complete, ideally online, for the prior calendar year. The university's legal department should originate biannual reminders of the reporting requirements under the Clery Act.

More urgently, if a serious crime that may cause an ongoing threat to the university community is reported to anyone defined as a campus security authority, that individual must immediately report the incident to campus police or security. Universities have a responsibility to notify the campus community about any crimes that pose a threat. If there is any question about whether an ongoing threat exists, the campus police or security authorities should be notified.

The university should provide contact numbers for CSAs or others who may have questions about whether specific persons, actions, behaviors, or situations are possible threats to others or to the campus community. The university should provide additional training regarding the Clery Act and the CSA responsibilities by means of annual compliance training. Mandatory reporting can be problematic, as discussed by Freyd (2016) and Holland, Cortina, and Freyd (2018) and as previously noted.

Exemptions and Exceptions

Mental health and religious counselors are exempt from Clery Act reporting requirements. However, the legislation encourages institutions to establish a confidential reporting procedure to which mental health and religious counselors may refer their clients. These exceptions complement the survivor-centered reforms to the mandatory reporting system as proposed by Holland, Cortina, and Freyd (2018). We do not see a secure, confidential reporting system as being in conflict with an official reporting system. The former offers victims the discretion to sort through alternative courses of action and associated consequences. Respect for the integrity and autonomy of the survivor or survivors must be weighed against the publicly available surveillance data that enable university decision-makers to see risks in the environment. We do not view these competing demands as irreconcilable.

Management of the Reporting System

While sexual assault data are clearly a component of Clery Act reporting, there are many more crimes, as just noted. The CSAP Board's focus is sexual assault and sexual violence. Specific authority and resources should be given to one or two individuals under team oversight to collect the sexual assault data.

The Faculty's Role in Reporting

While some faculty members are designated as CSAs due to their advisory position with student organizations or clubs, most do not fall into this required reporting category. As a result of trusted relationships with colleagues and students, however, faculty may inadvertently become first responders. They may be approached by survivors, by third-party witnesses, or even by perpetrators conflicted over what to do next. Since these faculty are not trained first responders, certified Title IX investigators, or event-certified Title IX judges, their most valuable contribution is in a triage function, serving as a referral source for the colleague or student in need—provided faculty know who to refer people to so the concern is not papered over or ignored. A trained authority can make a far more discerning judgment about the appropriate moral, ethical, and legal disposition of the issues presented. Faculty with good intentions but outsized presumption can do more harm than good and even compromise a case because it hasn't been handled with expert knowledge and skill.

What faculty can do when approached by colleagues or students is to listen closely, to help clarify any doubt or confusion. They can offer feedback to focus the message. Knowledgeable faculty may even serve on discipline panels. More powerfully, qualified faculty can engage in research on campus sexual assault. While much has been written on the subject, the foundation of high-quality research is paper thin. (The University of Texas System, across its thirteen medical and academic components, is exceptional in its commitment to apply scientific rigor to this serious public health problem.) The companion expertise to research for faculty is of course teaching, so those members so qualified and motivated may play a role in providing training on campus sexual assault and reporting procedures.

Faculty members who have a conversation with a student or colleague regarding sexual assault should know that they can be called to testify in a criminal proceeding about that assault. Faculty do not have the legal protections afforded mental health and religious counselors. Professional liability insurance is one safeguard.

Investigation and Response Alternatives

The investigation of incidents should be exhaustive and should done by at least two persons in a gender-diverse team under guidance of the CSAP Board. The rights of survivor or survivors and of the accused must be guarded throughout the process. The investigation picks up where the recording and reporting end, but there may be some overlap in these two post-incident phases. The CSAP Board should specify a process whereby the SART does not assume that a crime has occurred or take actions that foreclose a criminal process if it is later determined that a crime has occurred. (We focus in chapter 9 on noncriminal processes that address the conflicts attendant to sexual harassment and sexual assault incidents.)

Some universities wisely employ legal counsel for accusers and accused alike. By ensuring that the rights of young women and men are protected, the process aims to achieve fair treatment for all. Individual cases can be very complex, so there are advantages to slowing the process and precluding a rush to judgment. The risk of not following a deliberative judicial process is to move toward convicting without due process or demonizing an innocent individual. Universities and colleges need to avoid rushing to judgment in accusations of sexual assault.

Paying attention to conflicting standards for rules of evidence, rights of the accused, and due process is essential. Because of the differences between most campus adjudication systems and the criminal justice system, campuses need clear, defensible rules about how they will engage the investigatory process. Protecting due process is essential to both good jurisprudence and fair treatment of all concerned (Johnson and Taylor, 2017). Once an ugly incident has occurred, there is no easy way through it; to avoid compounding injuries or creating new victims in the interest of retribution or to achieve quick resolution, a college or university must put safeguards in place at the core of its process. Staying with the suffering of the event is painful, but from that process can come strengths that the parties involved did not know they possessed.

Investigation Process

Chapter 7 details how to conduct an effective investigation. We see this as the responsibility of the Title IX coordinator and the CSAP Board but separate from the SART first responders. One of the first determinations to be made is whether the victim/survivor is reporting a formal complaint and seeks to have a formal investigation. Acting on the expressed wishes of the complainant is essential; Holland, Cortina, and Freyd (2018) emphasize that doing so is one important survivor-centered reform of the ubiquitous mandate reporting system in universities. This may involve a pro-and-con discussion with the victim/survivor so that the investigation process is clear, along with the prospective response alternatives available for adjudicating the incident. There are critically important factual as well as cognitive and emotional dimensions to this decision process.

If the complainant wishes to file a formal complaint, then a formal interview for the record should be conducted with the complainant that includes at least two interviewers, ideally one male and one female. A separate similar formal interview should be conducted with the accused, again with two interviewers of different genders. To the extent possible, bystanders and witnesses should be identified and separately interviewed. Archival data (cellphone videos, audio recordings, related evidence) should be collected. Any sexual assault investigation has pitfalls that can be consequential.

Implicit Bias Problem

Everyone carries within himself or herself biases that go beyond conscious awareness (Dovidio and Gaetner, 1986). Implicit bias, prejudice, and stereotypical beliefs can impact how parties to a sexual assault are treated and how adjudicators form and apply judgments. The investigation phase is the phase of the post-incident process in which interpretations arise. Negative and positive evaluations of survivors and perpetrators are influenced by stereotypical myths and biases (Clarke and Stermac, 2010). Even with no malicious intent, a person's memory can be faulty and unreliable (Shaw, 2018), which introduces unconscious errors into the process. Implicit bias has the potential to impact how first responders approach the parties to an incident. Gender stereotypes, racial stereotypes, and religious stereotypes come directly into play. These stereotypes are psychological shorthand for classifying people and can be huge stumbling blocks for establishing as accurate a portrayal of what transpired as possible.

The discovery process should build a profile or reconstruction of the event and the actors in context. Suspending judgment and accepting conflicting points of view is essential. Implicit bias operates within the individuals involved in the sexual assault as well as within the interviewers and investigators. The key here is that what is not known about the participating individuals' implicit bias can seriously diminish the investigation. Dovidio and Gaetner (1986) formed their theory of aversive racism in the context of racial prejudice, which sadly can have implications in sexual assault cases. Their theory and evidence extend beyond racism, however. While explicit biases and prejudicial behaviors are often more discernible, the implicit biases that individuals harbor, often beyond their awareness, may be especially consequential in the investigation.

What is more concerning is that some professionals hold certain convictions that are wrong. Chaplin and Shaw (2016) found in one study that law enforcement officers were confident yet wrong about a number of psychological issues related to the legal system. While a sexual assault investigation on a university campus will not necessarily enter the legal system, the point about the potential for law enforcement professionals to be confidently wrong is relevant. Ensuring that investigators are open to doubt is crucial.

Implicit bias causes both internal conflict and interpersonal conflict, given that no individual is wholly internally consistent or self-aware. Self-awareness is among the most difficult emotional competencies to earn, yet it's among the most important, because without good self-awareness, it is difficult to self-regulate behavior and to empathize. Self-awareness attunes investigators to their own prejudices, thus mitigating the implicit bias problem.

Investigation as Incident Discovery

The investigation is a discovery process. No one individual in an incident may know what "really" happened. Investigators can never assume that the parties involved are reporting accurately, or even truthfully. (See Shaw, Porter, and ten Brinke, 2013, concerning high-stakes lies.) There are three aspects of an incident to be discovered, beginning with the intent of the parties involved (and it must never be assumed that the parties were clear about their intentions). The second aspect is the set of acts and behaviors engaged in during the assault. The third aspect involves the consequences of the event. Each party will have a story to tell, with agreement on some points and disagreement on others. Interviewing the parties may make leave the impression that the individuals were in entirely independent situations.

Bazelon (2017) discusses the difficulties in understanding a legal case where initially John Doe and Jane Roe had agreement about exploring a sexual relationship. Things quickly became complicated, with implicit bias likely intruding on the reconstruction of events, given Roe's Mormon heritage, the role of alcohol in the relationship, and, finally, the sex itself. From a consensual beginning came dramatically different trajectories—thus the need to explore the incident in an attempt to understand it. The process can become extremely complex. (This case is discussed further in chapter 9.)

Another problem in the investigation is the seductive nature of the science and data, which plays in concert with implicit bias and stereotyping. Considerable scientific information exists about the problem of sexual assault on campuses (Cantor et al., 2015), specifically about who suffers (women, usually) and who are the primary perpetrators (men). A host of additional science on group-level differential risks also is available. All of this information falls within the domain of nomothetic science. Much of this is very good science, perfect for illuminating intervention programs and high-risk situations, but as group-level science it paints only one picture of the sexual assault problem, and that is a picture within the social context. The seduction of the science comes when we translate it to individual cases.

Such translational thinking has a fatal flaw. We may be drawn to make conclusions about a case and the individuals in it based on what we "know" from the scientific body of knowledge. The reasoning goes like this:

Fact: Women are primarily the victims of a sexual assault, by a man.
Fact: The incident in question involves a woman and a man.
Conclusion: The woman is the victim and the man is the perpetrator (aggressor).

Well, not necessarily. The logic is faulty. This is where idiographic or case-based science proves valuable to the investigative process.

When investigating a case, it is most important to understand that the greatest variance is within the group. Specifically, there is more variance among women than there is between women and men (likewise, more variance among men than between men and women). This same principle applies to all groups, however they identify or are identified. Because group-level data cannot be applied to individuals, a thorough and complete investigation requires a very different form of scientific inquiry.

With idiographic science, focusing on the individual, investigators build the case from the ground up, one data element at a time. The scientific body of knowledge cannot be applied to the individual case. Because the incident involves people, the case profile will never be exact or, for that matter, finished. The purpose is to describe, to deconstruct, to pull it apart and put it back together. This is a very different kind of scientific inquiry than natural science.

Cognitive Gap between the Genders

A complication associated with building a profile of what happened in an incident is the cognitive or perceptual gap between the genders. There will always be some variance in incident reports, but it is compounded because women and men differ most when perceiving behaviors to be sexual harassment (Quick and McFadyen, 2017). Cognitively, women and men see things differently. Some of the difference may be hardwired in the genders, socially constructed, or learned. Regardless of its origins, the gender gap hampers an in-depth understanding of the incident.

Idiographic Science and In-Depth Case Study

Idiographic science relies on interpretations of the evidence, not just the evidence alone. It is hermeneutic. One of the challenges in constructing a case is the information and interest asymmetries of the parties involved. The investigation should focus less on agreements and more on the discrepancies. Pushing out the boundaries of the pool of knowledge promotes a fuller understanding of what happened. This goes against the desire for quick, conclusive closure.

The idiographic process also takes advantage of the differences between investigators. The investigators may agree on some aspects of the case, but it is essential that they cross-challenge their interpretations. They likely will have incomplete or ambiguous information, murky non-data that defy validation. Continuing to ask questions is critical. Then there is the emotional overload of the especially difficult cases. Jon

Krakauer's book *Missoula* (2015) can be hard to read due to the graphic nature of the reporting (by at least one female doctoral student). The details and description can be draining. Good investigators must be able to process that emotion in healthy ways. Expressive writing or journaling is an excellent way to process these emotions so they do not congest the investigator's own limbic system (Pennebaker, 2004).

Adjudication

In the adjudication phase of the investigation the accumulated evidence and argumentation are presented so as to render judgment about the rights and obligations of the parties involved. Chapter 7 outlines the trained competencies that should be expected in adjudicators. Selecting adjudicators and choosing the resolution model to be used are important processes. Chapter 7 presents alternative models for resolving the complaint: the administrative model and the panel model. With the former, an administrator serves as the adjudicator, which has advantages of standardization and convenience. We suggest that at least two administrators be involved, one male and one female. If the university chooses the panel model and student adjudicators, an advantage is greater acceptance by the student body, but we have concern over the selection of adjudicators.

The student adjudicators should be racially, ethnically, and gender diverse, with additional consideration given to deep-level diversity (opinions, attitudes, values). Deep-level diversity can affect team performance over time (Harrison, Price, Gavin, and Florey, 2002), and an adjudication panel may certainly be viewed through a team lens.

Related to deep-level diversity, in both the panel and administrative models, are the issues of bias and history. Individuals form opinions based on experience, and these opinions may contain embedded bias, pro or con, toward groups of people or identity categories. Awareness of prejudice offers the opportunity to counter it in decision-making. Likewise, unacknowledged bias can influence the process in unseen ways. One of the methods to surface and identify such potentially disruptive forces is through personal histories. Interviews that identify critical life events and relationships can reveal issues that may impact the decision process in adjudication. Individuals who grow through traumatic events and therefore master themselves after the event are potentially strong panel members so long as they do not overlay their own experiences onto the hearing.

Both adjudication models are based in a legal framework. Specifically, they are variations on the civil and criminal justice models for administering punishment to those who have done wrong. In the next chapter we explore a restorative justice model that may align more with the forgiveness and resilience processes within our tertiary prevention framework (figure 2.1).

Quick, McFadyen, and Nelson's (2014) approach to tertiary prevention of chronic disorders in organizations, of which campus sexual assault is one, has four steps: containment, caregiving, forgiveness, and resilience. This chapter focused on containment and caregiving along with the post-incident processes of recording, reporting, and investigating. We take into consideration the study of mandated reporting by Holland, Cortina, and Freyd (2018), who argue for survivor-centered reforms to the recording and reporting process that increase victim/survivor discretionary control. In chapter 9 we address the third and fourth steps— forgiveness and resilience—plus the longer-term issues of recovery and healing. Chapter 9 also weighs the consequences of the actions that are taken during the adjudication phase of the investigation.

Tertiary prevention is necessary but never the preferred point of intervention from a public health standpoint. The preferred intervention is always primary (figure 2.1). Secondary prevention is designed to address issues that have not been averted by primary prevention. Finally, tertiary prevention aims to help survivors and to adjudicate wrongdoing. Sexual assaults are failures of the system and ultimately must be used to improve the campus culture, which is really the domain of primary prevention. A positive campus culture is the focus of chapter 4.

CHAPTER NINE

Healing and Seeking Justice

ONCE A SEXUAL assault has occurred and the immediate issues have been addressed, the next stages of tertiary prevention should begin. After caring for the victim or victims and containing the offender or offenders (as described in chapter 8) come these next stages of tertiary prevention. They involve healing and seeking justice, resting in part on the psychological processes of forgiveness and resilience.

Long after a sexual assault and consequent investigations and other actions, however, the end of the incident still may not be in sight, depending on a number of factors. Bazelon (2017) reports one landmark Title IX case in its third post-incident year. Some might suggest that the university and the individuals involved should put the trauma behind them. We do not believe that is possible. A traumatic event such as a campus sexual assault creates a bifurcation in experience: before and after. What is important during the "after" period are the twin processes of healing and seeking justice, which can be long and arduous. Each is important. They may be measured in years and lifetimes. Some might suggest forgive and forget. We do not agree. Forgiveness can be instrumental in both healing and seeking justice, but forgetting leads to amnesia about what happened. We say never forget. The process of remembering is the fundamental basis for growing into a new future for all parties concerned.

A sexual assault may be considered a failure on the part of the university as well as the offender or offenders. Learning from failure becomes crucial to the campus and its members who are engaging in a systematic process of reflection. Finding a scapegoat is an ancient social process that short-circuits the learning process (Laing, 1971). The scapegoat may be chosen through a variety of social, legal, or other means, but once chosen, the blame for whatever has gone wrong goes there. Then everyone is relieved that the problem has been solved—except that it has not. Blaming is a disempowering process, one that leaves a community diminished to the extent to which blame is used as a problem-solving device.

Assessing social dynamics is a complex task. A campus community may be considered an extended family, with parental responsibilities taken on by the university (*in loco parentis*). Laing (1971) wrestled with the best ways to intervene in social situations, a university campus being one such social context. He began a typology of situations that is thought provoking with regard to the problem of sexual assault. He enumerated four situations:

1. Something is the matter with someone. We just have to identify the "someone."
2. Nothing is the matter with anyone, but nothing's working properly.
3. Something is the matter with everyone, according to everyone else. (This may sound like the contemporary assessment on many university campuses.)
4. Nothing is the matter, with us or with the situation. Don't bother us. Why are you interfering? Everything is fine as far as we are concerned. (But it might not be fine as far as the police are concerned, or the campus authorities.)

The problem with scapegoating is that it shifts responsibility and assigns blame. Do not blame the victim! The alternative to blaming is the acceptance of personal responsibility in a given social situation. The social process of blaming is distinct from the process of holding a person accountable for their actions and behaviors. Personal accountability is behaviorally specific in words said and deeds done. In the context of sexual assaults, it may be difficult for some to accept personal responsibility, especially for the harm they have caused. However, it is important for young men and women to do just that: accept personal responsibility. Accepting personal responsibility includes understanding the impact, even if unintended impact, of one's words and deeds on others, through empathy and compassion.

Reflecting on the varied responsibilities that members of the campus community have for a sexual assault takes time and effort. There is significant emotional and psychic hard work for everyone following a sexual assault. There is significant gain to be made when everyone is asking: What might I have done differently? What can I learn from this? Especially challenging is that there is no textbook answer. Figure 2.1 sets out our tertiary prevention approach to campus sexual assaults:

- Containment. The focus here is on restraining offenders and putting boundaries around the problem to limit contagion at all levels.
- Caregiving. The focus here is on caring for all those who have been injured or harmed, to include attention to secondary victims, tertiary victims, and others touched by the incident.
- Forgiveness. The focus here is on forgiving oneself and forgiving others, which should not be confused with reconciliation or with absolution.
- Resilience. The focus here is on what we call the *bounce back* from the incident, for individuals and for the campus community. This is not a rapid bounce back: achieving it takes time, effort, and energy.

Chapter 8 focused on containment and caregiving. Healing and seeking justice for the wrong that has been done rest in part on the processes of forgiving and seeking renewed life, on resilience and bounding back.

After-Incident Analysis: Learning from Failure

A key aspect of campus response to sexual assault is reflecting on every incident as a wake-up call. During any academic year, 2.8 percent of women will experience a completed or attempted rape (Fisher, Cullen, and Turner, 2000), and 27 percent are likely to experience unwanted touching (Gross, Winslett, Roberts, and Gohm, 2006). The Campus Sexual Assault Prevention (CSAP) Board, led by the Title IX coordinator, should address these failures, though not overreact to any one of them. Reminder: These are neither accidents nor random events but malicious, motivated acts (Quick, McFadyen, and Nelson, 2014). Weick and Sutcliffe (2015) offer insight into learning from failures and staying focused on the data. Failures harm the victim or victims as well as the larger campus community. The historic $500 million that Michigan State University paid into a settlement fund for the victims of Dr. Larry Nassar's sinister abuse of young women, along with the $4.5 million fine paid to the US Department of Education, should send a message to senior campus administrators everywhere about their culpability in the campus sexual assault problem.

Never Oversimplify or Dismiss

Weick and Sutcliffe (2015) say that high-performance, high-reliability organizations follow common practices to achieve a high degree of excellence. A university campus is a complex system. The Title IX coordinator and CSAP Board appreciate this rich complexity while taking note of the smallest incident report. Therefore, regular meetings of the board should focus on behavioral reports of all kinds from all across the campus. What the CSAP Board should be monitoring on a regular basis are those students, faculty, staff, and administrators who "stand out" for one reason or another. CSAP Board members should challenge assumptions, stereotypes, and implicit biases. Examining conditions throughout the campus is important because a minor event in one area may link to a minor event in another area, which can be discovered through the board's observation process.

Who Missed What?

When a sexual assault occurs, a key question is *Who* missed *what* that allowed this to happen? The campus surveillance system managed by the CSAP Board should pick up early indicators that someone is going off track. Campus surveillance and personal survival signals are essential to prevention efforts. Therefore, sexual harassment, assault, or rape represent the failure of one or more elements in the system. The campus must use the incident as a learning opportunity to reexamine the fabric of surveillance systems and improve them to catch a problem before serious harm is done. The aim should be to educate, change bad behaviors, and expel from the campus those unwilling to get healthy.

Crime Control and Criminal Justice Approach

Universities were not designed to be an element within the correctional system, but many universities now play police, prosecutor, judge, and jury with campus sexual assaults. Taking on these roles can be problematic. The legal system, including the criminal justice components, is designed to adjudicate crimes, civil wrongs, and illegal behavior. Universities have historically incorporated student conduct offices that have expertise in disciplinary matters; for sexual assault cases, however, the standards used may conflict with those in the legal system outside the campus. On September 7, 2018, the Sixth Circuit Court of Appeals, in *John Doe v. University of Michigan*, issued a rebuke to Title IX proceedings aimed at serving as police, prosecutor, judge, and jury. The conflict between the university and legal systems in the sixth circuit case centered on due process rights for the accused.

In some ways, the criminal justice approach to adjudicating campus sexual assault often results in unsatisfactory outcomes for the victim-survivor, the accused, or both. Herman (2005) found in in-depth interviews with twenty-two victims of violent crime that survivors' views of justice do not fit well into either retributive or restorative justice models. Latimer, Dowden, and Muise's (2005) meta-analysis attempted to synthesize the existing research on restorative justice, aggregated from studies that compared restorative justice programs to traditional criminal justice programs. They considered victim and offender satisfaction, restitution compliance, and recidivism as outcome measures. While restorative programs were significantly more effective, that result must be considered in the context of self-selection bias inherent in restorative justice research.

Here we discuss first the criminal approach to seeking justice under the law and then the restorative approach, which may be deployed either in concert with or separate from the justice system. The goals of any approach to seeking justice should be to achieve fair and transparent processes with agreed-upon rules and practices. The extent to which universities aim to achieve certain outcomes, such as verdicts of guilty or innocent, from the aforementioned processes is problematic. The procedural justice of the process should precede distributive justice.

Criminal Justice under the Law

One of the thorniest issues for universities in sexual assaults is the adjudication within a criminal, legal, and correctional framework. The crime control perspective on sexual assault prevention rests on a criminal justice model with its primary focus on the offender (McCall, 1993). Within this framework, primary prevention aims to attack the conditions fostering crimes of sexual assault, reduce the opportunities for sexual assaults to occur, and engage legislative and social prevention. These primary approaches are complemented by secondary prevention intended to achieve early identification and intervention of potential offenders. At the tertiary prevention level, the crime control perspective emphasizes treatment and rehabilitation of convicted offenders. This perspective is a questionable fit for universities, which are not set up either as correctional institutions or as criminal justice organizations. That does not mean that the legal and criminal justice system has no role in campus sexual assaults.

Busch-Armendariz and the University of Texas Research Team (2017a, 2017b) bring explicit focus to the differences across domains with comparisons of the Texas Penal Code, Student Judicial Services, and Title IX when it comes to dating and domestic abuse violence on each of six subscales: cyber abuse, psychological abuse, physical violence, unwanted sexual touching, rape, and attempted rape. (Rather than looking at campus sexual assault as a single construct, the UT Research Team deconstructed the behavior into these subscales.) While the item agreement between Student Judicial Services and Title IX is essentially identical, there is a lack of agreement between these two domains and the Texas Penal Code. This is a problem. Do we want universities to become the law unto themselves? We do not!

The fundamental challenge for university leaders is daunting given the conflicts between domains. The federal government chose to use Title IX in 2011 as the basis for issuing administrative guidance to universities for the resolution of sexual assault complaints on campus. Failure to comply with this administrative guidance would lead the university to put at risk all of its federal funding. Title IX exerts significant leverage to comply. The aim of the administrative guidance is to increase the probability of holding offenders accountable for their actions. However, there is far from uniform agreement that this is a legal approach, let alone a wise approach, to the problem of campus sexual assault. Coray (2016) believes that many universities have failed to meet their legal obligations in responding to sexual assault complaints, and suggests that law enforcement should be integrated into campus response procedures.

Johnson and Taylor (2017) argue that universities are in a moral frenzy akin to the panic in 1692 within the Massachusetts Bay Colony over witchcraft, where subjective testimony from children and "spectral" evidence "seen" by the accusers served as the basis for arresting 140 innocents, 19 of whom were hanged. In the process of critiquing the campus assault issue, these researchers run the risk of inflaming the debate while at the same time addressing serious issues for consideration by proponents of both legal approaches. A fundamental critique concerning the definition of rape is the argument about the redefinition of the word by a feminist scholar. The UT Research Team has displayed strong scientific rigor in its systematic approach to definitions of the actions and behaviors under the rubric of dating and domestic abuse and violence. Without scientifically grounded definitions, the process of adjudicating disputes becomes unhinged. While universities can help with the science, they cannot render the final judgments. These judgments are ultimately in either legislative or judicial hands, beyond the control of the universities to determine.

Three other conflicted issues that Johnson and Taylor (2017) bring to the fore are due process, burden of proof, and standard of proof. These issues are at the heart of the debate about the adjudication of campus sexual assault complaints.

Due process. University disciplinary and correctional processes are not courts of law and therefore are not obligated to adhere to the same standards that govern the legal process. Within the legal framework, due process is a basic procedural right preserved by the American constitutional system. As noted in chapter 8, Braceras (2016) is concerned that if universities fail to secure this basic right for the accused, they run the risk of creating Star Chambers such as those used in sixteenth- and seventeenth-century England for crushing political and religious dissent. The Star Chamber has become a euphemism for a system of justice that is arbitrary and unfair. One justice on the California Court of Appeals characterized the University of California, San Diego, system for dealing with the John Doe v. Jane Roe case (*John Doe v. Regents of the University of California*) as a kangaroo court (Bazelon, 2017), only to subsequently rule for the university. Such legal outcomes miss the mark in resolving the issue. From the plaintiff's perspective, due process rights for the accused entail the painful experience of directly confronting an offender and being cross-examined. Victims have a challenging hill to climb in reliving the painful events through the adjudication process. Angling to achieve justice, mercy, and fair treatment to all concerned is nearly impossible in many campus sexual assault cases. The legal system is predicated on open, transparent, and examinable processes.

Burden of proof. Within the American legal tradition, burden of proof rests with the plaintiff, the one bringing the charges (Johnson and Taylor, 2017). Within some university systems, burden of proof falls on the accused, who is put in the position of defending himself first. In fact, the allegations, possibly even the accuser, may not always be known to the accused. Labeling issues ("accuser," "accused," and so on) are significant for the fairness of the process. Implicit bias and stereotype come into play once a label has been affixed to each party to the conflict. What appears to be, may not be. The Innocence Project has gone a long way to demonstrate the limitations of our legal system for achieving accurate judgments for those accused in all cases. Where universities are operating under administrative guidance versus legal or statutory authority, they are in a precarious position to sort through this conflicted issue. Due to the varied interests of the parties, the university's central concern may well be risk management. Failure to comply with Title IX guidance exposes the university to heavy federal penalties. Failure to attend to rights of the accused exposes the university to civil litigation. Regardless of the outcome of the civil litigation, the process is expensive and lengthy. Bazelon's (2017) report of the John Doe and Jane Row litigation is a case in point.

Standard of proof. The standard of proof is the third conflicted issue addressed by Johnson (2017) as well as Johnson and Taylor (2017). Based on a previous US Department of Education directive, many universities are assigning blame based on a preponderance of the evidence standard, which means there's a 51 percent chance that the accuser is telling the truth (Johnson and Taylor, 2017). These are the primary standards of proof:

- Beyond a reasonable doubt (most rigorous standard)
- Clear and convincing evidence (medium rigor)
- Preponderance of the evidence (least rigorous standard)

The preponderance of evidence standard is lowest of the three standards. The clear and convincing evidence standard shifts the probability from 51 percent to highly probable. Both of these are lower standards of proof than beyond a reasonable doubt.

There is no agreement within the legal community, let alone across universities, concerning which standard of proof is the right one for sexual abuse cases. Universities are left in the position of determining the best and also the most defensible procedure for adjudicating these cases. The federal Title IX guidance is probably the right place within the law to position these cases because they are predominantly gender based. There is the clear need for legal protection and redress for victims, especially when the offensive behaviors rise to the level of criminal acts. Adjudication within the university relieves the victim of the burdens associated with criminal or civil litigation and the rights afforded defendants within those systems. The argument for resolving disputes within the college or university is that it is a quicker process that leads to more case resolutions.

Restorative Justice

Restorative justice certainly may be a model to consider for campus sexual assaults. Koss and Achilles (2008) suggest that considerable literature advances restorative justice options as satisfying and empowering for crime victims. These researchers examine restorative justice for sexual assault in particular; they use the term *survivor/victim* in order to retain the empowerment conveyed by *survivor* and the outrage implied by *victim*. They suggest that restorative interventions may be used at many possible points following a sexual assault whenever the survivor/victim desires resolution outside the justice system. Restorative justice, then, may precede the charging of an accused, may occur after a defendant has been convicted, may occur after a convicted defendant is in prison, may occur after the defendant is released from prison, or may occur even years following the incident.

Umbreit, Vos, Coates, and Lightfoot (2006) identify sharing circles, victim-offender dialogue, victim impact panels, community reparation boards, circles of support, sentencing circles, conferencing (developed specifically for sexual assault), and restorative discipline in educational settings as among the restorative options. Koss and Achilles (2008) focus on three of these restorative justice alternatives: victim-offender dialogue, sentencing circles, and conferencing. In considering these alternatives to criminal justice, the goals of healing and seeking justice are foremost.

Victim-offender dialogue. Also known as mediation, this restorative justice intervention has been used for sexual assault when a survivor wants to meet with the offender and the offender agrees. This form of restorative justice intervention aims to empower the survivor/victim; therefore, he or she is the one who sets the agenda for the meeting. Often the agenda includes the survivor/victim stating the personal impact of the sexual assault, asking questions of the offender, and seeking acknowledgement of responsibility. One of the limitations of victim-offender dialogue is that mediation rests on an assumption of equal power between the parties. That is often not the case in sexual assaults. Victim-offender dialogue may be considered an appropriate option for campus incidents where both parties are students or campus members of equal social stature.

The benefit of dialogue may be found when the survivor/victim desires additional perspective on the incident from the viewpoint of the offender. In addition, the offender must be genuinely remorseful, must fully accept responsibility, and must be motivated to repair the damage. The restorative justice option may not be appropriate for especially violent sexual assaults and is inappropriate to use unless the survivor/victim seeks it.

Sentencing circles. Koss and Achilles (2008) explain that sentencing circles were developed primarily in Canada and have been most widely used among First Peoples and American Indians. Sentencing circles involve a large group of individuals who are invested in the resolution of an incident and who come together to determine a plan for the offender. This circle concept has ancient roots and is manifest in a variety of indigenous societies. Because college and university campuses are constrained social systems, there is potential to adapt this restorative justice intervention in the campus setting.

Umbreit, Vos, Coates, and Lightfoot (2006) present the Hollow Water First Nation Community Holistic Circle Healing approach as appropriate for sexual offenders, their victims, and the families of both. While there are advantages in a broad community voice seeking justice, the lack of privacy, potential embarrassment working with fellow students and colleagues, unprofessional conduct on the part of some individuals, and potential coercion of the survivor pose limitations. Coker (2004) does not see sentencing circles as a restorative justice intervention, because circles may include the same community members involved in the conventional sentencing of the criminal justice system.

Conferencing. Conferencing is widely used and has been specifically adopted for sexual assault. The conference occurs when there is consensual agreement among the survivors/victims, offenders, and their family and friends. The conference and the resultant redress plan constitute restorative punishment. In contrast to the dialogue intervention, conferencing acknowledges the broad impact of the sexual assault in the larger social context, specifically related to family and friends.

Conferences are often sited in police stations for safety, but within the campus community conferences may be facilitated by social service professionals, trained volunteers, campus security personnel, or even student conduct professionals, any of whom have received specialized training in a scripted process, be it a strict or loose scripting. Offenders must take responsibility for the acts they committed. All parties must engage in thorough preparation in advance, often involving weeks or months. A facilitator guides the conference to make sure that key points are covered, speech is not abusive, and everyone has a chance to speak. A typical agenda:

- The offender describes the acts and takes responsibility for them
- The survivor/victim voices the impact of the assault
- Family and friends of both the offender and the survivor/victim speak
- The offender responds to what has been said about the harm that resulted from the acts

The concluding discussions in the conference formalize a programmatic, survivor/victim-driven plan that the offender accepts to make amends and repair harm to the survivor, family and friends, and the campus community. In contrast to a criminal justice approach, conferencing aims for individualized restorative punishment for the offender and empowers the survivor and the campus in the process of determining justice.

Forgiveness, Responsibility, and Resilience

Restorative justice has a unique potential to repair emotional damage for victims, yet the role of forgiveness is not simple. Not all campus sexual assaults are maliciously intentional, especially where no comorbid problem of alcohol or substance abuse is involved. Armour and Umbreit (2006) delineate the unique dimensions of forgiveness in restorative justice and make recommendations for advancing research on forgiveness in ways that protect the uniqueness of each victim's process and guard against imposing moral or religious imperatives to forgive.

When harm is done, acceptance of responsibility is called for and forgiveness is an option that may help the actors and the campus heal. Vengeance and revenge are nonrestorative. Punishment is often appropriate, as in the case of restorative punishment or in the case of criminal incarceration. Forgiveness should not be confused with pardoning, condoning, excusing, forgetting, denying, minimizing, or trusting. Forgiveness does not necessarily lead to reconciliation, nor does it preclude litigation and legal action where that may be warranted and appropriate. Intertwining healing with seeking justice is a complex process, and forgiveness can be therapeutic and restorative, but it cannot be decoupled from the need for offenders to take responsibility.

Harm and damage are inevitable characteristics of organizational and community life (Cameron, 2007). Forgiveness is critically important in universities with regard to a sexual assault, a clear case where harm and damage have been done. Anger, resentment, and bitterness are among the most destructive and unending emotional cycles in human experience. To respond to harm with harm is to enter a black hole that consumes all. Human excellence and flourishing are often the products of difficult and challenging circumstances (Cameron, 2007). What could be more difficult and challenging than to respond to being raped by engaging in the forgiveness process?

It is crucial to distinguish forgiveness from related, yet conceptually distinct, concepts. Forgiveness does not mean to pardon someone. Pardoning spares the offender of punitive consequences, including legal consequences. An offender may be forgiven and simultaneously burdened with an appropriate punishment for the sexual assault. Forgiveness is not condoning. To condone is to offer approval, and that is absolutely not acceptable in a sexual assault case. Forgiveness is not excusing. Excusing someone for a minor offense may be appropriate, but certainly not for a sexual assault and especially its most serious forms. Forgiveness is not forgetting. Forgetting would lead to lack of learning, and the entire community needs to learn from a single incident. In fact, encouraging the remembering and recollection process is vital but does not require that one relive the experience. The function of remembering is not to re-traumatize. Forgiveness is not denying. Denying is a psychological adaptive mechanism that ultimately distorts reality. Forgiveness is not minimizing. Minimizing does not embrace the full pain and suffering of sexual assault. Forgiveness is not trusting. Trusting only can occur with trustworthy persons, and a person who commits a sexual assault is not trustworthy.

Forgiveness is the process of replacing negative, hurtful, and destructive thoughts and emotions, toward self and toward others, with positive, affirming, and life-giving emotions that are the foundation of human flourishing. Having healthy self-regard is healing and restorative. Offering positive regard even to the offender is counterintuitive and may only be appropriate under certain conditions acceptable to the survivor. For some, extraordinary acts of forgiveness are healing, such as the mother who not only forgives the person who murdered her son but takes the next step to embrace the murderer with unmerited positive regard—with love. Compelling examples of the healing power of forgiveness are just that: individual examples.

At the campus level, forgiveness and the resulting positive emotions help to restore, revitalize, and enhance the resilience of the community. Forgiveness is more than a personal cognitive-affective process. Forgiveness is a collective process that aims to offer grace, mercy, and unearned positive regard for members of the community. The absence of forgiveness leads to life-depleting recrimination, retribution, bitterness, anger, hostility, and a host of negative experiences that may have spawned the sexual assault in the first place. Denying negative emotions and behaviors can be delusional, but having a firm grasp of the reality of sexual assault and its negative outcomes does not preclude a more positive pathway forward that rests on healing, recovery, and renewal. The key actors in the forgiveness drama following a sexual assault are the victim, the offender, university leadership, and the university community.

Victim

For victims to forgive themselves and others does not require them to pardon the offender, condone the actions of the offender, excuse the offender, or deny what happened. Forgiveness is a choice for the victim, not an obligation. Forgiveness may enable the victim to begin the process of releasing the anger, bitterness, and negativity that arose in response to the assault. Remembering and forgiving can occur simultaneously. To remember does not require one to relive. The recollection of events, apart from the associated emotions and affective responses, offers a basis for learning a different path. This forgiveness process for victims needs to separate out what they did not have any control over just prior to and during the incident from what they did have control over. Blaming the victim for the assault is disempowering for the victim, whereas asking a victim to partake of self-forgiveness can be empowering for the victim. While empowerment is good, there can be limits to defensive coping and resistance training (Macy, Nurius, and Norris, 2007). The victim did not cause the sexual assault and may have been powerless to prevent it, but the victim is not powerless to learn from what happened. That learning process is complicated by the pain and suffering that attend such an event. A key issue here is the differences among victims. Not all victims are the same, nor are their circumstances the same. Thus there is no one best way to live following a sexual assault. There are multiple pathways for recovery and resilience, and forgiveness is one of them.

Offender

Just as victims are not all alike, neither are offenders. Some are malicious individuals whose sexual assault acts are intentional. Others are individuals who have lost self-control and had their inhibitions compromised by alcohol or drugs. The individual circumstances of the offender are crucial in considering forgiveness. Not all offenders are forgivable; some even spurn forgiveness. A precondition for even considering forgiving offenders is their acceptance of responsibility for the harm their acts have caused; their experience of remorse; their desire to repair the damage; and their desire to seek rehabilitation while accepting punishment. Offenders who want to be forgiven must do the work required to be forgivable. They should suffer no illusion that they will escape punishment for what they have done. Accepting responsibility for one's actions entails accepting punishment for those actions, to include the natural, disciplinary, or legal consequences. Thus, offenders may be forgiven only when they have become fully accountable.

Offenders who have abused their power (positional, physical, or social power) and any trust invested in them can begin the healing process with lessons in discipline and self-regulation. Offenders may not understand their own strength and power. Humility is at the core of the judicious use of power in all its forms. So the forgiveness process for offenders begins, not ends, with them asking for and receiving forgiveness. What's next is a change in behavior. How will they reform? How will they act differently?

The offender needs a context in which to combine internal effort with external leverage to ensure that reformation does occur. University supervision of students through faculty and staff advising is a standard form of oversight that is ingrained in the academy. Having an accountability partner is another mechanism by which the offender can reform with help from a stronger authority.

University Leadership

Cameron (2007) brings attention to leadership roles and responsibilities often associated with high-performing organizations characterized by institutional forgiveness and other virtues.

First, leaders acknowledge the trauma and injustice that organization members experience. In the university context, this means that university leaders acknowledge the problem of sexual assault on campus, embracing ways to study the problem, understand the problem, and resolve the problem, much as Chancellor William McRaven (2017) did within the University of Texas System. When the university's senior leaders acknowledge the problem, they make it possible to address the problem. Leaders who distance themselves from campus sexual assaults are engaging in denial.

Second, leaders focus the organization's outcomes (its products and services) on a higher purpose, diverting any focus on the leader himself or herself. In universities, this valuable emphasis on a higher calling focuses on the positive. To allow the university to be consumed by the wrongdoing of a few is to surrender to the pathologic minority. To retain the focus on the positive, however, it is essential that the university have explicit and visible means for redressing wrongdoing.

Third, leaders cannot compromise high standards. Forgiveness is not synonymous with tolerating campus sexual assault. Quite the contrary, forgiveness is the university embracing an intolerance by leaders of this violation of human dignity. Forgiveness by leaders should acknowledge the wrong and facilitate the aspiration for all that the university is better than its members' worst acts.

University Community

Following the lead of its leaders, the university community that embraces the forgiveness process acknowledges that sexual assaults occur but will not be tolerated. The university must be better than that. Forgiveness aims to heal the brokenhearted and harmed while ensuring a just and equitable adjudication. The uniting forces within the community and the higher aspirations of the university should be the overarching basis for energy going forward. Chapter 4 addresses building a university culture that is intolerant of sexual abuse and violence.

Public Health Approach

The public health approach includes public health surveillance, risk factor research, development and evaluation of prevention programs, and dissemination of information about what works (McMahon, 2000). While the crime control perspective places the spotlight on the offender, the public health perspective places the spotlight on the victim (see Bachar and Koss, 2001; McMahon, 2000). Personal exposure to sexual violence appears in three forms: knowing a victim, being a victim, and attending a presentation that "gives a face to the statistics" (Deeds, 2009). Long-term care for the victims of rape is the focus of tertiary prevention within the public health model. While an act that has been done cannot be undone, an important question about the public health model is whether as a community and as individuals we want to define members by one incident.

We note above that Koss and Achilles (2008) use the term *survivor/ victim* in their work. Some universities label victims of sexual violence *survivors*. While surviving a violent sexual attack is a powerful first statement of resilience, it may be best for someone who has been victimized by sexual abuse and violence to think of survival not as the end objective but rather as the first step on a journey to thriving and living life abundantly once again. Once someone has survived, shouldn't he or she want more than that? To thrive after a violent event is only possible, of course, after survival. But both thriving and post-traumatic growth are possible for those who have survived. The victim role then becomes a transitory role through which an individual grows.

Revictimization is a risk for survivors that university communities should invest heavily in helping avoid. It is a special concern for women who were sexually abused in childhood (Noll and Grych, 2011). Avoiding revictimization may involve directing attention to drinking and alcohol-related problems that predict future victimization (Messman-Moore et al., 2014).

While perpetrating a sexual assault can never be eradicated from one's record, it can be tuition paid for learning a life lesson so as to grow beyond the event and find new life. The community has an opportunity to repudiate the act without permanently castigating the actor. If the victimizer is willing to accept responsibility, engage in self-forgiveness, and take a healthier direction in life, then the community can contribute to the rehabilitation process through support, guidance, and positive reinforcement of new, constructive actions on the victimizer's part.

Educational Approach

While the crime control and public health approaches are active models used by many universities, the educational approach seems especially appropriate for educational institutions. An educational model would place the emphasis on learning from experience. What is the lesson to be learned from a sexual assault? Learning can fall into two broad categories, one being the acquisition of objective or scientific knowledge, the other being the development of skills. Gaining objective or scientific knowledge and developing skills are equally applicable to offenders and victims and to other members of the university community. Sexual assault resistance education, for developing those specific skills, may be especially appropriate given that one in six women will be sexually assaulted, most by men they know (Senn et al., 2013).

In 2017 the Institute on Domestic Violence and Sexual Assault University at the University of Texas prepared two reports on sexual violence titled *Cultivating Learning and Safe Environments* (Busch-Armendariz et al., 2017a, 2017b). We believe that title places the emphasis where it clearly should be: on learning and on safety. UT's academic institutions produced one report, and its health institutions produced the other. One of the differences to note between the two reports is in the incident rates of unwanted sexual contact (touching, attempted rape, and rape). In the academic institutions, 10 percent of females and 4 percent of males at the undergraduate level report being raped, while 5 percent of females and 2 percent of males at the graduate and professional level report being raped. In the health science centers and medical schools, 4 percent of females and 1 percent of males report being raped. In addition, 10 percent of LGBTQ individuals report being raped in the health institutions. The age differences between students in the institutions is consequential, with the average student about five years older in the health institutions, and certainly the graduate and professional students are older than the undergraduate students.

Our interpretation of these data is that undergraduate students are at greater risk of being victimized; they are known to be less developed cognitively, socially, and emotionally than older students. Peer education is the most commonly used method of teaching sexual violence prevention to college students (Deeds, 2009). One caveat is that our general conclusions do not acknowledge the significant within-group variance for each of these groups of students, which is the more significant variance.

Educational institutions should provide stronger safeguards, more oversight, and a higher concentration of mentors or supervisors throughout undergraduate student populations, because they are at greater risk. These mentors and supervisors should be specifically trained to guide students so they become neither victim nor offender. In addition, they can intervene if a sexual assault does occur, to use it as a catalyst for learning and development, not simply punishment. While the forgiveness process can address the relationship between the two parties, the learning and development process focuses on the victim and the offender individually. At the graduate and professional student level, the expectations are higher and a disciplinary approach to violations is more appropriate than an educational approach, though the latter should not be rejected.

Psychology within the Educational Model

Psychology has three missions that come into play in this educational model. One is the prevention of mental health problems and behavioral disorders. That mission is resonant with the public health model previously discussed. The second mission is the repair of damage, a mission that is relevant to the tertiary prevention of sexual assault. Psychological therapy and counseling for primary, secondary, and other victims as well as for offenders is highly relevant to treatment of injuries and damage after the fact. The purpose is, first, to prevent any psychological or behavior problems from worsening, and, second, to seek improvement in function.

The third mission of psychology is equally relevant to the educational model and is the core of the domain of positive psychology. That mission is to identify and build on unique strengths, abilities, and capacities. Thus, the post-incident assessment should develop a profile of the victim's strengths, abilities, and capacities as the foundation for recovery while at the same time acknowledging the harm and problem or problems that need to be treated.

Learning from Sexual Assault

A victim's first focus should be on survival and healing, counting the costs associated with the assault as well as what to be grateful for following the incident. A balanced scorecard takes both into consideration. At some point in successful recovery, the victim may continue to process lessons learned. One of the most powerful sources of learning comes from those who have survived and are thriving in a new life trajectory. That is very difficult psychological and emotional work to do, but it is work that can be done. Empathetically studying people who have survived trauma will cultivate assault survivors' empathy and coping skills. For example, assault survivors can find inspiration by looking to the large population of war wounded who have recovered in healthy ways, learned to pick up the pieces, and built new lives. Underestimating the challenge in doing so would be a mistake. Not seeing life's possibilities after the incident would be tragic.

Recognizing victim variance in the aftermath of a sexual assault is important as a type of triage concerning the victim's needs. Victim history with regard to vulnerability and stress factors (major life events, medical history, physical symptoms, psychological symptoms, behaviors, and emotions) as well as coping skills and strength factors (health habits, social supports, responses to stress, life satisfactions, purpose, and connections) can yield a balanced framework for understanding the whole person (Rahe, 2009). Universities that favor precautionary education, especially with young women, engage this type of framework by focusing on parental and social support as guards against predatory offenders who aim to groom a person for victimization. While predatory rapists may account for a small percentage of campus sexual assaults, they are a potentially dangerous group of offenders to identify early and remove from the campus.

Learning to be Respectful

While not the victim of sexual assault, Gavin de Becker (1997) charts, as the backdrop for his work, the violent and abusive childhood that he survived. The scientific research on those from abusive homes would put him on a path to an abusive, violent adulthood. That is not the path he walked. Teaching our young men how to harness their urges in constructive outlets is the educational challenge with abusers. Learning theory would suggest that rather than just having them learn to stop specific actions and behaviors, the strategy should be to replace those actions with positive alternatives. Rather than being abusive, young men need to learn to respect others, especially women.

An educational model emphasizes the rehabilitation and reclamation of an offender. The alternative would be to identify the offender, convict the offender, and outplace the offender—expel him from the university. This approach is clearly appropriate in some cases, but not all. So, while an unreformed offender is no longer the university's problem, the unreformed offender becomes a problem for the larger society, including if he is incarcerated. Educational systems are set up to educate and to train. Conceptualizing the approach as one of reeducation and retraining may offer the potential to help the individual become a better person.

There is a parallel model within the criminal justice system for young offenders who display violence in the home or at school. Court-ordered anger management classes provide a pathway for the offender to experience the consequences of his or her actions while at the same time self-identifying and then self-regulating his or her anger before it becomes destructive. Anger is a common and, when regulated, constructive emotion with the potential to do good, such as righting wrongs. So courts do not assign youth to anger management classes for being angry. Rather, youths are assigned by the courts for anger management because they strike a sibling or parent, because they destroy property, because they sabotage schools or places of employment—because they act out the anger destructively. The behavior is the problem, not the emotion. For young males, whose brain development is not complete until around 25 years of age, the self-regulation of emotion and of physical strength can be a particular challenge with which they need external support through mentors and guides.

Polizzi, MacKenzie, and Hickman (1999) found that a cognitive-behavior treatment approach for adult sex offenders had positive effects while also reducing crime in non-prison-based programs. Sex offender rehabilitation and treatment programs have proliferated through departments of corrections in many states. Understanding the differences between adult sex offenders and the university sexual assault offender should be one objective as universities consider an educational model for dealing with the problem.

Because universities have a core educational and training mission, the rehabilitation approach for a select set of abusers offers potential. This educational approach is likely best suited for motivated offenders who want to change. A campus program might consider three substantive stages of treatment intervention following an assessment, orientation, and preparatory period.

Stage 1: Early treatment. During this stage the offender learns to give and receive feedback; learns to use self-regulation and interpersonal skills; and fully accepts responsibility for the offense and its effects on victims. The combination of self-awareness and self-monitoring needs to be complemented with external support systems.

Stage 2: Internalization. During this stage the offender revisits the proximate and early precursors to the specific incident and develops cognitive-behavioral skills for enhanced self-management of risk factors. These may include family, self, and sociocultural risk factors (Sutton and Simons, 2015). This stage emphasizes the internalization of skills development through stages 1 and 2. This is a combination of education and training, because the ultimate goal is behavioral change.

Stage 3: Generalization. During this stage the emphasis is on the application and generalization of skills to new settings and situations.

This stage aims to solidify and extend the education and training processes that have occurred through the previous stages.

Not all offenders are good candidates for learning and changing. Predators who are may be hard-core cases need to be removed from the university. This is one place where the interface between the university and the larger social context is important. The point of interface in this case may be with the criminal justice system.

Behavioral Intervention

Frank Lamas pioneered the behavioral intervention approach as part of a team at the Rochester Institute of Technology, later leading behavioral interventions approaches at the University of Texas at Arlington and California State University, Fresno. This educational approach rests on a Behavioral Intervention Team (BIT), which is a cross-functional team responsible for assessing reports of troubling behavior on the part of students, faculty, or staff. The BIT website at UT Arlington (https://www.uta.edu/bit/) describes the BIT and how it works; provides information and tips about how to deal with incidents; and provides additional resources for a campus and its community. When activated, the BIT implements interventions that are in the best interest of the university and the individual. The approach features prevention, assessment, and intervention for situations that may pose a threat to the safety and well-being of the university community. The BIT is a concept that resonates with the CSAP Board described in chapter 4.

Inspired by the subsequent work done at CSU Fresno, figure 9.1 displays a three-team integrated model for behavioral intervention. The three teams focus on distinct behavioral domains and work in concert. The SART (Sexual Assault Response Team, first introduced in chapter 4) is at the heart of the model and focuses on sexual assaults, relationship violence, and stalking. The SART's point person should be a trained victim advocate who will ensure that victims receive the resources they need for recovery. Members of the SART are the first responders. The CARE (Campus Assessment and Response) team focuses on students

Three-Team Model for Behavioral Intervention

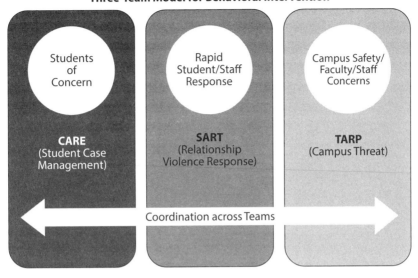

Figure 9.1. An Integrated Three-Team Model for Behavioral Intervention

with significant personal struggles, students in distress, or students of concern who may benefit from additional support. The CARE team is functionally a surveillance team on the lookout for those in need within the campus community. TARP (Threat Assessment and Risk Prevention) is the third team within this integrated model. The TARP team focuses on threats to faculty and staff. Campus safety is a key concern for TARP. Together, these three teams offer a comprehensive campus behavioral intervention and educational approach to sexual assaults and related behavioral issues.

The BIT and the teams composing the three-team integrated model should report directly to the vice president for student affairs, giving them very high level visibility and reach within the campus community. The vice president, with direct access to the president or chancellor of the university, can ensure that the most senior administrative council within the university is fully informed about the sensitive and critical issues of sexual assault.

Comorbidity Treatment

One of the complicating behavioral problems associated with campus sexual assault is alcohol and substance abuse. High-risk drinking is particularly serious, with implications for campus sexual assault (see Laufer Green Isaac Marketing Consultants, n.d.). One problem with excessive drinking and substance abuse is the compromising of the natural self-protective mechanism of impulse control. Pennebaker's (2004) research identifies this natural mechanism as a double-edged sword. Specifically, the blocking of thoughts, feelings, and behaviors enables a person to engage in socially acceptable behavior. That's the good news. The bad news is that pent-up feelings can be the basis for internal turmoil. Hence, Pennebaker's healthy process of expressive writing or confession (confiding in trusted others our most troubling thoughts). Modest alcohol consumption can facilitate the healthy release of pent-up feelings, as recommended for physiological reasons by the American Heart Association. However, when consumption becomes excessive, impulse control as well as good judgment are compromised.

The effects of high-risk drinking range from chronic conditions and impairments to deadly accidents and unintentional harm (Laufer Green Isaac Marketing Consultants, n.d.). This is where high-risk drinking can cross over with the problem of campus sexual assault. The non-predatory college student or faculty member who becomes intoxicated may engage in sexual assault when he would not consider doing so were it not for the excess of drink. Saying that "the alcohol made me do it" is patently unacceptable. This comorbid problem of excessive drinking is significant. The market research firm Laufer Green Isaac (n.d.) has produced clear findings that a majority of college students do not engage in high-risk drinking. However, the firm also reports that 31 percent of all college students engage in behavior that fits the definition for alcohol abuse in the American Psychiatric Association's *Diagnostic and Statistical Manual of Mental Disorders* (American Psychiatric Association, 2013). In addition, about 6 percent meet the criteria for alcohol dependence.

From the tertiary prevention standpoint, pathologic drinking has two important implications for campus sexual assault. First, during the assessment and triage of those in a campus or off-campus incident, there should be screening for alcohol abuse, dependence, or substance abuse. There are many cases where alcohol or other substances were instrumental in the incident and where there is not a known history of abuse or dependence. However, the campus sexual assault may be the presenting issue that reveals other serious problems.

If the latter is the case, then there is a need for independent treatment of the comorbid problem. Like campus sexual assault, high-risk drinking falls in the category of chronic problems in universities. Chronic problems are not resolved easily or quickly. More importantly, they are not manageable solely at the individual level. While a person may be diagnosed with the disorder, the treatment and solution reside in a multipronged approach. Laufer Green Isaac (n.d.) use a three-in-one framework that is compatible with a public health program of intervention and that targets individual-level interventions, environmental-level interventions, and campus-level interventions. By actively and aggressively addressing high-risk drinking, the university is having a positive contextual impact on the risk of campus sexual assault.

The preferred points of intervention for preventing campus sexual assaults are primary prevention through a campus culture characterized by strong policies and procedures and accompanied by enforcement mechanisms for wrong behaviors, and secondary prevention through training of campus constituents. Primary and secondary prevention do not prevent all campus sexual assaults, however. For that reason, tertiary prevention is necessary, as we have seen in chapters 8 and 9. This chapter has focused primarily on the long term—what happens months and years after a campus sexual assault. Healing and seeking justice rest in part on forgiveness and lead to resilience in the campus community. Campus sexual assaults should be remembered so they are not repeated.

CHAPTER TEN

Three Institutional Cases

SEXUAL ASSAULT IS ONE of several serious health risks faced by late adolescent and young adult college, graduate, and professional students, as well as their faculty. Other leading health risks for young women and men include vehicular accidents and access to firearms, both of which can lead to suicide or homicide mortality, as well as substance abuse, teen pregnancy, sexually transmitted diseases, and obesity, all of which can lead to morbidity. As we demonstrated earlier in this book, sexual assault and violence are serious problems that are also preventable. In this chapter we examine sexual assault cases and their aftermath at the University of Montana, the University of Texas, and Marist College.

University of Montana, Missoula: Coming Back from the Edge

The sexual assaults that took place at the University of Montana, Missoula, in 2011 were widely reported and are the subject of Jon Krakauer's 2015 book, *Missoula*. We look at those assaults in this chapter not to continue the blame and negativity, but to demonstrate that even colleges with major problems can—and must—change the campus and the culture, crafting a safe place of learning for all students.

Examining sexual assault on a campus is useful for a host of reasons already discussed in this book. The sexual assaults at the university at Missoula allowed us to examine the issue from a macro perspective, taking into account the engagement with these incidents by the entire community. UM was investigated by the US Department of Justice (DOJ) and the US Department of Education (DOE). There was an investigation by the National Collegiate Athletic Association into the football program and its compliance with NCAA rules. And there was a US Department of Justice investigation of the Office of Public Safety at the University of Montana, the Missoula police department, and the Missoula County Attorney's Office.

Examining this tragic situation gave us significant insight into the mindset of the rape culture discussed throughout this book. We are not indicting those involved in investigating or adjudicating the rapes at UM. That has been effectively handled by others. What we are saying is that even good people, when caught up in a cultural mindset, can do things that in retrospect they might not have done.

The History of the Sexual Assaults in Missoula

The issues at Missoula first came to light in December 2011 when the *Missoulian*, the local newspaper, published a tip from an anonymous source that three University of Montana football players were the alleged assailants in a sexual assault investigation being conducted by the Missoula police department (Florio, 2011). On December 15, 2011, then UM president Royce Engstrom hired former Montana supreme court justice Diane Barz to review two recent allegations of sexual assault on the UM campus. By the end of the month, Engstrom had received a status report informing him that UM appeared to "have gaps in reporting sexual assaults" (Barz, 2011).

In January 2012, Beau Donaldson, quarterback for the UM Grizzlies football team, was arrested and charged with sexual assault (Moore, 2012). Engstrom held an open forum where he stated that the university would aggressively educate students about sexual assaults and would review reports of past incidents. He also stated that Jim Foley, UM's vice president, and David Aronofsky, UM's chief legal counsel, would review university sexual assault policies for needed revisions. That same month, the *Montana Kaimin*, the University of Montana's student-run newspaper, published an article indicating that students who had been sexually assaulted while attending UM had reported to local media that the policies of the university and the Missoula Police Department disenfranchised victims and did not adequately punish assailants.

By the end of January the NCAA had launched an investigation into the football program. In March, Engstrom announced via campus-wide email that Athletic Director Jim O'Day and football head coach Robin Pflugrad's contracts would not be renewed. By May 2012, the US Department of Justice and the US Department of Education had launched an investigation and compliance review of the university's handling of allegations of sexual assault and harassment. And with all of this going on, on May 8, a student reported being raped in her Miller Hall dorm room on campus—and still no Clery Act warning was sent out to students.

The Culture in Missoula

Few cultures exemplify a rape culture as much as Missoula in 2011. This culture was demonstrated in the actions of the school and the surrounding community. Not the school, the police, the county attorney, or the community took sexual assault seriously.

The attitudes and actions of the people of Missoula seem to indicate immersion in the rape culture. Katie Baker, a journalist for Jezebel.com, reported that the people of Missoula she interviewed in the spring of 2012 agreed on three things (Baker, 2012). The first was that the police department was a joke; they were ill equipped to deal with the heavy interstate narcotics flow in the area or the drunk driving and sexual assaults that occurred on a regular basis. The second point people in Missoula agreed on was that rape was a very bad thing. And the third thing was that girls in Missoula are the type who would make things up for the attention. They believed that girls who cry rape were sluts for getting themselves in sketchy situations with guys.

Even the Missoula County Attorney's Office was under fire, although Fred Van Valkenburg, county attorney, adamantly denied any wrongdoing or gender discrimination by himself or his department. In response to the announcement by US Assistant Attorney General Thomas Perez that after a preliminary investigation the federal government would be launching a full probe into wrongdoing, Van Valkenburg called the investigation overreaching and deeply disturbing (Associated Press, 2012). He also accused the feds of trying to bully him into enacting sexual assault reform.

The Culture of the University of Montana

Under scrutiny, the culture of the university does not fare much better. That culture was revealed in emails retrieved through a suit filed jointly by the *Wall Street Journal* and the *Missoulian* under the Freedom of Information Act (Work, 2013). The emails bring to light how administrators thought about and handled the sexual assault claims filed.

In an email, Charles Couture, University of Montana Dean of Students, indicated that four UM football players were among the five men who had allegedly gang raped a student. In response to this message Vice President Foley questioned Couture's use of the term *gang rape*. Couture responded that he used the term because that is what is was. In an equally disturbing email, Foley, in an attempt to punish a student for speaking out about the attack, asked Couture if the student's public discussion of her sexual assault was not a violation of the student conduct code.

A draft of public remarks that President Engstrom planned to deliver also appeared in uncovered emails. It stated that the football coach, Pflugrad, had disciplined some football players accused of raping a woman but had failed to report the incident to his supervisors. This draft was sent out to several people, including Athletic Director O'Day. O'Day responded that he did not think the administration should provide more information than was already public and confirmed. He also advised Engstrom that this information might come out in Diane Barz's report and that if the administration released it before she filed her report it would look like they had wasted a lot of money hiring a consultant. O'Day also counseled against including a part of the report making reference to "when we do [find those guilty of the assault]." He made this suggestion because he believed that making such a statement indicated that the administration knew who the perpetrators were and that the administration was going to prove it.

The DOJ and DOE Investigation of the University of Montana

On May 9, 2013, the Department of Justice and the Department of Education released the findings of their investigation of UM (US Department of Justice, 2013a). The report stated that the university's sexual harassment and assault policies required revision to provide clearer notice of the conduct prohibited by the university. It also found that the university's grievance policy must be improved and that its policy prohibiting retaliation was inadequate.

The report stated that although the university had made attempts at correcting the problems, it had not taken sufficient effective actions to eliminate a sexually hostile environment, prevent its reoccurrence, and address the problems effectively. Finally, the report found that the university needed to coordinate its Title IX enforcement better, provide more training to those tasked with coordination and enforcement of Title IX, devise a system of tracking Title IX complaints, and revise its notice of nondiscrimination (DOJ, 2013a).

Along with this report the DOJ and DOE published a sixteen-page resolution agreement between the University of Montana and the federal government (DOJ, 2013b). In the terms of the agreement, the government laid out exactly what UM had to do to address the concerns expressed in the findings of their investigation report. The agreement stated in great detail, and with delivery dates, exactly what the university was mandated to do.

The University of Montana had to, first, hire an equity consultant. The university and the consultant would then revise the identified policies and procedures. The university must notify all constituents of these changes. The agreement detailed how and when the university must address issues of its Title IX coordinator and how it must notify the community of the changes to this position. The university must train all existing and new employees. UM was required to develop a system for tracking complaints as well as a resource guide that would be disseminated to all students. And the university was required to develop and deliver a campus climate survey to all students every year. The agreement was to remain in force for no fewer than three academic years with reporting ongoing through the first semester of the 2015–2016 academic year.

The NCAA Investigation of the University of Montana Athletic Department

The NCAA's Division I Committee on Infractions' investigation into wrongdoing in the UM football program found that the university and its former head coach failed to monitor the program (National Collegiate Athletic Association, 2013). They found that university boosters offered extra benefits to players, in direct violation of NCAA rules. Players received extra meals, free legal representation, and bail bond payments, among other things. The NCAA also found that the school had violated the coaching limits and had two players compete while they were ineligible to play.

As a result of these findings, the NCAA put Montana on three years of probation. In addition to probation, the team had to forfeit five wins, including one against Montana State and two playoff victories. The college was also banned from off-campus recruiting for the first three weeks of the fall semester in 2013. Representatives from UM were also required to attend the 2014 rules seminar held by the NCAA.

Two other major sanctions were handed down by the NCAA. One was directed at the university and one at the former head coach. The university received a reduction in the number of scholarship equivalents, down from the usual sixty-five to fifty-nine, for the entire three-year probation. The head coach was suspended from coaching for the first game of the 2013 football season.

The DOJ Investigation into the University of Montana's Office of Public Safety

The DOJ's investigation found that the UM Office of Public Safety (OPS) did not adequately respond to reports of sexual assault (DOJ, 2013c). It also found that the OPS's policies and training related to sexual assault response were insufficient and at times nonexistent. In addition, the DOJ found that there were no legitimate law enforcement or other reasons for these inadequacies. The final finding was that OPS officers' statements demonstrated sex-based stereotypes and thus constituted discrimination which is prohibited by the equal protection clause of the Fourteenth Amendment.

Based on the DOJ's findings, the DOJ and UM reached an agreement that UM would undertake the following corrections. To correct its response to reports of sexual assault, the OPS should develop better policies and procedures. These policies and procedures should enhance training on response to sexual assault reports for all officers and should clarify the inconsistent and inadequate response to reports of sexual assaults. Finally, the agreement asserted that the university needed to address the gender-based stereotypes prevalent in the OPS.

The DOJ Investigation of the Missoula Police Department and Missoula County Attorney

The findings of the DOJ investigation into the practices of the Missoula Police Department indicated that some of the MPD investigative practices significantly compromised the quality and effectiveness of the department's response to sexual assaults (DOJ, 2013d). The investigation failed to find any law enforcement reasons or other reasons for these inadequacies. Here, like with the university's Office of Public Safety, the DOJ found evidence of sex-based biases which constituted discrimination.

The DOJ's agreement with the city of Missoula set out very similar recommendations as those put forth by the agreement between the DOJ and the university's OPS. The MPD needed to develop policies and procedures that would allow them to better respond to reports of sexual assault. They also agreed that the city of Missoula must address the role that gender stereotypes play in potentially compromising law enforcement's response to sexual assault claims.

In a separate report, the DOJ addressed its investigation of the Missoula County Attorney's Office (DOJ, 2014a). In a memo of understanding reached between the DOJ, Montana's attorney general, and the Missoula County Attorney's Office (MCAO), the Montana attorney general and MCAO agreed to improve policies and practices related to sexual assault prosecution in Missoula County. To achieve this, the attorney general and MCAO agreed to hire a technical adviser to assist in the training of attorneys in acceptable standards of handling sexual assault cases and to assist with the assessment of the MCAO's performance under this agreement.

With the help of the technical adviser, the MCAO was to develop new written policies and procedures for handling all aspects of sexual assault cases. The MCAO would also ensure the initial and ongoing training of all personnel in the handling of sexual assault cases. And finally, the MCAO agreed to improve communication with law enforcement and community partners.

Missoula: Rape and the Justice System in a College Town

The findings of the government's investigations into the Missoula situation were delivered in June 2014. The city and the university were busy working on the things that needed to be corrected, with an eye to the future and getting things back to normal. Just when it looked like everything was settling down, Jon Krakauer's book *Missoula* hit the shelves in April 2015, and the entire disaster became prime news again.

While those interested in or concerned with sexual assault may already have known about the situation in Missoula, Krakauer's book brought the subject to the world. This needed to happen—not to make Missoula or the University of Montana look bad or to relive the events but rather for the world to recognize that Missoula was not an outlier and that there are many US college towns just like Missoula.

When asked why he wrote the book, Krakauer stated that he had found out that someone close to him had been raped by an acquaintance (Martin, 2015). After learning about this crime, he began tracking rape cases around the country and went to Missoula for the sentencing of Beau Donaldson, the UM quarterback, who pled guilty to raping Allison Huguet, his childhood friend.

Krakauer said that he was riveted watching Huguet's testimony. Once he started digging into the situation he found a pattern of rape cases falling through the justice system cracks at UM and in Missoula. He decided he needed to tell the story from the victim's view. And the victim's view was something that needed to be told. This book brought much-needed attention to the crisis of sexual assaults on college campuses. Unfortunately, this attention came at the expense of those living and working in Missoula and at the University of Montana.

The University of Montana and the City of Missoula Make Changes

Even before the Department of Justice investigations began, the university and the city of Missoula had begun making changes. And in their findings letters, the DOJ commented on the work that had already taken place. Both the city and the university also willingly agreed to make the changes that the DOJ thought necessary.

In a news conference held on May 11, 2015, Vanita Gupta, head of the Department of Justice's Civil Rights Division, stated that the Missoula Police Department was a "success story" (Szpaller, 2015). She stated that the police department had fully implemented its agreement with the DOJ and had put all reforms in place. Gupta also stated that she felt that the University of Montana and its police department had made important strides in addressing and preventing sexual assaults on campus.

The University of Montana police department got good news again just two month later. On July 10, 2015, the DOJ announced that the UM police department had met all of its obligations as set out in the agreement with the DOJ (DOJ, 2015). The DOJ stated in its announcement that the agreement had resulted in historic advances in the university's response to sexual assault.

The final announcement of accomplishment to date came on August 16, 2016. At this time, Tim Fox, Montana attorney general, announced that the Missoula County attorney's office was in full compliance with the agreement reached between his office and the US Department of Justice. Fox said that the MCAO had worked very hard and had accomplished a lot under the leadership of Kristin Pabst, Missoula county attorney. Pabst, along with the technical adviser and other members of the office, had created a Special Victims Unit that uses best practices to better serve victims of sexual assault crimes.

The University of Montana Today

Today UM and Missoula is a much safer place to be. The university's 2016 Annual Campus Security and Fire Safety Report showed a significant decrease in campus sexual violence even during the period when they were under close scrutiny by the DOJ. The university may still be paying a price for its past actions, however.

In the fall of 2011, the University of Montana hit a new enrollment record, with 15,669 students (University of Montana, 2011). It was the second consecutive fall in which UM reached new enrollment levels—but that was before the football team scandals hit the news in December that year. By 2017, enrollments were down to 11,615 (Szpaller, 2017). While there are many possible reasons for such a decrease in enrollment, many believe it may be an outcome of the sexual assault scandals.

In a study conducted on the top one hundred US schools, scandals with a high level of media coverage resulted in a reduction in enrollment (Luca, Rooney, and Smith, 2016). Results indicated that a major scandal would, on average, cause a 10 percent drop in applications. This effect on enrollment is equivalent to the impact of dropping ten places on the *US News and World Report* college rankings.

Even with the drop, the leadership of the University of Montana were pleased with the enrollment numbers for the spring of 2017. Both President Sheila Stearns and Vice President for Enrollment Tom Crady are optimistic about the future (Szpaller, 2017). VP Crady is shooting for a 3 percent increase in entering freshmen for the fall of 2017. While overall enrollment may still be down, the administration is encouraged and hopeful that the university is back on the right track.

The University of Texas: Proactive Planning Leadership

Cantor, Fisher, Chibnall, Townsend, Lee, Bruce, and Thomas (2015) reported the results of a campus climate survey on sexual assault and sexual misconduct sponsored by the Association of American Universities (AAU). Twenty-seven institutions of higher education were surveyed, including seven Ivy League schools (for example, Harvard and Yale) and such leading public institutions as the University of Texas at Austin, the University of North Carolina at Chapel Hill, the University of Michigan, and the University of Oregon. (The University of California campuses did not appear in the report.) The prevalence of sexual assault varied markedly at these institutions, from Cal Tech and Texas A&M University at 13 percent and 15 percent respectively to a high of 30 percent reported by Michigan and the University of Southern California. What was not reported was the wide variance in the cultures of these universities, the context within which they are situated, and their system of operation. Looking across institutions is one thing, and looking within one's own institution is another. It is both challenging and worthwhile to do so, as some institutional leaders have demonstrated.

At about the same time this national survey was released in 2015, the University of Texas System's chancellor and board of regents made a significant commitment to provide transformative leadership within one of the nation's largest public university systems and to study the problem of campus sexual assault with scientific rigor and depth. Two years after making this commitment, the chancellor introduced the first two reports from the *Cultivating Learning and Safe Environments* (CLASE) project (Busch-Armendariz et al., 2017a, p. 9; 2017b, p. 11).

> If we want to change our campus culture, then we have to be open and honest about our students' experiences, no matter how uncomfortable it

is. Our UT System institutions have numerous effective programs to serve victims of sexual assault and misconduct, yet we can and must do better because even one incident is too many. These findings provide specific data to more deeply understand our students' experiences, and address the problem.

William H. McRaven

Chancellor, The University of Texas System

The 2015 reports provide significant benchmarking, details, sources, and data from the thirteen UT System institutions that provided the data for these reports. They are our two primary sources in preparing this institutional case. The academic institutions report is based on data from eight component institutions: UT Arlington, UT Austin, UT Dallas, UT El Paso, UT Permian Basic, UT Rio Grande Valley, UT San Antonio, and UT Tyler (Busch-Armendariz et al., 2017a). The health institutions report is based on data from five component institutions: UT Health Houston, MD Anderson Cancer Center, UTMB Health, UT Health San Antonio, and UT Southwestern.

The CLASE Project

Preventing sexual assault begins with committed leadership, which within the UT System has been demonstrated by the chancellor and the board of regents. That leadership commitment aligns well with leadership-driven policy starting at the national level, with federal legislation and the White House Task Force to Protect Students from Sexual Assault. That task force's report *Not Alone* called for benchmarking surveys to assess efforts that build on knowledge and improve prevention and interventions (Busch-Armendariz et al., 2017a).

The University of Texas System takes a leadership role in this national agenda with its commitment of resources and the institution's focus on sexual abuse. Its scope is restricted to the forms of violence that are prohibited under Title IX. Four forms of violence specified in the Education Amendment of 1972 are sexual harassment, stalking, dating and domestic violence, and sexual assault.

CLASE project conceptual design. UT's *Cultivating Learning and Safe Environments* project has a robust conceptual design to study these four specified forms of sexual violence, initially through a web-based survey that is the foundation for the first two reports we discuss here. The CLASE project's web-based survey asked three guiding research questions:

1. What is the prevalence and rate of sexual harassment, stalking, dating/domestic abuse and violence, and unwanted sexual contact of students since their enrollment at a UT System institution?
2. What are the students' perceptions of institutional responses to these issues?
3. How do UT System institutions use findings to enhance existing programs and services and identify next steps?

The second component of the CLASE project's design is an in-depth empirical investigation phased in with all institutions across four years. This component will enable the collection of archival and institutional data that is not perception based.

The third component of the design is a four-year cohort study at UT Austin, the flagship campus in the UT System. This third component offers very long term research potential akin to that in Harvard's Grant Study that began in 1940 with the class of 1942 as sophomores and extended into the twenty-first century (Vaillant, 2012), when the study's subjects were in their nineties.

CLASE project scientific rigor. Conceptual designs must be implemented with scientific rigor. For example, how are we to understand the variance across institutions in the AAU report by Cantor and colleagues (2015)? How are we to understand the differences in prevalence rates reported by diverse scholars within the domain of sexual assault research (see, for example, Snyder, Fisher, Scherer, and Daigle, 2012)? How do we make sense of the conflicting claims and allegations from the accused, from the accuser, or from different investigators? These are questions the underlying science must address. Scientific rigor is essential to any debates about significant and controversial topics such as sexual assault. We find the CLASE project especially strong in its scientific rigor, which puts strong legs under the conceptual design. The project anchors its reports in solid evidence.

Nothing can be known based on something being "obvious," because dogmatism is inadequate grounds for knowledge. Evidence must be public and challengeable. What is obvious to one may not be obvious to another. Therefore, there are important roles in any domain of knowledge for the skeptic, who raises doubts and questions, as well as for the critic, who conducts analyses and makes judgments (Quick et al., 2010). There is a legitimate place for debate over the interpretation of the evidence, but above all research must provide sound scientific evidence, because that is the one valid pathway for advancing knowledge and, we would argue, advancing professional practice. Further, public health and epidemiology are strengthened when the evidence is anchored in the physical world rather than in a world of social construction. The CLASE project is anchored within the natural science paradigm rather than within the humanities.

Busch-Armendariz and her colleagues (2017a, 2017b) argue for the validity of their CLASE project statistics based on three grounds, with which we concur. First, the CLASE project uses behaviorally specific definitions focused on unwanted, nonconsensual behaviors. We have previously reported the variance in definitions of victimization and concur that behaviorally specific definitions result in more accurate reports of victimization. Asking a person if they were sexually harassed, stalked, abused, or sexually assaulted is not behaviorally anchored, thus offering the respondent a basis for projection and interpretation. This is an issue where it is important to stick closely with the evidence, the data, and what is verifiable.

Second, the CLASE project limits its scope to the issues protected under Title IX. Thus, the measures are circumscribed by the law and further circumscribed by events that students have experienced since enrollment at a UT System institution. Finally, however, CLASE prevalence data are not limited to formal reports to institutional services, such as police or health centers. We have stated earlier that sexual assaults are among the most underreported crimes in the United States. Busch-Armendariz and her colleagues (2017a, 2017b) indicate that only

9 percent of adult sexual assault victims reported their victimization to law enforcement in Texas. Therefore, the voluntary and anonymous web-based survey offers confidentiality for accurate self-report data about which investigators can have confidence.

Power Dynamics in Relationships

The health institutions report recognizes that sexual harassment in particular is characterized by power dynamics in relationships (Busch-Armendariz et al., 2017b; see also Quick and McFadyen, 2017, for a discussion of hierarchical power dynamics in sexual harassment). The CLASE health institutions review of previous research notes that the majority of perpetrators of sexual harassment or abuse in health care education are in hierarchical relationships with students. While the hierarchical structure provides authority-based power for a potential perpetrator of abuse, it is not the only basis of social power that poses a risk for individuals in academic and health institutions. Expert and referent power, anchored in professional expertise in the one case and charisma in the other, are equal in force to legitimate power anchored in hierarchical authority (French and Raven, 1959). Both are individual power attributes, based neither on organizational position nor on affiliation. Given the nature of the peer system in academic and health institutions, expert and referent power are consequential. The University of Texas System, for example, recognizes the expert power of its most prized faculty in three distinct top tiers, the first and most prestigious tier being the Nobel Laureates, the second most powerful tier being members of the National Academies, and the third most prestigious tier being the fellows of national scientific associations, societies, and organizations. This hierarchy of expertise and professional stature stands apart from the authority-based administrative structure of a university. Members of these prestigious faculty tiers have a responsibility not to abuse the power that comes with the status.

Key Findings within the Academic Institutions

Busch-Armendariz and her colleagues (2017a) report eight key findings from the web-based survey of students' experiences since their enrollment at a UT System academic institution:

Sexual harassment
- 14 percent of all students reported experiencing faculty-/staff-perpetrated sexist gender harassment
- 25 percent of all students reported experiencing student-perpetrated sexual harassment
Stalking
- 13 percent of students reported stalking victimization *Dating/domestic abuse and violence*
- 12 percent of students who had been in a dating or marital relationship while at a UT academic institution reported experiencing cyber abuse
- 10 percent of students who had been in a dating or marital relationship while at a UT academic institution reported experiencing physical violence
Unwanted sexual contact
- 12 percent of students reported experiencing unwanted sexual touching
- 6 percent of students reported experiencing rape since enrolling at a UT academic institution
Vulnerable groups
- 43 percent of undergraduate and 41 percent of graduate students who identified as LGBTQ report student-perpetrated sexual harassment

In addition, the CLASE project found over 50 percent of victims and over 75 percent of perpetrators of unwanted sexual contact used alcohol or drugs at the time of victimization. Most instances of dating/domestic abuse and violence and unwanted sexual contact occurred off campus. Over 50 percent of unwanted sexual contact victims had a close relationship with the perpetrator. Only 28 percent of victims of sexual harassment, stalking, dating/domestic violence, or unwanted sexual contact disclosed the incident or incidents to someone prior to taking the survey.

In terms of students' perceptions of institutional response, the CLASE project results for academic institutions appear quite favorable. Specifically,

- 76 percent of victims and 80 percent of non-victims feel safe on their campus
- 75 percent of victims and 84 percent of non-victims believe their academic institution would take a report of sexual harassment, stalking, dating/domestic abuse or violence, or unwanted sexual contact seriously
- 68 percent of victims and 82 percent of non-victims reported feeling safe from sexual harassment

Key Findings within the Health Institutions

Busch-Armendariz and her colleagues (2017b) report six key findings from the web-based survey of students' experiences since their enrollment at a UT System health institution:

Sexual harassment
- 18 percent of students experienced sexist gender harassment by faculty/staff
- 20 percent of students reported having experienced student-perpetrated sexual harassment
Stalking
- 8 percent of student reported stalking victimization
Dating/domestic abuse and violence
- 5 percent of students who had been in a dating or marital relationship while at a UT health institution reported having experienced physical violence

Unwanted sexual contact
- 3 percent of students reported experiencing rape since enrolling at a UT health institution

Vulnerable groups
- 22 percent of students who identified as LGBTQ+ report student-perpetrated sexual harassment

In addition, the CLASE project found over 62 percent of victims and 83 percent of perpetrators of unwanted sexual contact used alcohol or drugs at the time of victimization. The vast majority of dating / domestic abuse and violence and unwanted sexual contact occurred off campus: 97 percent of both physical violence and unwanted sexual contact incidents occurred off campus. Seventy-two percent of perpetrators of unwanted sexual contact were not other students. Only 23 percent of victims of sexual harassment, stalking, dating / domestic violence, or unwanted sexual contact disclosed the incident or incidents to someone prior to taking the survey.

In terms of students' perceptions of institutional response, the CLASE project results appear quite favorable for health institutions. Specifically, 89 percent of victims and 92 percent of non-victims reported feeling safe on their campus. In addition, 81 percent of victims and 92 percent of non-victims believe their academic institution would take a report of sexual harassment, stalking, dating / domestic abuse or violence, or unwanted sexual contact seriously.

Looking at the academic and health key finding comparatively, a pattern emerges of lower rates of sexual abuse in the health institutions versus the academic institutions. In addition, there are more students reporting feeling safe on the health institution campuses. These within-system differences make sense to us based on the age difference in the student populations, with the average age difference in the range of five years. The developmental differences that accompany the chronological differences place the younger students at risk. The CLASE website provides a detailed review of the CLASE data from the web-based survey (www.utsystem.edu/CLASE).

From Data to Action and Advancement

The UT System's use self-examination and benchmarking as a basis for refining the culture of its component institutions sets a compelling and positive example for other institutions of higher education. The intention of the CLASE project is to use the evidence and data as the basis for action. The three arenas for planned action are in leadership, intersectionality, and, finally, programs, services, and policies.

While the leadership of the UT System has taken a clear position to address the problem of sexual assault within its component institutions, there is the continuing need to engage institutional leaders in annual strategic goals to advance the agenda. Goal-driven agendas are among the most effective in elevating performance and achieving results—hence the value in component institutional leader engagement—but the process should not stop there. As noted earlier in this case, institutions of higher education in the United States are characterized by shared faculty governance, and expert power resides within, especially, the prized faculty groups of the UT System. Therefore, faculty leadership, responsibility, engagement, and accountability for the goal of taking incidents of sexual assault to zero is essential. Finally, the response of parents, alumni, and other nonresidential stakeholders to the leadership initiatives within the system are crucial. Leadership without followership and collaboration is ineffective.

The second action area is intersectionality. Earlier in the book and then again within this case we have seen that alcohol and substance abuse interplay with sexual assault. The problems of high-risk drinking, binge drinking, and underage drinking, alcohol use, and substance use are all of concern within the arena of sexual abuse. The intoxicating effect of power is another associated issue of concern. Power differences are inevitable within both administrative hierarchies and professional human systems. Programs aimed at educating those who acquire positions of power and privilege are essential. We discussed in chapter 9 the importance of restraint when learning to manage emerging power that comes with growth and maturation. Building structures and relationships that complement the development of self-regulatory controls and help individuals grow responsibly in their use of power is essential to avoiding the abuse of power. Open systems of accountability can facilitate this process while building innovative reporting pathways for not only sexual abuse but also the abuse of power and authority. Teaching those in positions of power and privilege to look down, not up (see Lynch, 2013), can enable them to use their positions to triage those in need to get the help and services they require to function at their best.

Finally, the UT System aims to reexamine and rethink the delivery of programs, services, and policies. Evidence and data serve as an effective platform for taking preventive or remedial action while solving problems. In epidemiology, the evidence when followed closely leads the investigator to the cause of the problem. From there, solutions, remediation, and prevention can be formulated. For sexual assault, it is not simple cause and effect. Educating everyone within the institution about the legal and statutory rules of engagement is an essential first step and can be done through mandatory compliance training on an annual basis.

One of the most effectual actions of an institution is formulating fair and just sanctions for behaviors that violate Title IX legislation as well as institutional codes of conduct, then applying those sanctions consistently across individuals and groups as well as over time. The high degree of visibility and predictability of the behavior-sanction connections send clear and compelling messages throughout the institution. This process of adjudication, however, is not inconsistent with our earlier discussion of the need for forgiveness. Institutions have a need for organizational justice that sets high standards for acceptable behavior without being harsh or mean spirited while at the same time displaying appropriate opportunities for rehabilitation and redemption when those are warranted.

Marist College: Buy-in at the Top

As discussed in chapter 4, for any institution of higher education to craft a safe campus, there must be complete support for the sexual assault prevention plan at the very top of the organization. This is the case with Marist College president Dennis Murray. President Murray shared his thoughts on the subject in an interview with the authors.

In terms of preventing sexual violence in their organizations, leaders have the power to set the tone from the top down, and they should use their influence to encourage ethical behavior. Good leadership resides within an appropriate ethical framework and is informed by values. An ethical leader

> helps his or her organization define its values,
> affirms those values in both words and deeds, and
> protects those values through the organization's policies and
>   procedures.

An organization's values may be based on a number of sources, including the law and the organization's history and core values, professional standards, and personal values. Articulating these principles in a written statement of values is a potent way for leaders to communicate and reinforce them.

When it comes to encouraging ethical behavior by others in the organization, the most important thing a leader can do is affirm the organization's values in word and deed. Ethical leadership is about setting an example for ethical behavior and fostering an ethical culture at all levels. Ethical leaders hold themselves to a high standard of conduct and consider the potential ethical implications of their decisions. They communicate and model their values through their words, what they celebrate, how they interact with others, and the decisions they make. They also reward and promote those in the organization who uphold the highest ethical standards.

Leaders protect the organization's values by putting in place systems to reduce the risk of unethical conduct. Examples include hiring those who will embrace the organization's values, orienting new members to the organization's code of conduct, engaging in ongoing training, and providing an effective compliance framework. Compliance includes establishing a system of checks and balances to ensure appropriate oversight, implementing a strong outside audit function, providing a clear and confidential process for reporting ethical breaches, and punishing unethical behavior firmly, consistently, and publicly.

President Dennis Murray has tried to fulfill these goals by sending the clear message that sexual violence of any form has no place at Marist College or indeed at any other responsible organization in the United States. Marist's values statement references the institution's "belief in the dignity and value of every human being." As president, Murray has ensured that a comprehensive set of policies has been implemented at the college to promote a safe campus. For example, all employees and students are required to complete a course on sexual harassment and violence prevention, and employees agree to the college's policies on the issue when they sign their employment contracts. The annual retreat of the president's cabinet begins with a reminder of each individual's responsibility to report misconduct if they become aware of it. Finally, because President Murray played football as a student, and because athletes are often involved in incidents of sexual violence, he personally speaks to members of the football team each fall regarding the appropriate behavior that is expected of them.

Marist has sent a clear message with respect to sexual violence, and this message has been reflected in student activism on the issue. Male student athletes have been involved in the White Ribbon Campaign, a global movement of men and boys working to end male violence against women and girls. A Marist student started an organization called the Purple Thread to raise awareness of dating violence.

In conclusion, we emphasize that while protecting members of the community against sexual harassment and violence is everyone's job, it is the leaders of organizations who must show people the way.

REFERENCES

Abbey, A., & Harnish, R. J. (1995). Perception of sexual intent: The role of gender, alcohol consumption, and rape supportive attitudes. *Sex Roles, 32*(5/6), 297–313.

Abbey, A., McAuslan, P., & Ross, L. (1998). Sexual assault perpetration by college men: The role of alcohol, misperception of sexual intent, and sexual beliefs and experiences. *Journal of Social and Clinical Psychology, 17*(2), 167–195.

Abbey, A., Ross, L. T., McDuffie, D., & McAuslan, P. (1996). Alcohol and dating risk factors for sexual assault among college women. *Psychology of Women Quarterly, 20*(1), 147–169.

Adkins, J. A. (1999). Promoting organizational health: The evolving practice of occupational health psychology. *Professional Psychology: Research and Practice, 30*(2), 129–137.

Adkins, J. A., Quick, J., & Moe, K. (2000). Building world-class performance in changing times. In L. Murphy & C. Cooper (Eds.), *Healthy and productive work: An international perspective* (pp. 107–131). London: Taylor & Francis.

Ali, R. (2011). Dear Colleague Letter. https://www2.ed.gov/about/offices/list/ocr/letters/colleague-201104.html

Ambrose, C. E., & Gross, A. M. (2016). Interpreting sexual dating encounters: Social information processing differences in men and women. *Journal of Family Violence, 31*(3), 361–370. https://doi.org/100020.1007/s10896-015-9757-z

Ambrose, S. A., Bridges, M. W., DiPietro, M., Lovett, M. C., & Norman, M. K. (2010). *How learning works: 7 research-based principles for smart teaching.* San Francisco, CA: Jossey-Bass.

American Association of University Professors (2012). AAUP Statement. Campus sexual assault: Suggested policies and procedures. https://www.aaup.org/report/campus-sexual-assault-suggested-policies-and-procedures

American Psychiatric Association (2013). *Diagnostic and statistical manual of mental disorders (DSM-IV-TR)* (5th ed.). Washington, DC: American Psychiatric Publishing.

Arain, M., Haque, M., Johal, L., Mathur, P., Nel, W., Rais, A., Sandhu, R., & Sharma, S. (2013). Maturation of the adolescent brain. *Neuropsychiatric Disease and Treatment, 9*, 449–461. https://doi.org/10.2147/NDT.S39776

Armour, M. P., & Umbreit, M. S. (2006). Victim forgiveness in restorative justice dialogue. *Victims and Offenders, 1* (July), 123–140.

Associated Press (2012). Feds examine response to Montana sexual assault. *Fox News*. http://www.foxnews.com/us/2012/05/01/feds-to-investigate-response-to-um-sexual-assaults.html

Association of School Conduct Administration (2014). Student conduct administration & Title IX: Gold standard practices for resolution of allegations of sexual misconduct on college campuses. http://theasca.org

Association of Title IX Administrators (2013). Investigation protocol checklist. https://www.atixa.org/wordpress/

Association of Title IX Administrators (2016). Position Statement. https://atixa.org/wordpress/wp-content/uploads/2015/03/2016NovemberATIXA-POSITION-STATEMENT-IN-FAVOR-OF-THE-SAFE-TRANSFER-ACT.pdf

Bachar, K., & Koss, M. P. (2001). From prevalence to prevention: Closing the gap between what we know about rape and what we do. In C. M. Renzetti, J. L. Edelson, & R. K. Bergen (Eds.), *Sourcebook on violence against women* (pp. 117–142). Thousand Oaks, CA: Sage.

Baker, K. (2012, May 10). My Weekend in America's So Called "Rape Capital." *Jezebel.com*, http://jezebel.com/5908472/my-weekend-in-americas-so-called-rape-capital

Balemba, S., & Beauregard, E. (2012). Reactions to Resistance: The Role of Contextual Factors in Sex Offending. *Violence and Victims*, 27(2), 148–165. https://doi.org/10.1891/0886-6708.27.2.148

Ball, V. (2013, February 12). Why would anyone oppose the Violence Against Women Act? *The Atlantic*. https://www.theatlantic.com/politics/archive/2013/02/why-would-anyone-oppose-the-violence-against-women-act/273103/

Banyard, V. (2011). Who will help prevent sexual violence: Creating an ecological model of bystander intervention. *Psychology of Violence*, 1(3), 216–229.

Banyard, V. L. (2015). *Toward the next generation of bystander prevention of sexual and relationship violence: Action coils to engage communities*. New York: Springer.

Banyard, V. L., Eckstein, R. P., & Moynihan, M. M. (2010). Involving community in sexual violence prevention: The role of stages of change. *Journal of Interpersonal Violence*, 25(1), 111–135. https://doi.org/10.1177/0886260508329123

Banyard, V. L., Moynihan, M. M., & Plante, E. G. (2007). Sexual violence prevention through bystander education: An experimental evaluation. *Journal of Community Psychology*, 35(4), 463–481.

Bart, P., & O'Brien, P. (1984). Stopping Rape: Effective avoidance strategies. *Signs*, 10(1), 83–101. http://www.jstor.org.online.library.marist.edu/stable/3174238

Barz, D. (2011). Status investigation report December 31, 2011. http://www.umt.edu/president/docs/Investigation%20Report%20December%2031%202011.pdf

Battle, S., & Wheeler, T. E. (2017). Dear Colleague letter. https://www2.ed.gov/about/offices/list/ocr/letters/colleague-201702-title-ix.docx

Bazelon, L. (2017, September 8). How to see justice done on campus sexual assault. *Politico Magazine*. https://www.politico.com/magazine/story/2017/09/08/devos-campus-sexual-assault-how-to-get-it-right-215585

Bennett, S., & Banyard, V. L. (2016). Do friends really help friends? The effect of relational factors and perceived severity on bystander perception of sexual violence. *Psychology of Violence*, 6(1), 64–72. https://doi.org/10.1037/a0037708

Bennett, S., Banyard, V. L., & Garnhart, L. (2013). To act or not to act, that is the question? Barriers and facilitators of bystander intervention. *Journal of Interpersonal Violence, 29*(3): 476–96. https://doi.org/10.1177/0886260513505210

Biden, J. (2014, September 10). 20 Years of change: Joe Biden on the Violence Against Women Act. *Time.* http://time.com/3319325/joe-biden-violence-against -women/

Black, M. C., Basile, K. C., Breiding, M. J., Smith, S. G., Walters, M. L., Merrick, M. T., Chen, J., & Stevens, M. R. (2011). The National Intimate Partner and Sexual Violence Survey (NISVS): 2010 summary report. National Center for Injury Prevention and Control, Centers for Disease Control and Prevention. http://www.cdc.gov/ViolencePrevention/pdf/NISVS_Report2010-a.pdf

Bogle, K. A. (2007). The shift from dating to hooking up in college: What scholars have missed. *Sociology Compass, 1/2,* 775–788.

Bogle, K. A. (2008). *Hooking up: Sex, dating, and relationships on campus.* New York: New York University Press.

Bohmer, C., & Parrot, A. (1993). *Sexual assault on campus: The problem and the solution.* New York: Lexington Books.

Borges, A. M., Banyard, V. L., & Moynihan, M. M. (2008). Clarifying consent: Primary prevention of sexual assault on a college campus. *Journal of Prevention & Intervention in the Community, 36*(1–2), 75–88. https://doi.org/10.1080 /10852350802022324

Borowski, S. (2012, Summer). Keeping college students safe: Sexual harassment and assault on campus. *INSIGHT into Diversity, 79*(4/5), 4.

Bosman, S. (2017, February 16). *Campus security authority reporting.* Arlington: University of Texas at Arlington.

Bowes-Sperry, L., & O'Leary-Kelly, A. M. (2005). To act or not to act: The dilemma faced by sexual harassment observers. *Academy of Management Review, 30*(2), 288–306.

Braceras, J. C. (2016, October 21). College sex meets the Star Chamber. *Wall Street Journal,* A13.

Bradshaw, C., Kahn, A. S., & Saville, B. K. (2010). To hook up or date: Which gender benefits? *Sex Roles, 62*(9/10), 661–669. doi:10.1007/s11199—010—9765—7

Brignone, E., Gundlapalli, A. V., Blais, R. K., Carter, M. E., Suo, Y., Samore, M. H., Kimerling, R., & Fargo, J. D. (2016). Differential risk for homelessness among U.S. male and female veterans with a positive screen for military sexual trauma. *JAMA Psychiatry, 73*(6), 582–589. doi:10.1001/jamapsychiatry.2016.0101. Retrieved June 26, 2018.

Brownmiller, S. (1975). *Against our will: Men, women, and rape.* New York: Ballantine.

Buddie, A. M., & Testa, M. (2005). Rates and predictors of sexual aggression among students and nonstudents. *Journal of Interpersonal Violence, 20*(6), 713–724.

Burd, S. (1999, May 28). Incidents that are not reported to police remain a thorny issue in crime reports. *Chronicle of Higher Education.* http://www.chronicle.com /article/Incidents-That-Are-Not/10659

Busch-Armendariz, N. B., Wood, L., Kammer-Kerwick, M., Kellison, B., Sulley, C., Westbrook, L., Olaya-Rodriguez, D., Hill, K., Wachter, K., Wang, A., McClain, T., &

Hoefer, S. (2017a). *Cultivating learning and safe environments: An empirical study of prevalence and perceptions of sexual harassment, stalking, dating/domestic abuse and violence, and unwanted sexual contact.* University of Texas System Academic Institutions. Institute on Domestic Violence & Sexual Assault, University of Texas at Austin.

Busch-Armendariz, N. B., Wood, L., Kammer-Kerwick, M., Kellison, B., Sulley, C., Westbrook, L., Olaya-Rodriguez, D., Hill, K., Wachter, K., Wang, A., McClain, T., & Hoefer, S. (2017b). *Cultivating learning and safe environments: An empirical study of prevalence and perceptions of sexual harassment, stalking, dating/domestic abuse and violence, and unwanted sexual contact.* University of Texas System Health Institutions. Institute on Domestic Violence & Sexual Assault, University of Texas at Austin.

Cameron, K. S. (2007). Forgiveness in organizations. In D. L. Nelson & C. L. Cooper (Eds.), *Positive organizational behavior* (pp. 129–142). Thousand Oaks, CA: Sage.

Campbell, B., Menaker, T., & King, W. (2015). The determination of victim credibility by adult and juvenile sexual assault investigators. *Journal of Criminal Justice, 43,* 29–39.

Campbell, R., & Johnson, C. (1997). Police officers' perceptions of rape: Is there consistency between state law and individual beliefs? *Journal of Interpersonal Violence, 12*(2), 255–274.

Cantor, D., Fisher, B., Chibnall, S., Townsend, R., Lee, H., Bruce, C., & Thomas, G. (2015). *Report on the AAU Campus Climate Survey on Sexual Assault and Sexual Misconduct.* Rockville, MD: Westat. http://www.upenn.edu/ir/surveys/AAU /Report%20and%20Tables%20on%20AAU%20Campus%20Climate%20Survey.pdf

Carey, K., Durney, S., Shepardson, R., & Carey, M. (2015). Precollege predictors of incapacitated rape among female students in their first year of college. *Journal of Studies on Alcohol and Drugs, 76*(6), 829–837.

Carlson, G. (2017). *Be fierce: Stop harassment and take your power back.* New York: Center Street.

Carter, A. C., Brandon, K. O., & Goldman, M. S. (2010). The college and noncollege experience: A review of the factors that influence drinking behavior in young adulthood. *Journal of Studies on Alcohol and Drugs, 71*(5), 742–750.

Cascio, W. F., & Boudreau, J. (2011). *Investing in people: Financial impact of human resources initiatives* (2nd ed.). Upper Saddle Ridge, NJ: Pearson Education/FT Press.

Cass, A. I. (2007). Routine activities and sexual assault: An analysis of individual- and school-level factors. *Violence and Victims, 22*(3), 350–366.

Castro, C. A., Kintzle, S., Schuyler, A. C., Lucas, C., & Warner, C. (2015). Sexual assault in the military. *Current Psychology Reports 17,* 54. https://doi.org/10.1007 /s11920-015-0596-7. Retrieved June 26, 2018.

Catalyst (n.d.). http://www.catalyst.org/knowledge/women-workforce-united -states

Centers for Disease Control and Prevention (2010). NISVS Survey. https://www.cdc .gov/violenceprevention/pdf/cdc_nisvs_victimization_final-a.pdf. Retrieved February 28, 2020.

Chaplin, C., & Shaw, J. (2016). Confidently wrong: Police endorsement of psycho-legal misconceptions. *Journal of Police and Criminal Psychology, 31*(3), 208–216.

Chasteen, A. L. (2001). Constructing rape: Feminism, change, and women's everyday understandings of sexual assault. *Sociological Spectrum, 21*(2): 101–139.

Chatterjee, R. (2018, February 21). A new survey finds 81 percent of women have experienced sexual harassment. NPR. https://www.npr.org/sections/thetwo-way/2018/02/21/587671849/a-new-survey-finds-eighty-percent-of-women-have-experienced-sexual-harassment. Retrieved June 21, 2018.

Child Welfare Information Gateway (n.d.). US Department of Health and Human Services. https://www.childwelfare.gov/topics/systemwide/laws-policies/state/. Retrieved September 28, 2018.

Clark-Flory, T. (2010, October 15). Yale fraternity pledges chant about rape. *Salon.* http://www.salon.com/2010/10/15/yale_fraternity_pledges_chant_about_rape/

Clarke, A. K., & Stermac, L. (2010). The influence of stereotypical beliefs, participant gender, and survivor weight on sexual assault response. *Journal of Interpersonal Violence, 26*(11), 2285–2302. https://doi.org/10.1177/0886260510383039

Coker, A. L., Bush, H. M., Fisher, B. S., Swan, S. C., Williams, C. M., Clear, E. R., & DeGue, S. (2016). Multi-college bystander intervention evaluation for violence prevention. *American Journal of Preventive Medicine, 50*(3), 295–302. https://doi.org/10.1016/j.amepre.2015.08.034

Coker, A. L., Cook-Craig, P. G., Williams, C. M., Fisher, B. S., Clear, E. R., Garcia, L. S., & Hegge, L. M. (2011). Evaluation of Green Dot: An active bystander intervention to reduce sexual violence on college campuses. *Violence Against Women, 17*(6), 777–796.

Coker, D. (2004). Race, poverty, and the crime-centered response to domestic violence; A comment on Linda Mills insult to injury: Rethinking our response to intimate abuse. *Violence Against Women, 10*(11), 1331–1353.

Cole, E. K., Hustoles, T. P., & McClain, J. R. (2006). How to conduct a sexual harassment investigation. National Association of College and University Attorneys Publication Series. http://www.cybermanual.com/how-to-conduct-a-sexual-harassment-investigation-2006-update.html

Cole, J. (2011). Victim confidentiality on Sexual Assault Response Teams (SARTs). *Journal of Interpersonal Violence, 26*(2), 360–376.

Cole, J., & Logan, T. K. (2008). Negotiating the challenges of multidisciplinary responses to sexual assault victims: Sexual assault nurse examiner and victim advocacy programs. *Research in Nursing & Health, 31*, 76–85.

Cole, J., & Logan, T. K. (2010). Interprofessional collaboration on Sexual Assault Response Teams (SARTs): The role of victim alcohol use and a partner-perpetrator. *Journal of Interpersonal Violence, 25*(2), 336–357.

Consent Tea (n.d.). https://www.youtube.com/watch?v=fGoWLWS4-kU

Cooper, C. L., & Quick, J. C. (2017). *The handbook of stress and health.* Chichester, England: Wiley Blackwell.

Copp, T. (2019, January 31) Academy sex assaults up 47% since 2016, DoD estimates. *Military Times*. https://www.militarytimes.com/news/your-military/2019/01/31/dod-estimate-academy-sex-assaults-up-47-since-2016/

Coray, E. (2016). Victim protection or revictimization: Should college disciplinary boards handle sexual assault claims. *Boston College Journal of Law & Social Justice, 36*, 59.

Corcoran, K. J., & Thomas, L. R. (1991). The influence of observed alcohol consumption on perceptions of initiations of sexual activity in a college dating situation. *Journal of Applied Social Psychology, 21*, 500–507.

Core Institute, Southern Illinois University (2014, August 25). Core alcohol and drug survey long form—Form 194. Carbondale. https://core.siu.edu/_common/documents/longform.pdf

Crandall, C. S., & Helitzer, D. (2003). Impact evaluation of a Sexual Assault Nurse Examiner (SANE) program (NCJ 203276). US Department of Justice. http://www.ncjrs.gov/App/Publications/abstract.aspx?ID=203276

Creeley, W. (2012). Why the Office for Civil Rights' April "Dear Colleague letter" was 2011's biggest FIRE fight. Foundation for Individual Rights in Education. https://www.thefire.org/why-the-office-for-civil-rights-april-dear-colleague-letter-was-2011s-biggest-fire-fight/

Crooke, C. (2013). Women in law enforcement. *Dispatch, 6*(7). https://cops.usdoj.gov/html/dispatch/07-2013/women_in_law_enforcement.asp

Crosset, T. W., Ptacek, J., McDonald, M. A., & Benedict, J. R. (1996). Male student-athletes and violence against women: A survey of campus judicial affairs offices. *Violence Against Women, 2*(2), 163–179.

Curcio, A. (2016, April 6). What schools don't tell you about campus sexual assault. https://theconversation.com/what-schools-dont-tell-you-about-campus-sexual-assault-57163

de Becker, G. (1997). *The gift of fear*. New York: Della.

de Keseredy, W. S., & Kelly, K. (1995). Sexual abuse in Canadian university and college dating relationships: The contribution of male peer support. *Journal of Family Violence, 10*(1), 41–53.

Deeds, J. M. (2009). *Attracting college men to sexual violence prevention: A multiple case study of male peer educators* (Doctoral dissertation). In *Educational Administration: Theses, Dissertations, and Student Research, 15*. https://digitalcommons.unl.edu/cgi/viewcontent.cgi?referer=&httpsredir=1&article=1015&context=cehsedaddiss

deHahn, P. (2017, May 11). Study: 89% of colleges reported zero campus rapes in 2015. *USA Today*. https://www.usatoday.com/story/college/2017/05/11/study-89-of-colleges-reported-zero-campus-rapes-in-2015/37431949/

DeMatteo, D., Galloway, M., Arnold, S., & Patel, U. (2015). Sexual assault on college campuses: A 50-state survey of criminal sexual assault statutes and their relevance to campus sexual assault. *Psychology, Public Policy, and Law, 21*(3), 227–238. http://dx.doi.org/10.1037/law0000055

Dey, E. L., Korn, J. S., & Sax, L. J. (1996). Betrayed by the academy: The sexual harassment of women college faculty. *Journal of Higher Education, 67*(2), 149. https://doi.org/10.2307/2943978

Dovidio, J. F., & Gaetner, S. L. (1986). *Prejudice, discrimination, and racism.* Orlando, FL: Academic Press.

Duhart, D. T. (2001). National Crime Victimization Survey: Violence in the workplace, 1993–99 (NCJ 190076). Office of Justice Programs, Bureau of Justice Statistics, US Department of Justice. https://www.bjs.gov/content/pub/pdf/vw99.pdf.

Eberhardt, D. N., Rice, D., & Smith, L. (2003). Effects of Greek membership on academic integrity, alcohol abuse, and risky sexual behavior at a small college, *NASPA Journal, 41*(1), 137–148. https://www.tandfonline.com/doi/abs/10.2202/1949-6605.1306

Erdely, S. (2014). A rape on campus: A brutal assault and struggle for justice at UVA. *Rolling Stone.* https://genius.com/Sabrina-rubin-erdely-a-rape-on-campus-a-brutal-assault-and-struggle-for-justice-at-uva-annotated. Archived from the original on November 19, 2014.

Erdreich, B., Slavet, B., & Amador, A. (1994). Sexual harassment in the federal workplace: Trends, progress, continuing challenges. https://www.mspb.gov/netsearch/viewdocs.aspx?docnumber=253661&version=253948. Retrieved June 21, 2018.

Estrich, S. (1987). *Real rape.* Cambridge, MA: Harvard University Press.

Fasting, K., Brackenridge, C. H., Miller, K. E., & Sabo, D. (2008). Participation in college sports and protection from sexual victimization. *International Journal of Sport and Exercise Psychology, 6*(4), 427–441.

Federal Bureau of Investigation (2017). National incident-based reporting system, 2012–2016.

Federal Bureau of Investigation (2018). Crime in the United States. Table 74, "Full-time law enforcement employees." https://ucr.fbi.gov/crime-in-the-u.s/2018/crime-in-the-u.s.-2018/topic-pages/tables/table-74

Feldblum, C., & Lipnic, V. (2016, June). Select task force on the study of harassment in the workplace. Report of co-chairs. https://www.eeoc.gov/eeoc/task_force/harassment/upload/report.pdf. Retrieved June 24, 2018.

Fielder, R. L., & Carey, M. P. (2010). Prevalence and characteristics of sexual hookups among first-semester female college students. *Journal of Sex & Marital Therapy, 36*, 346–359. https://doi.org/10.1080/0092623X.2010.488118

Fischer, P., Greitemeyer, T., Pollozek, F., & Frey, D. (2006). The unresponsive bystander: Are bystanders more responsive in dangerous emergencies? *European Journal of Social Psychology, 36*, 267–278.

Fisher, B. S., Cullen, F. T., & Turner, M. G. (2000). The sexual victimization of college women. Research report. http://eric.ed.gov/?id=ED449712

Fisher, M. L., Worth, K., Garcia, J. R., & Meredith, T. (2012). Feelings of regret following uncommitted sexual encounters in Canadian university students. *Culture, Health & Sexuality, 14*, 45–57. https://doi.org/10.1080/13691058.2011.619579

Flack, W. F., Jr., Daubman, K. A., Caron, M. L., Asadorian, J. A., D'Aureli, N. R., Gigliotti, S. N., Hall, A., Kiser, S., & Stine, E. R. (2007). Risk factors and consequences of unwanted sex among university students: Hooking up, alcohol, and stress response. *Journal of Interpersonal Violence, 22*(2), 139–157.

Flack, W. F., Jr., Hansen, B. E., Hopper, A. B., Bryant, L. A., Lang, K. W., Massa, A. A., & Whalen, J. E. (2016). Some types of hookups may be riskier than others for campus sexual assault. *Psychological Trauma: Theory, Research, Practice, and Policy, 8*(4), 413-420. https://psycnet.apa.org/doiLanding?doi=10.1037%2Ftra0000090

Florio, G. (2011, December 20). Missoula police: 2nd attack may be linked to alleged sex assault involving UM football players. *Missoulian.* http://missoulian.com/news/local/missoula-police-nd-attack-may-be-linked-to-alleged-sex/article_d261cb6e-2aca-11e1-9033-0019bb2963f4.html

Foshee, V. A., Bauman, K. E., Ennett, S. T., Suchindran, C., Benefield, T., & Linder, G. F. (2005). Assessing the effects of the dating violence prevention program "Safe Dates" using random coefficient regression modeling. *Preventive Science 6*(3), 245-258.

Foubert, J. (2011). *The men's and women's programs.* New York: Routledge, Taylor & Francis.

Foubert, J., Langhinrichsen-Rohling, J., Brasfield, H., & Hill, B. (2010). Effects of a rape awareness program on college women: Increasing bystander efficacy and willingness to intervene. *Journal of Community Psychology, 38*(7), 813-827.

Foubert, J. D., Newberry, J. T., & Tatum, J. L. (2007). Behavior differences seven months later: Effects of a rape prevention program on first-year men who join fraternities. *Journal of Student Affairs Research and Practice, 44,* 728-749.

Foubert, J. D., Tatum, J. L., & Donahue, G. A. (2006). Reactions of first-year men to a rape prevention program: Attitude and predicted behavior changes. *Journal of Student Affairs Research and Practice, 43,* 578-598.

Frankl, V. (2006, 1946). *Man's search for meaning.* Boston: Beacon Press.

Franklin, T., Taylor, D., & Beytagh, A. (2017). Addressing conflicts of interest in the context of campus sexual violence. *Brigham Young University Education & Law Journal, 1.* http://digitalcommons.law.byu.edu/cgi/viewcontent.cgi?article=1392&context=elj

Freeh, L. (2012). Remarks of Louis Freeh in conjunction with announcement of publication of report regarding the Pennsylvania state university. https://www.insidehighered.com/sites/default/server_files/files/99901024-Freeh-Report-Release.pdf

French, J. R. P., Jr., & Raven, B. (1959). The bases of social power. In D. Cartwright (Ed.), *Studies in social power* (pp. 259-269). Ann Arbor, MI: Institute for Social Research.

Freyd, J. J. (2016, April 25). The problem with "required reporting" rules of sexual violence on campus. *Huffington Post.*

Fusilier, M., & Penrod, C. (2015). University employee sexual harassment policies. *Employee Responsibilities and Rights Journal, 27*(1), 47-60. https://doi.org/10.1007/s10672-014-9255-0

Gains, C. (2016, October 14). The difference in how much money schools make off of college sports is jarring, and it is the biggest obstacle to paying athletes. *Business Insider.* http://www.businessinsider.com/ncaa-schools-college-sports-revenue-2016-10

Garcia, J. R., Reiber, C., Massey, S. G., & Merriwether, A. M. (2012). Sexual hookup culture: A review. *Review of General Psychology: Journal of Division 1 of the American Psychological Association, 16*(2), 161–176. http://doi.org/10.1037/a0027911

Garvey, J. (2011, June 13). Why we're going back to single-sex dorms. *Wall Street Journal.* https://www.wsj.com/articles/SB10001424052702304432304576369843592242356. Retrieved July 2, 2018.

George, W. H., Cue, K. L., Lopez, P. A., Crowe, L. C., & Norris, J. (1995). Self-reported alcohol expectancies and postdrinking sexual inferences about women. *Journal of Applied Social Psychology, 25,* 164–186.

Gidycz, C., Lynn, S., Rich, C., Marioni, N., Loh, C., Blackwell, L., Stafford, J., Fite, R., & Pashdag, J. (2001). The evaluation of a sexual assault risk reduction program: A multi-site investigation. *Journal of Consulting and Clinical Psychology, 69,* 1073–1078.

Gidycz, C., Orchowski, & L., Berkowitz, A. (2011). Preventing sexual aggression among college men: An evaluation of a social norms and bystander intervention program. *Violence Against Women, 17*(6), 720–742.

Gidycz, C. A., & Dardis, C. M. (2014). Feminist self-defense and resistance training for college students: A critical review and recommendations for the future. *Trauma, Violence, & Abuse, 15*(4), 322–333. https://doi.org/10.1177/1524838014521026

Gidycz, C. A., McNamara, J. R., & Edwards, K. M. (2006). Women's risk perception and sexual victimization: A review of the literature. *Aggression and Violent Behavior, 11*(5), 441–456. https://doi.org/10.1016/j.avb.2006.01.004

Gosen, J., & Washbush, J. (2004). A review of scholarship on assessing experiential learning effectiveness. *Simulation & Gaming, 35*(2), 270–293.

Gray, D. M., Lesser, D., Quinn, E., & Brounds, C. (1990). The effectiveness of personalizing acquaintance rape prevention: Programs on perception of vulnerability and on reducing risk-taking behavior. *Journal of College Student Development, 31,* 217–220.

Gray, J. (2011). Rape myth beliefs and prejudiced instructions: Effects on decisions of guilt in a case of date rape. *Legal and Criminal Psychology, 11*(1), 75–80.

Green, A. E., Potts, D., Treichler, P. A., & Levy, A. (2013). Campus sexual assault: Suggested policies and procedures. Washington, DC: American Association of University Professors.

Gross, A. M., Winslett, A., Roberts, M., & Gohm, C. L. (2006). An examination of sexual violence against college women. *Violence Against Women, 12*(3), 288–300. https://doi.org/10.1177/1077801205277358

Grube, J. W., Mayton, D. M., & Ball-Rokeach, S. J. (1994). Inducing change in values, attitudes, and behaviors: Belief system theory and the method of value self-confrontation. *Journal of Social Issues, 50*(4), 153–173.

Harrell, E. (2011). Workplace violence, 1993–2009: National Crime Victimization Survey and the census of fatal occupational injuries (NCJ 233231). Office of Justice Programs, Bureau of Justice Statistics, US Department of Justice. https://www.bjs.gov/content/pub/pdf/wv09.pdf. Retrieved June 24, 2018.

Harris, J., & Linder, C. (2017). *Intersections of identity and sexual violence on campus: Centering minoritized students' experiences*. Sterling, VA: Stylus.

Harrison, D. A., Price, K. H., Gavin, J. A., & Florey, A. T. (2002). Time, teams, and task performance: Changing effects of surface- and deep-level diversity on group functioning. *Academy of Management Journal, 45*, 1029–1045.

Hendershott, A. (2016, December 30). "Safe Transfer Act" would brand transcripts of students ensnared in campus sex-crimes tribunals. http://www.nationalreview .com/article/443413/campus-sexual-assault-accusations-students-deserve-due -process

Hendershott, A. (2017, January 4). Denying due process for sexual assault cases. *Washington Post.* http://www.washingtontimes.com/news/2017/jan/4/denying -due-process-for-campus-sex-assault-cases/

Herman, J. L. (2005). Justice from the victim's perspective. *Violence Against Women, 11*(5), 571–602.

Hockett, J. M., Smith, S. J., Klausing, C. D., & Saucier, D. A. (2016). Rape myth consistency and gender differences. *Violence Against Women, 22*(2), 139–167.

Holland, K. J., Cortina, L. M., & Freyd, J. J. (2018). Compelled disclosure of college sexual assault. *American Psychologist, 73*(3), 256–268.

Hopper, J. (2015). The impact of trauma on brain, experience, behavior, and memory. https://www.jimhopper.com/pdf/Handout_for_Interviewers.pdf

Hopper, J. (2015, June 23). Why many rape victims don't fight or yell. *Washington Post.* https://www.washingtonpost.com/news/grade-point/wp/2015/06/23/why -many-rape-victims-dont-fight-or-yell/?utm_term=.745ff0b8fbbe

Hummer, J. F., Pedersen, E. R., Mirza, T., & LaBrie, J. W. (2010). Factors associated with general and sexual alcohol related consequences: An examination of college students while studying abroad. *Journal of Student Affairs Research and Practice, 47*, 427–444.

Inciardi, J. (2009). *Criminal justice* (9th ed.). New York: McGraw-Hill.

Jacobs, P. (2014). The "red zone" is a shockingly dangerous time for female college freshmen. *Business Insider*, July 14, 2014. http://www.businessinsider.com/red -zone-shockingly-dangerous-female-college-freshmen-2014-7. Retrieved July 2, 2018.

Johnson, K. C. (2017, July 5). Will Trump end campus kangaroo courts? *Wall Street Journal*, A17.

Johnson, K. C., & Taylor, S., Jr. (2017). *The campus rape frenzy: The attack on due process at America's universities*. New York: Encounter Books.

Jones, J., Alexander, C., Wynn, B., Rossman, L., & Dunnuck, C. (2009). Why women don't report sexual assault to the police: The influence of psychosocial variables and traumatic injury. *Journal of Emergency Medicine, 36*(4), 417–424.

Jordan, J. (2004). Beyond belief? Police, rape, and women's credibility. *Criminal Justice, 4*, 29–59. http://dx.doi.org/10.1177/1466802504042222

Jozkowski, K., & Ekbia, H. (2015). Campus Craft: A game for sexual assault prevention in universities. *Games for Health Journal: Research, Development, and Clinical Applications, 4*(2), 95–106.

Kearns, M. C., & Calhoun, K. S. (2010). Sexual revictimization and interpersonal effectiveness. *Violence and Victims, 25*(4), 504–517. http://dx.doi.org/10.1891/0886 -6708.25.4.504

Kelley, E. L., Orchowski, L. M., & Gidycz, C. A. (2016). Sexual victimization among college women: Role of sexual assertiveness and resistance variables. *Psychology of Violence, 6*(2), 243–252. http://dx.doi.org/10.1037/a0039407

Kennedy, A. C., Adams, A., Bybee, D., Campbell, R., Kubiak, S. P., & Sullivan, C. (2012). A model of sexually and physically victimized women's process of attaining effective formal help over time: The role of social location, context, and intervention. *American Journal of Community Psychology, 50*(1–2), 217–228. https://doi.org/10.1007/s10464-012-9494-x

Kerstetter, W. A. (1990). Gateway to justice: Police and prosecutorial response to sexual assaults against women. *Journal of Criminal Law and Criminology, 81*(2), 267–313.

Kimble, M., Flack, W. F., Jr., & Burbridge, E. (2013). Study abroad increases risk for sexual assault in female undergraduates: A preliminary report. *Psychological Trauma: Theory, Research, Practice, and Policy, 5*(5), 426–430. http://dx.doi.org/10 .1037/a0029608

Kimble, M., Neacsiu, A. D., Flack, W., & Horner, J. (2008). Risk of unwanted sex for college women: Evidence of the red zone. *Journal of American College Health, 57*(3), 331–337.

Kingkade, T. (2013, November 26). Georgia Tech frat email about "luring your rapebait" condemned by everyone. *Huffington Post.* http://www.huffingtonpost .com/2013/10/08/georgia-tech-frat-email-rapebait_n_4063101.html

Kipnis, L. (2017). *Unwanted advances.* New York: Harper.

Kitchener, C. (2014, December 17). When helping rape victims hurts a college's reputation. *The Atlantic.* https://www.theatlantic.com/education/archive/2014 /12/when-helping-rape-victims-hurts-a-universitys-reputation/383820/

Kleinsasser, A., Jouriles, E. N., McDonald, R., & Rosenfield, D. (2015). An online bystander intervention program for the prevention of sexual violence. *Psychology of Violence, 5*(3), 227–235. http://dx.doi.org/10.1037/a0037393

Koss, M., & Achilles, M. (2008). Restorative justice approaches to sexual violence. Harrisburg, PA: VAWnet, a project of the National Resource Center on Domestic Violence / Pennsylvania Coalition Against Domestic Violence. http://www .vawnest.org

Koss, M. P., Leonard, K. E., Beezley, D. A., & Oros, C. J. (1985). Nonstranger sexual aggression: A discriminant analysis of the psychological characteristics of undetected offenders. *Sex Roles, 12*(9/10), 981–992.

Krakauer, J. (2015). *Missoula: Rape and the justice system in a college town.* New York: Doubleday.

Krebs, C., Lindquist, C., Warner, T., Fisher, B., & Martin, S. (2007). The Campus Sexual Assault Study. National Institute of Justice. https://www.bjs.gov/content /pub/pdf/rsavcaf9513.pdf

Laing, R. D. (1971). *The politics of the family and other essays.* New York: Pantheon Books.

Langhinrichsen-Rohling, J., Foubert, J. D., Brasfield, H., Hill, B., & Shelley-Tremblay, S. (2011). The Men's Program: Does it impact college men's bystander efficacy and willingness to intervene? *Violence Against Women, 17*(6), 743–759.

Latane, B., & Darley, J. M. (1970). *The unresponsive bystander: Why doesn't he help?* New York: Appleton-Century-Crofts.

Latimer, J., Dowden, C., & Muise, D. (2005). The effectiveness of restorative justice practices: A meta-analysis. *Prison Journal, 85*, 127–144.

Laufer Green Isaac Marketing Consultants (n.d.). *High risk drinking on college campuses.* http://docs.sumn.org/College_Students/lgihighriskdrinkingoncollegecampuses.pdf

Legal Momentum (n.d). The history of the Violence Against Women Act. https://www.legalmomentum.org/history-vawa

Leonard, K. E. (1989). The impact of explicit aggressive and implicit nonaggressive cues on aggression in intoxicated and sober males. *Personality and Social Psychology Bulletin, 15*, 390–400.

Levine, M., & Crowther, S. (2008). The responsive bystander: How social group membership and group size can encourage as well as inhibit bystander intervention. *Journal of Personality and Social Psychology, 95*, 1429–1439.

Levinson, H. (2002). *Organizational assessment.* Washington DC: American Psychological Association.

Lewis, M. A., Granato, H., Blayney, J. A., Lostutter, T. W., & Kilmer, J. R. (2011). Predictors of hooking up sexual behavior and emotional reactions among US college students. *Archives of Sexual Behavior, 41*(5), 1219–1229. https://doi.org/10.1007/s10508-011-9817-2

Lhamon, C. E. (2015). Dear Colleague letter. https://www2.ed.gov/about/offices/list/ocr/letters/colleague-201504-title-ix-coordinators.pdf

Lhamon, C. E., & Gupta, V. (2016). Dear Colleague letter. https://www2.ed.gov/about/offices/list/ocr/letters/colleague-201605-title-ix-transgender.pdf

Lievore, D. (2004). Victim credibility in adult sexual assault cases. *Trends & Issues in Crime and Criminal Justice, 288*, 1–6.

Linder, C. (2018). Sexual violence on campus: Power-conscious approaches to awareness, prevention, and response. Bingley: Emerald Publishing.

Lisak, D., Gardinier, L., Nicksa, S. C., & Cote, A. M. (2010). False allegations of sexual assault: An analysis of ten years of reported cases. *Violence Against Women, 16*(12), 1318–1334.

Lisak, D., & Miller, P. (2002). Repeat rape and multiple offending among undetected rapists. *Violence and Victims, 17*(1), 73–84.

Littel, K. (2001). Sexual Assault Nurse Examiner (SANE) programs: Improving the community response to sexual assault victims (OVC Bulletin, NCJ 186366). US Department of Justice. http://www.vawnet.org/Assoc_Files_VAWnet/OVC_SANE0401-186366.pdf

Littleton, H. L., Grills, A. E., & Drum, K. B. (2014). Predicting risky sexual behavior in emerging adulthood: Examination of a moderated mediation model among child sexual abuse and adult sexual assault victims. *Violence and Victims, 29*(6), 981–998. https://doi.org/10.1891/0886-6708.VV-D-13-00067

Livingston, J. A., Testa, M., & VanZile-Tamsen, C. (2007). The reciprocal relationship between sexual victimization and sexual assertiveness. *Violence Against Women, 13*(3), 298–313. https://doi.org/10.1177/1077801206297339

Loh, C., Gidycz, C., Lobo, T., & Luthra, R. (2005). A prospective analysis of sexual assault perpetration: Risk factors related to perpetrator characteristics. *Journal of Interpersonal Violence, 20*(10), 1325–1348.

Lonsway, K. A., & Fitzgerald, L. F. (1994). Rape myths: In review. *Psychology of Women Quarterly, 18*(2), 133–164.

Lonsway, K. A., Srchabault, J., & Lisak, D. (2009). False reports: Moving beyond the issue to successfully investigate and prosecute non-stranger sexual assault. *The Voice, Newsletter of the National Prosecutors Research Institute.* http://ndaa.org/pdf/the_voice_vol_3_no_1_2009.pdf

Luca, M., Rooney, P., & Smith, J. (2016, June 20). The impact of campus scandals on college applications. Harvard Business School NOM Unit working paper no. 16-137. http://hbswk.hbs.edu/item/the-impact-of-campus-scandals-on-college

Lynch, R. (2013). *Adapt or die: Leadership principles from an American general.* Grand Rapids, MI: Baker Books.

Macy, R. J., Nurius, P. S., & Norris, J. (2007). Latent profiles among sexual assault survivors: Implications for defensive coping and resistance. *Journal of Interpersonal Violence, 22*(5), 543–565. https://doi.org/10.1177/0886260506298841

Malamuth, N. M., Linz, D., Heavey, C. L., Barnes, G., & Acker, M. (1995). Using the confluence model of sexual aggression to predict men's conflict with women: A 10-year follow-up study. *Journal of Personality and Social Psychology, 69,* 353–369.

Malamuth, N. M., Sockloskie, R. J., Koss, M. P., & Tanaka, J. S. (1991). Characteristics of aggressors against women: Testing a model using a national sample of college students. *Journal of Consulting and Clinical Psychology, 59,* 670–681.

Martin, R. (2015, April 19). Jon Krakauer tells a "depressingly typical" story of college town rapes. NPR. http://www.npr.org/2015/04/19/400185648/jon-krakauer-tells-a-depressingly-typical-story-of-college-town-rapes. Retrieved July 24, 2017.

Maschke, K. J. (1997). *The legal response to violence against women.* New York: Garland.

McCall, G. J. (1993). Risk factors and sexual assault prevention. *Journal of Interpersonal Violence, 8*(2), 277–295.

McCall-Hosenfeld, J. S., Freund, K. M., & Liebschutz, J. M. (2009). Factors associated with sexual assault and time to presentation. *Preventive Medicine, 48*(6), 593–595. https://doi.org/10.1016/j.ypmed.2009.03.016

McCallion, G. (2014). History of the Clery Act: Fact sheet. https://www.hsdl.org/?view&did=759350

McCaskill, C. (2017). Bipartisan coalition of senators renew legislation to combat sexual assault on college & university campuses. https://www.mccaskill.senate.gov/media-center/news-releases/bipartisan-coalition-of-senators-renew-legislation-to-combat-sexual-assault-on-college-and-university-campuses

McDonald, P. (2012). Workplace sexual harassment 30 years on: A review of the literature. *International Journal of Management Reviews, 14*(1), 1–17.

McLaughlin, H., Uggen, C., & Blackstone, A. (2017). The economic and career effects of sexual harassment on working women. *Gender & Society, 31*(3), 333–358.

McMahon, P. M. (2000). The public health approach to the prevention of sexual violence. *Sexual Abuse: A Journal of Research and Treatment, 12*(1), 27–36.

McMahon, P. P. (2008). Sexual violence on the college campus: A template for compliance with federal policy. *Journal of American College Health, 57*(3), 361–366.

McMahon, S., Allen, C. T., Postmus, J. L., McMahon, S. M., Peterson, N. A., & Hoffman, M. L. (2014). Measuring bystander attitudes and behavior to prevent sexual violence. *Journal of American College Health, 62*(1), 58–66.

McMahon, S., Winter, S. C., Palmer, J. E., Postmus, J. L., Peterson, N. A., Zucker, S., & Koenick, R. (2015). A randomized controlled trial of a multi-dose bystander intervention program using peer education theater. *Health Education Research, 30*(4), 554–568. https://doi.org/10.1093/her/cyv022

McNeal, L. (2007). Clery Act: Road to compliance. *Journal of Personnel Evaluation in Education, 19*(3), 105–113.

McRaven, W. (2017, April 28). Cultivating learning and safe environments. Chancellor's Council Meeting, University of Texas at Austin.

Merkin, R. S., & Shah, M. K. (2014). The impact of sexual harassment on job satisfaction, turnover intentions, and absenteeism: Findings from Pakistan compared to the United States. *SpringerPlus, 3*, 215. http://doi.org/10.1186/2193-1801-3-215

Merry, S. (2016, June 4). Her shocking murder became the stuff of legend. But everyone got the story wrong. *Washington Post.* https://www.washingtonpost.com/lifestyle/style/her-shocking-murder-became-the-stuff-of-legend-but-everyone-got-the-story-wrong/2016/06/29/544916d8-3952-11e6-9ccd-d6005beac8b3_story.html

Mervosh, S. (2017, January 27). New Baylor lawsuit alleges 52 rapes by football players in 4 years, "show 'em a good time" culture. *Dallas Morning News.* https://www.dallasnews.com/news/baylor/2017/01/27/new-baylor-lawsuit-describes-show-em-good-time-culture-cites-52-rapes-football-players-4-years

Messman-Moore, T., Ward, R. M., Zerubavel, N., Chandley, R. B., & Barton, S. N. (2014). Emotion dysregulation and drinking to cope as predictors and consequences of alcohol-involved sexual assault examination of short-term and long-term risk. *Journal of Interpersonal Violence, 30*(4), 601–621. https://doi.org/10.1177/0886260514535259

Messman-Moore, T. L., Ward, R. M., & Walker, D. P. (2007, November). Sexual assertiveness in relational context: Development and psychometric properties of the Sexual Assertiveness Questionnaire for Women (SAQW). Paper presented at the 50th annual meeting of the Society for the Scientific Study of Sexuality, Indianapolis, IN.

Minow, J. C., & Einolf, C. J. (2009). Sorority participation and sexual assault risk. *Violence Against Women, 15*(7), 835–851.

Mohler-Kuo, M., Dowdall, G. W., Koss, M. P., & Wechsler, H. (2004). Correlates of rape while intoxicated in a national sample of college women. *Journal of Studies on Alcohol, 65*(1), 37–45.

Monroe, S. (2006). Dear Colleague letter. https://www2.ed.gov/about/offices/list/ocr/letters/sexhar-2006.html

Moore, M. (2012, January). UM football player in court to answer rape charge. *Missouria.* http://missoulian.com/news/state-and-regional/um-football-player -in-court-to-answer-rape-charge/article_aa241723-4cea-5274-a9f6-3743bfb8f24d .html

Morse, A., Sponsler, B., & Fulton, M. (2015). State legislative developments on campus sexual violence: Issues in the context of safety. https://www.ecs.org /wp-content/uploads/ECS_NASPA_BRIEF_DOWNLOAD3.pdf

Moylan, C. A., & Lindhorst, T. (2015). "Catching flies with honey": The management of conflict in sexual assault response teams. *Journal of Interpersonal Violence, 30*(11), 1945–1964.

National Collegiate Athletic Association (2013, July 26). Montana failed to monitor football team. http://www.ncaa.org/about/resources/media-center/press -releases/montana-failed-monitor-football-program

National Women's History Project (n.d.). http://www.nwhp.org/resources /womens-rights-movement/history-of-the-womens-rights-movement/

Nelson, D. L., & Quick, J. C. (2013). *Organizational behavior: Science, the real world, and you* (8th ed.). Mason, OH: Cengage/South-Western.

New, J. (2015, November 5). Court wins for accused. *Inside Higher Ed.* https://www .insidehighered.com/news/2015/11/05/more-students-punished-over-sexual -assault-are-winning-lawsuits-against-colleges

New York State Unified Court System (2018). Basic steps in a criminal case. https://www.nycourts.gov/courthelp/Criminal/caseBasicsCriminal.shtml

Noll, J. G., & Grych, J. H. (2011). Read-react-respond: An integrative model for understanding sexual revictimization. *Psychology of Violence, 1*(3), 202–215. https://doi.org/10.1037/a0023962

Norris, J., Nurius, P. S., & Dimeff, L. A. (1996). Through her eyes: Factors affecting women's perception of and resistance to acquaintance sexual aggression threat. *Psychology of Women Quarterly, 20*(1), 123–145. https://doi.org/10.1111%2Fj.1471 -6402.1996.tb00668.x

Nurius, P. S., & Norris, J. (1996). A cognitive ecological model of women's responses to male sexual coercion in dating. *Journal of Psychology & Human Sexuality, 8,* 117–139. http://dx.doi.org/10.1300/J056v08n01_09

Oehme, K., Stern, N., & Mennicke, A. (2014, November 13). A deficiency in addressing campus sexual assault: The lack of women law enforcement officers. *Harvard Journal of Law and Gender, 38.* https://ssrn.com/abstract=2523935

Office for Civil Rights (2001, January). US Department of Education. Revised sexual harassment guidance: Harassment of students by school employees, other students, or third parties. https://www2.ed.gov/offices/OCR/archives/pdf /shguide.pdf

Office for Civil Rights (2014). US Department of Education. Questions and answers on Title IX and sexual violence. https://www2.ed.gov/about/offices/list/ocr/docs/qa-201404-title-ix.pdf

Office of Justice Programs (2014). Bureau of Justice Statistics, US Department of Justice. Rape and sexual victimization among college-aged females, 1995–2013. https://www.bjs.gov/content/pub/pdf/rsavcaf9513.pdf

Office of Justice Programs (2015). Bureau of Justice Statistics, US Department of Justice. National Crime Victimization Survey, 2010–2014. https://www.bjs.gov/index.cfm?ty=dcdetail&iid=245

Office of Justice Programs (2017). National Institute of Justice, US Department of Justice. National best practices for sexual assault kits: A multidisciplinary approach (NCJ 250384). https://nij.ojp.gov/topics/articles/national-best-practices-sexual-assault-kits-multidisciplinary-approach

Office on Violence Against Women (2009). US Department of Justice. Violence Against Women Act: 15 years working together to end violence. http://www.ncdsv.org/images/OVW_HistoryVAWA.pdf

Office on Violence Against Women (n.d.). Minimum standards for creating a coordinated community response to violence against women on campus. https://www.justice.gov/sites/default/files/ovw/legacy/2008/01/11/standards-for-ccr.pdf

Owen, J., Fincham, F. D., & Moore, J. (2011). Short-term prospective study of hooking up among college students. *Archives of Sexual Behavior, 40,* 331–341. https://link.springer.com/article/10.1007%2Fs10508-010-9697-x

Palm Reed, K. M., Hines, D. A., Armstrong, J. L., & Cameron, A. Y. (2015). Experimental evaluation of a bystander prevention program for sexual assault and dating violence. *Psychology of Violence, 5*(1), 95–102. http://dx.doi.org/10.1037/a0037557

Parenti, M. (2005). The global rape culture. In *The cultural struggle* (pp. 71–79). New York: Seven Stories Press.

Parks, K. A., Romosz, A. M., Bradizza, C. M., & Hsieh, Y. P. (2008). A dangerous transition: Women's drinking and related victimization from high school to the first year of college. *Journal of Studies on Alcohol and Drugs, 69*(1), 65–74.

Paul, E. L., & Hayes, K. A. (2002). The casualties of "casual" sex: A qualitative exploration of the phenomenology of college students' hookups. *Journal of Social and Personal Relationships, 19,* 639–661. https://doi.org/10.1177/026540750 2195006.

Pennebaker, J. W. (2004). *Writing to heal: A guided journal for recovering from trauma and emotional upheaval.* Oakland, CA: New Harbinger Press.

Peri, C. (1991, March). Below the belt: Women in the martial arts. *Newsletter of the National Women's Martial Arts Federations,* 6–14.

Perry, M. (2015, September 17). Women earned majority of doctoral degrees in 2014 for 6th straight year, and outnumber men in grad school 136 to 100. *American Enterprise Institute.* https://www.aei.org/publication/women-earned-majority-of-doctoral-degrees-in-2014-for-6th-straight-year-and-outnumber-men-in-grad-school-136-to-100/

Petty, R. E., & Cacioppo, J. T. (1986a). *Communication and persuasion: Central and peripheral routes to attitude change.* New York: Springer.

Petty, R., & Cacioppo, J. (1986b). The elaboration likelihood model of persuasion. *Advances in Experimental Social Psychology, 19*, 123–205.

Polizzi, D. M., MacKenzie, D. L., & Hickman, L. J. (1999). What works in adult sex offender treatment? A review of prison- and non-prison-based treatment programs. *International Journal of Offender Therapy and Comparative Criminology, 43*(3), 357–374.

Potter, S. J., & Banyard, V. L. (2011). The victimization experiences of women in the workforce: Moving beyond single categories of work or violence. *Violence and Victims, 26*(4), 513–532. https://doi.org/10.1891/0886-6708.26.4.513. Retrieved June 21, 2018.

Potter, S. J., Moynihan, M. M., Stapleton, J. G., & Banyard, V. L. (2009). Empowering bystanders to prevent campus violence against women: A preliminary evaluation of a poster campaign. *Violence Against Women, 15*(1), 106–121. https://doi.org/10.1177/1077801208327482

Quick, J. C., Cooper, C. L., Gibbs, P. C., Little, L. M., & Nelson, D. L. (2010). Positive organizational behavior at work. In G. P. Hodgkinson & J. K. Ford (Eds.), *International review of industrial and organizational psychology, 25*, 187–216. Chichester, England: Wiley.

Quick, J. C., & Goolsby, J. L. (2013). Integrity first: Ethics for leaders and followers. *Organizational Dynamics, 42*(1), 1–7.

Quick, J. C., & Klunder, C. (2000). Preventive stress management at work: The case of the San Antonio air logistics center, Air Force Materiel Command (AFMC). *Proceedings of the Eleventh International Congress on Stress.*

Quick, J. C., & McFadyen, M. A. (2017). Sexual harassment: Have we made any progress? *Journal of Occupational Health Psychology, 22*(3), 286–298.

Quick, J. C., McFadyen, M. A., & Nelson, D. L. (2014). No accident: Health, well-being, performance . . . and danger. *Journal of Organizational Effectiveness: People and Performance, 1*(1), 98–119.

Quick, J. C., Tetrick, L. E., Adkins, J. A., & Klunder, C. (2003). Occupational health psychology. In I. Weiner (Ed.), *Comprehensive handbook of psychology* (pp. 569–589). New York: John Wiley.

Quick, J. C., Wright, T. A., Adkins, J. A., Nelson, D. L., & Quick, J. D. (2013). *Preventive stress management in organizations* (2nd ed.). Washington, DC: American Psychological Association.

Quizon, D. (2015, January 31). UVA's Sullivan reflects on tenure, *Rolling Stone* controversy, student privacy laws. *The Daily Progress.* http://www.dailyprogress.com/news/uva-s-sullivan-reflects-on-tenure-rolling-stone-controversy-student/article_02a641f8-a9bf-11e4-b304-cbbab2d2f2f5.html

Rahe, R. H. (2009). *Paths to health and resilience.* Reno, NV: Health Assessment Programs.

Rape, Abuse & Incest National Network (n.d.). Victims of sexual violence: Statistics. https://www.rainn.org/statistics/victims-sexual-violence

Rape, Abuse & Incest National Network (n.d.). What consent looks like. https://www.rainn.org/articles/what-is-consent

Rape Crisis (2017). Rape crisis syndrome. http://rapecrisis.org.za/rape-trauma-syndrome/

Redden, M. (2017, June 24). "No doesn't really mean no": North Carolina law means women can't revoke consent for sex. *Guardian*. https://www.theguardian.com/us-news/2017/jun/24/north-carolina-rape-legal-loophole-consent-state-v-way

Rennison, C. A. (2002). Rape and sexual assault: Reporting to police and medical attention, 1992–2000. Office of Justice Programs, Bureau of Justice Statistics, US Department of Justice. https://www.bjs.gov/content/pub/pdf/rsarp00.pdf

Rich, K., & Seffrin, P. (2012). Interviews of sexual assault reporters: Do attitudes matter? *Violence and Victims, 27*(2), 263–279.

Rollè, L., Giardina, G., Caldarera, A. M., Gerino, E., & Brustia, P. (2018). When intimate partner violence meets same sex couples: A review of same sex intimate partner violence. *Frontiers in Psychology*. https://doi.org/10.3389/fpsyg.2018.01506

Rossi, V. (2016, March 1). The road to zero: Inside the university's fight against sexual assault. *The Alcalde*, 51–59. https://medium.com/the-alcalde/the-road-to-zero-b4fbf9828aa6

Rozee, P. D., & Koss, M. P. (2001). Rape: A century of resistance. *Psychology of Women Quarterly, 25*(4), 295–311. https://doi.org/10.1111/1471-6402.00030

Rubin, L. J., & Borgers, S. B. (1990). Sexual harassment in universities during the 1980s. *Sex Roles, 23*(7/8), 397–411.

Rutherford, A. (2011). Sexual violence against women: Putting rape research in context. *Psychology of Women Quarterly, 35*(2): 342–347.

Salazar, L. F., Vivolo-Kantor, A., Hardin, J., & Berkowitz, A. (2014). A web-based sexual violence bystander intervention for male college students: Randomized controlled trial. *Journal of Medical Internet Research, 16*(9), e203. https://doi.org/10.2196/jmir.3426

Salmon, M. (2015). Safe Campus Act of 2015. Congress.gov.

Schein, E. H. (1999). *Process consultation revisited*. Saddle Ridge, NJ: Prentice Hall.

Schein, E. H. (2017). *Organizational culture and leadership* (5th ed.). San Francisco: Jossey-Bass/Wiley.

Schewe, P. (2002). Preventing violence in relationships: Interventions across the life span. Washington, DC: American Psychological Association.

Schewe P. A., & O'Donohue, W. T. (1993). Rape prevention: Methodological problems and new directions. *Clinical Psychology Review, 13*, 667–682.

Senn, C. (2013). Education on resistance to acquaintance sexual assault: Preliminary promise of a new program for young women in high school and university. *Canadian Journal of Behavioural Science, 45*(1), 24–33.

Senn, C. Y., Eliasziw, M., Barata, P. C., Thurston, W. E., Newby-Clark, I. R., Radtke, H. L., & Hobden, K. L. (2013). Sexual assault resistance education for university women: Study protocol for a randomized controlled trial (SARE trial). *BMC Women's Health, 13*(1), 1. http://www.biomedcentral.com/1472-6874/13/25

Senn, C. Y., & Forrest, A. (2016). "And then one night when I went to class . . .": The impact of sexual assault bystander intervention workshops incorporated in academic courses. *Psychology of Violence, 6*(4), 607–618. http://dx.doi.org/10.1037/a0039660

Serna, J. (2014, August 26). Rapist first sentenced to 31 days gets 10 years. *Los Angeles Times*. http://www.latimes.com/nation/nationnow/la-na-nn-montana-rapist-resentencing-judge-20140926-story.html

Shapiro, T. (2016, May 9). "Catfishing" over love interest might have spurred U-Va. gang-rape debacle. *Washington Post*. https://www.washingtonpost.com/news/grade-point/wp/2016/01/08/catfishing-over-love-interest-might-have-spurred-u-va-gang-rape-debacle/?utm_term=.f729b6e8f219

Shaw, J. (2018). How can researchers tell whether someone has a false memory? Coding strategies in autobiographical false memory research. A reply to Wade, Gary, and Pezdek. *Psychological Science, 29*(3), 477–480.

Shaw, J., Campbell, R., Cain, D., & Feeney, H. (2017). Beyond surveys and scales: How rape myths manifest in sexual assault police records. *Psychology of Violence, 7*(4), 602–614.

Shaw, J., Porter, S., & ten Brinke, L. (2013). Catching liars: Training mental health and legal professional to detect high-stakes lies. *Journal of Forensic Psychiatry and Psychology, 24*(2), 145–159.

Shotland, R. L., & Straw, M. K. (1976). Bystander response to an assault: When a man attacks a woman. *Journal of Personality and Social Psychology, 34*, 990–999. https://doi.org/10.1037/0022-3514.34.5.990

Smith, C. P., & Freyd, J. J. (2014). Institutional betrayal. *American Psychologist, 69*(6), 575–587.

Smith, M. D. (2004). *Encyclopedia of rape* (p. 174). Westport, CT: Greenwood Press.

Snyder, J. A., Fisher, B. S., Scherer, H. L., & Daigle, L. E. (2012). Unsafe in the camouflage tower: Sexual victimization and perceptions of military academy leadership. *Journal of Interpersonal Violence, 27*(16), 3171–3194. https://doi.org/10.1177/0886260512441252

Solomon, R. C. (1992). *Ethics and excellence*. New York: Oxford University Press.

Sommers, B. H. (2014, June 23). Title IX: How a good law went terribly wrong. *Time*. http://time.com/2912420/titleix-anniversary/

Speier, J. (2016). The Safe Transfer Act, H.R. 6523. https://www.congress.gov/bill/114th-congress/house-bill/6523?q=%7B%22search%22%3A%5B%22safe+transfer+act+HR6523%22%5D%7D&s=2&r=1

Spencer, C., Stith, S. Durtschi, J., & Toews, M. (2017, June). Factors related to college students' decisions to report sexual assault. *Journal of Interpersonal Violence*, 1–20. https://doi.org/10.1177/0886260517717490

Spohn, C., & Tellis, K. (2012). Policing and prosecuting sexual assault in Los Angeles City and County: A collaborative study in partnership with the Los Angeles Police Department, the Los Angeles County Sheriff's Department, and the Los Angeles County District Attorney's Office. https://www.ncjrs.gov/pdffiles1/nij/grants/237582.pdf

State University of New York (n.d.). Definition of affirmative consent. http://
system.suny.edu/sexual-violence-prevention-workgroup/policies/affirmative
-consent/

Steele, C. M., & Southwick, L. (1985). Alcohol and social behavior I: The psychology
of drunken excess. *Journal of Personality and Social Psychology, 48*, 18–34.

Stewart, A. L. (2014). The Men's Project: A sexual assault prevention program
targeting college men. *Psychology of Men & Masculinity, 15*(4), 481–485. http://dx
.doi.org/10.1037/a0033947

Suarez, E., & Gadalla, T. M. (2010). Stop blaming the victim: A meta-analysis on
rape myths. *Journal of Interpersonal Violence, 25*(11), 2010–2035.

Sutton, T. E., & Simons, L. G. (2015). Sexual assault among college students: Family
of origin hostility, attachment, and the hook-up culture as risk factors. *Journal
of Child and Family Studies, 24*(10), 2827–2840. https://doi.org/10.1007/s10826
-014-0087-1

Swiss, K. (2014). Confined to a narrative: Approaching rape shield laws through
legal narratology. *Washington University Jurisprudence Review, 6*(2), 397–420.

Szpaller, K. (2015, May 11). DOJ: Missoula police make "tremendous" progress on
rape response. *Missoulian.* http://missoulian.com/news/local/doj-missoula
-police-make-tremendous-progress-on-rape-response/article_aco3a9b6-dc45
-5fe4-ae9a-5301404e623f.html

Szpaller, K. (2017, March 2). University of Montana enrollment drops, but officials
optimistic. *Missoulian.* http://missoulian.com/news/local/university-of
-montana-enrollment-drops-but-officials-optimistic/article_fe0d494b-d38e
-5445-99a1-a905953c945c.html

Taylor, B. G., Stein, N. D., Mumford, E. A., & Woods, D. (2013). Shifting boundaries:
An experimental evaluation of a dating violence prevention program in middle
schools. *Preventive Science, 14*(1), 64–76.

Teasdale, E. L., & McKeown, S. (1994). Managing stress at work: The ICI-Zeneca
Pharmaceuticals experience, 1986–1993. In C. L. Cooper & S. Williams (Eds.),
Creating healthy work organizations (pp. 133–165). Chichester, England: Wiley.

Thuma, E. (2015). Lessons in self-defense: Gender violence, racial criminalization,
and anticerebral feminism. *Women's Studies Quarterly, 43*(3/4), 52–71.

Tosti-Vasey, J. (2014, August 31). The rape myth problem within the judicial system.
Pennsylvania State National Organization for Women. http://pennsylvanianow
.org/the-rape-myth-problem-within-the-judicial-system/

Tuttle, G. (2013, August 26). Former high school teacher gets 30 days for rape of
student. *Billings Gazette.* http://billingsgazette.com/news/local/crime-and
-courts/former-senior-high-teacher-gets-days-for-rape-of-student/article
_b1f84190-ef23-5868-8799-b779c0421dc1.html

Ullman, S., & Knight, R. (1993). The efficacy of women's resistance strategies in
rape situations. *Psychology of Women Quarterly, 17*(1), 23–28.

Ullman, S. E. (1997). Review and critique of empirical studies of rape avoidance.
Criminal Justice and Behavior, 24, 177–204. https://doi.org/10.1177/009385489702
4002003

Umbreit, M. S., Vos, B., Coates, R. B., & Lightfoot, E. (2006, January 11). Restorative justice in the twenty-first century: A social movement full of opportunities and pitfalls. *Marquette Law Review* (online), 253–304.

Uniform Crime Reporting/FBI (2013). Summary Reporting System (SRS) user manual. https://ucr.fbi.gov/nibrs/summary-reporting-system-srs-user-manual

United Educators (2015). Understanding how and why Title IX regulates campus sexual violence. https://www.ue.org/uploadedFiles/History%20of%20 Title%20IX.pdf

University of Montana (2011). http://www.umt.edu/home/stories/2011/10 /enrollfall11.php

US Department of Education (2014). US Department of Education releases list of higher education institutions with open Title IX sexual violence investigations. https://www.ed.gov/news/press-releases/us-department-education-releases -list-higher-education-institutions-open-title-i

US Department of Education (2015). Campus safety and security. https://ope.ed .gov/campussafety/#/

US Department of Education (2019). National Center for Education Statistics. "Postsecondary Education." In *Digest of Education Statistics, 2017* (NCES 2018-070). https://nces.ed.gov/pubs2018/2018070.pdf

US Department of Justice (2013a). DOJ case no. DJ 169-44-9 findings. http://www .higheredcompliance.org/resources/publications/um-ltr-findings.pdf

US Department of Justice (2013b). DOJ case no. DJ 169-44-9 resolution agreement. https://www.justice.gov/iso/opa/resources/52820135914432954596.pdf

US Department of Justice (2013c). Findings letter—University of Montana Office of Public Safety. https://www.justice.gov/sites/default/files/crt/legacy/2013/05/09 /missoulafind_5-9-13.pdf

US Department of Justice (2013d). Missoula Police Department—Findings letter. https://www.justice.gov/sites/default/files/crt/legacy/2013/05/22 /missoulapdfind_5-15-13.pdf

US Department of Justice (2014a). DOJ investigation of Missoula County Attorney's Office—Settlement agreement. https://www.clearinghouse.net/chDocs/public /CJ-MT-0003-0004.pdf

US Department of Justice (2014b). Rape and sexual victimization among college-aged females, 1995–2013. https://www.bjs.gov/index.cfm?ty=pbdetail&iid=5176

US Department of Justice (2015). Justice Department announces University of Montana Police Department has fully implemented agreement to improve response to reports of sexual assault. *Justice News.* https://www.justice.gov/opa /pr/justice-department-announces-university-montana-police-department -has-fully-implemented

US Department of Justice (2016). Special report: Female victims of sexual violence, 1994–2010 (revised). https://www.bjs.gov/content/pub/pdf/fvsv9410.pdf

US Department of Justice (2018). Office of the United States Attorneys. Steps in the federal criminal process. https://www.justice.gov/usao/justice-101/steps -federal-criminal-process

US Government (1997). Title IX: A sea change in gender equity in education. In *Title IX: 25 years of progress.* https://www2.ed.gov/pubs/TitleIX/part3.html

Vaillant, G. E. (2012). *Triumphs of experience: The men of the Harvard Grant Study.* Cambridge, MA: Belknap Press of Harvard University Press.

Van Airsdale, S. (2002, October 23). Crime reporting law ambiguous, according to critics. *The State Hornet.* http://statehornet.com/2002/10/crime-reporting-law -ambiguous-according-to-critics/

Walsh, J. F., & Foshee, V. (1998). Self-efficacy, self-determination, and victim blaming as predictors of adolescent sexual victimization. *Health Education Research, 13*(1), 139–144. http://dx.doi.org/10.1093/her/13.1.139

Warshaw, R. (1988). *I never called it rape.* New York: Harper & Row.

Watkins, M. (2016, October 19). Feds investigating Baylor University for handling of sexual assault. *Texas Tribune.* https://www.texastribune.org/2016/10/19 /federal-agency-investigating-baylor-university-han/

Weick, K., & Sutcliffe, K. M. (2015). *Managing the unexpected* (3rd ed.). San Francisco: Jossey-Bass.

Wilkie, R. (2018). Department of Defense annual report on sexual assault in the military: Fiscal year 2017. http://sapr.mil/public/docs/reports/FY17_Annual /DoD_FY17_Annual_Report_on_Sexual_Assault_in_the_Military.pdf. Retrieved on June 26, 2018.

Wilson, L. C., & Miller, K. E. (2016). Meta-analysis of the prevalence of unacknowl- edged rape. *Trauma, Violence, and Abuse, 17*(2), 249–159.

Winslow, B. (n.d.). The impact of Title IX. The Gilder Lehrman Institute of American History. https://www.gilderlehrman.org/history-by-era/seventies /essays/impact-title-ix

Wolohan, J. T. (1995). Sexual harassment of student athletes and the law: A review of the rights afforded students. *Seton Hall Journal of Sport and Entertainment Law, 5,* 339.

Woodhams, F. (1999, January 15). Colleges complain of paperwork and confusion over new rules on crime reports. *Chronicle of Higher Education,* A37. http://www .chronicle.com/article/Colleges-Complain-of-Paperwork/12237

Work, C. (2013). *WSJ* reporter aids *Missoulian* in requesting University of Montana's information. *Montana Journalism Review* archives. http://mjr.jour.umt.edu/wall -street-journal-reporter-aids-the-missoulian-in-requesting-university-of -montanas-information/

Yoffe, E. (2014. December 7). The college rape overcorrection. *Slate.com.* http://www .slate.com/articles/double_x/doublex/2014/12/college_rape_campus_sexual_ assault_is_a_serious_problem_but_the_efforts.html

Yoffe, E. (2015, September 15). A campus rape ruling, reversed, *Slate.com.* http:// www.slate.com/articles/double_x/doublex/2015/09/drew_sterrett_and_ university_of_michigan_the_school_vacates_its_findings.html

Young, B. R., Desmarais, S., Baldwin, J., & Chandler, R. (2016). Sexual coercion practices among undergraduate male recreational athletes, intercollegiate athletes, and non-athletes. *Violence Against Women, 23*(7), 795–812.

Yung, C. (2014). How to lie with rape statistics: America's hidden rape crisis. *Iowa Law Review, 99*(3), 1197–1256.

Yung, C. (2015). Concealing campus sexual assault: An empirical examination. *Psychology, Public Policy and Law, 21*(1), 1–9.

Yung, C. (2017). Rape law gatekeeping. *Boston College Law Review, 58*(6), 205–256.

Zillman, C. (2017, October 17). A new poll on sexual harassment suggests why "me too" went so insanely viral. http://fortune.com/2017/10/17/me-too-hashtag -sexual-harassment-at-work-stats/. Retrieved June 21, 2018.

INDEX

Page numbers in *italics* refer to figures.

protection. *See* university protection
programs

protection surveillance, 66

psychology within educational approach,
204–5

public, sexual assault prevention
workshops for, 127

public health perspective, 164–65, 170–71,
201–3

Questions & Answers on Title IX and
Sexual Violence (Office of Civil Rights),
14, 20

Quick, J. C., 66, 87, 184

Rambold v. Montana, 3

rape: definition of and laws related to,
38–39; law enforcement and, 42–44;
myths about, 40; by spouses and
acquaintances, 41–42

Rape, Abuse & Incest National Network
(RAINN), 47, 161–62

rape crisis centers, 42

rape culture, 39–40, 51, 214–15

rape kits, 102–3

rape myth biases, 3, 42, 43–44, 150

rapists, profiles of, 97–99

Real Consent program, 12

recording incidents, 170

red zone, 7, 10

Rehnquist, William, 23

relabeling sexual violence, 45

reluctance to simplify, 165

reporting incidents: barriers to, 44–47;
channels for, 71–73, 173; data completeness
and accuracy in, 172–73; faculty role in,
119–20, 122–24, 176–77; guidelines and
protocols for, 171–72; to law enforcement,
42–43; overview of, 170–71; system
management and, 175; to track risks, 173

reporting requirements: complexity of, 22,
23; mandatory, 71–72, 77, 169–70;
responses to, 29–31

research by faculty, 128, 176–77

resilience, 187, 202

resistance strategies, 84, 152

resolution models, 144–45

resources, 161–63

respect, learning, 206–8

responsibility (personal), acceptance of,
187, 197

responsible employees: definition of, 117;
education of students about, 119, 123;
training of, 118, 136

restorative justice programs, 189–90,
194–96. *See also* forgiveness

restraining forces, 76–77

reverse discrimination in sports, 22

revictimization, 40–41, 202

Revised Sexual Harassment Guidance of
2001, 19

rights, education in, 153–55

risk factors for sexual assault: emotional
vulnerability, 8, 46; overview of, 32–33,
82. *See also* alcohol use; high-risk
situations

risky behaviors, 9–10. *See also* alcohol use

Rochester Institute of Technology, 208

Rolling Stone on University of Virginia
allegations, 24

Safe Campus Act, 25–26

Safe Campus Week, 125–26

Safe Dates program, 12

Safe Transfer Act, 26

Sandusky, Jerry, 12, 29–30

SARTs. *See* Sexual Assault Response Teams

scapegoating, 186–87

Schein, E. H., 62, 63, 64, 65, 71, 165

Scherer, H. L., 61–62, 78

Schuyler, A. C., 5–6, 62

science, seduction of, 181–82

screening potential employees, 66

secondary prevention, 13, 34–35, 190.
See also education and training

self-awareness of investigators, 180

self-defense strategies, 84, 152

sentencing circles, 195–96

sex-segregated activities and facilities, 21

sexual abuse, history of, 76

sexual assault: as chronic health problem,
31; on college campuses, 6–8; costs of, 86;
enrollment and, 221–22; learning from,
205–6; in military, 5–6; scope of, 2–4; at
work, 4–5. *See also* aftermath of assaults;
model to prevent sexual assault; risk
factors for sexual assault; Title IX
legislation

Assault Prevention (CSAP) Boards; policies and procedures; socialization practices
US Merit Systems Protection Board, 5
US Military Academy at West Point, 7, 73

values, in campus culture, 63, 232–33
Van Valkenburg, Fred, 215
victim empathy training, 150
victim-offender dialogues, 195
victims/survivors: blaming, 10–11, 40–41; Brownmiller on, 40; definition of, 14; educational approach to, 205–6; faculty as, 84; forgiveness as choice for, 199; as helpless, 168–69; men as, 55; negative outcomes for, 5; public health approach to, 202; scapegoating and, 186–87; training in helping, 103–4. *See also* accusers; complainants
Violence Against Women Act of 1994, 18–19, 23, 41

Vos, B., 194, 195
vulnerability, emotional, 8, 46

Warner, C., 5–6, 62
warning signs of serious issues, 33, 120–24
Weick, K., 86, 88, 165, 172, 188
White House Task Force to Protect Students from Sexual Assault, 223
White Ribbon Campaign, 104–5, 233
Williams, C. M., 78, 80, 108
witnesses, interviews with, 141–42
Wonrow, Yvonne, 41–42
workplace, sexual assault/harassment in, 4–5
workshops on sexual assault prevention, faculty role in, 127–28

Yale University, Delta Kappa Epsilon at, 51

zero tolerance policy and culture, 59–60, 61–62